W9-BHH-357

REAL ESTATE BROKERAGE

FREDERICK E. CASE
UNIVERSITY OF CALIFORNIA AT LOS ANGELES

PRENTICE-HALL, INC. Englewood Cliffs, New Jersey

PRENTICE-HALL SERIES IN REAL ESTATE

Current printing (last digit):
11 10 9 8 7 6 5 4 3 2

PRENTICE-HALL INTERNATIONAL, INC., *London*
PRENTICE-HALL OF AUSTRALIA, PTY., *Sydney*
PRENTICE-HALL OF CANADA, LTD., *Toronto*
PRENTICE-HALL OF INDIA (PRIVATE) LTD., *New Delhi*
PRENTICE-HALL OF JAPAN, INC., *Tokyo*

Library of Congress Catalog Card No.: 65-18499

Printed in the United States of America

76233-C

PREFACE

Success is a "will-of-the-wisp" that we often pursue and rarely catch, particularly in the real estate brokerage business. The purpose of this book is to analyze the reasons why so few real estate brokerage offices are truly successful. In doing this, we have focused on the managerial principles and techniques that successful real estate brokerage offices use to support their sales efforts. Analyses of successful practices have not been made in a systematic manner for real estate brokerage offices, although the foundations for the practice of medicine, law, engineering, and accounting have been known, studied, improved, and presented in numerous ways for years.

Experience is often the best guide to successful business operations, therefore, this book presents detailed studies of varieties of successful and unsuccessful real estate offices. In many cases these offices had public images of success but proved to be doing poorly when their inner workings were analyzed. The analyses of many types of firms did yield a number of important principles, ideas and data that can aid other offices in improving their profit and production levels.

The major hypothesis of this book is that successful real estate brokerage operations involve much more than competent, technical sales abilites. A real estate office achieves above average levels of profit and continuity of operations primarily because of the business "know-how" and managerial ability of its chief executive and because it provides necessary, unique services to the local community. The manner in which managerial ability, selling, and community service may be combined to provide successful brokerage operations is presented in detail in the chapters that follow.

Real estate brokers often insist that public interest is served best if an experienced, trained, successful real estate broker is used in every property transfer. To that end they have been seeking to have themselves recognized as "professional." The standards of "professional" competency and the quality of services that "professionals" can and should offer are discussed at some length in this book. The book concludes with some speculation about the future of a "professional" real estate brokerage industry.

The data from which this book was written were selected from information supplied by 89 real estate brokerage offices doing business between 1954 to 1962 and a re-examination of their operations in 1962 and 1963. Each of the firms studied had to meet the following requirements:

1. The members of the firm had participated actively in organized real estate activity and community and political service, or in other ways had given evidence of public contributions commensurate with a "professional" level of operations.
2. The firm was acknowledged by its competitors to be an outstanding real estate brokerage firm in its community in terms of business ethics, volume of sales, competitive ability, and methods of doing business.
3. The firm consisted of more than one person, and all members of the firm were willing to submit to interviewing.
4. The owner of the firm was willing to answer all questions for which they had information in the 13-page questionnaire used for the study and was also willing to participate in a series of recorded interviews of two hours or more.

The cooperation of practitioners was most gratifying because reasonably complete case records were compiled for all 89 brokerage offices. These firms were located in both rural and urban communities. They were large and small, very old and very new in terms of business life, but all met the criteria for inclusion in this study. Because the identity of these firms must be protected, their assistance cannot be acknowledged except in a general way.

All the data from the research study were summarized in a series of mimeographed volumes published by the Real Estate Research Program at the University of California, Los Angeles. Not all the data collected were used in writing this book, but they do provide the factual base on which were built the analyses and conclusions in this book. In fact the emphasis in this book is on the meaning of the data rather than a mere recounting of the findings in numerical terms. Those who wish to review the complete data should communicate with the Real Estate Research Program, University of California, Los Angeles.

Funds for much of the research were provided through the Real Estate Research Program at U.C.L.A. These funds are derived from amounts set aside by the California Legislature from real estate license fees and appropriated to the University of California for real estate research and education. Numerous graduate assistants aided in the collection of data and many U.C.L.A. faculty members made comments on this manuscript. Among those whose special aid should be acknowledged are Dr. Leo Grebler, Dr. Leland S. Burns, and Mr. Frank Mittelbach. The analyses and the conclusions in the book are entirely those of the author.

F. E. C.

CONTENTS

Chapter 1

THE EVOLVING REAL ESTATE BROKERAGE OFFICE

The sellers' market in real estate brokerage in the decade following the close of World War II permitted almost anyone with some real estate selling experience and a real estate license to open an office and maintain a reasonably satisfactory profit level. As early as 1950, the opportunities for "easy" profits declined, but the number of persons opening real estate brokerage offices did not. As the rate of growth in many real estate markets declined, the number of persons entering real estate selling and the number of small real estate offices that were opened continued to increase.

The more successful real estate offices searched for ways to maintain and improve their shares of the real estate markets and turned more and more to the idea of "professionalizing" their activities. Some who followed this trend were merely searching for means of increasing profits and eliminating competition. Many others, however, recognized that "professionalization" could be the means of stabilizing their operations, improving their client services, contributing to the orderly growth of their local communities, and gaining acceptance of real estate brokerage offices as well-managed business enterprises. Whether those who want "professionalization" will achieve their goal is not certain, but their leadership is changing the nature of real estate brokerage operations.

THE TYPICAL REAL ESTATE BROKER IN 1954

In the United States, hundreds of thousands of persons are licensed to sell real estate, and the ubiquitous real estate office annually accounts for billions of dollars in business; yet the manner in which these offices make a profit is still somewhat of an enigma. For instance, in California, where there is approximately one person licensed to sell real estate for each 100 to 150 persons living in the state, real estate licenses have been required since 1927, but a study of real estate brokerage operations in that state was not undertaken until 1954.[1] Not only was this the first such study in California, but it was also the only study on either a national or state basis that had ever attempted to present a reasonably complete statistical analysis of real estate brokerage operations.

The California study, and others that were less complete, present a startling picture of wasted human and economic resources in the number of persons who enter and then soon leave real estate selling. Very few of those who remain in the business ever achieve much more than a very modest financial success. Furthermore, the waste and inefficiency in so many real estate brokerage operations suggest that the public serviced by these persons may be losing millions of dollars annually. Additional millions might be lost because of unwise land uses or property purchases undertaken on the advice of the inexperienced and incompetent real estate salespersons.

THE TYPICAL REAL ESTATE BROKER TODAY

A thoroughly definitive study of real estate brokerage operations has not been undertaken since the 1954 California study. There are many clues to indicate that significant changes are occurring in an increasing number of real estate brokerage offices. In 1954, for example, only two or three offices in any state had regional or state-wide reputations. Today many such firms are emerging in all of the major urban centers of the United States. As was true in 1954, unfortunately, the percentage of licensed persons working as full-time real estate salespersons is still not large, and not too many of these are outstandingly successful in their sales work.

Perhaps the most significant difference between the typical real estate broker in 1954 and the broker of 1964 is the degree to which a few offices in each major market area are obtaining a greater and greater share of all sales and, in the process, attracting and developing much more effective and efficient salespersons. In addition, in the major urban areas, the system of multiple listing is dominating many markets to an increasing degree, so that more and more offices must perform much more efficiently and in conformance with higher standards of service. The multiple-listing system provides all offices with the same inventory to sell, so that survival in these

---

[1] Sherman J. Maisel and Albert H. Schaaf, *Characteristics and Performance of Real Estate Brokers and Salesmen in California* (Berkeley, California: Real Estate Research Program, Bureau of Business and Economic Research, University of California, 1956).

markets depends upon a better quality of service to clients and the development of a community-wide reputation for "professional"-quality services.

There are, however, still many marginal offices selling real estate, and they continue to damage the reputation of the better offices. However, today hundreds of thousands of dollars are being spent for real estate education and research, with the result that standard courses in basic real estate subjects are available in state universities, state colleges, junior colleges, and adult evening schools. The number of persons with college degrees who are now in real estate brokerage is also increasing rapidly, and they are setting new standards of performance which the not-so-well-educated are finding that they must meet. As more and more persons become educated in the fundamentals of real estate brokerage and its related fields, the goals of professionalization becomes closer, so that by 1974 a high level of "professional" and "managerial" competence will be needed for survival in real estate brokerage operations.

The achievement of professionalization in real estate brokerage must, however, be accompanied by the development of "professional management" in operating real estate offices. Real estate, as a small business, is subject to the same ills and faults as are most small businesses, and any advance on the professional brokerage level must be matched by advancement in professional business management.

SMALL-BUSINESS MANAGERIAL PROBLEMS

The problems which a small business, such as a real estate brokerage office, faces in mere survival are, as will be emphasized in later chapters, a function of the owner-manager's characteristics. For example, the owner-manager of the typical real estate office has had little formal education beyond high school, he is middle-aged, and he has had almost no business experience except in selling. There are exceptions, however, and generally it is these exceptional firms which have been most successful.

The real estate brokerage firms that are successful achieve this status because they are managed in one of two ways. The most numerous of the successful offices are managed by owners who recognize their lack of business ability in any field except that of selling and, therefore, organize and operate their businesses so that they are little more than sales organizations. The second group, representing the evolving real estate office, anchor their activities in selling but, having done this, either develop or acquire the necessary general-managerial functions which must accompany growth.

That this problem is not unique to the real estate brokerage business is indicated by studies in the closely allied field of residential construction. Technical skills are not lacking throughout the industry, but failures reached an annual rate in excess of 13,000 firms in recent years and represented an average financial liability per failure of $44,784. In the majority of cases, it was found that there was a significant lack of managerial capacity and skill. Causes of failure were almost universally traced directly to lack of planning, undercapitalization, and inefficient keeping of records.

Similar deficiencies have been found in small businesses in general. For instance, the University of Pittsburgh, after examining the operations of several small manufacturing firms in the area, found that failures were due to three principal factors:

1. Poor financial planning because of inadequate records.
2. Poor sales management, including deficient product planning and market analysis.
3. Poor general administration, culminating in expenses not covered by revenues.

Thus, failures in almost any type of small business can be traced to deficiencies in managerial skills in both general and special areas of operations. Unfortunately, industries in which such skills are lacking have not received the full attention of students of management. One of the most apparent reasons is that such businesses give only limited scope to managerial ability because technical skills loom large as primary requisites for success; their organization and operation are relatively small and simple; and the executive is closer to the operations of his firm. However, the weight of research evidence indicates that this neglect is no longer warranted.

ATTITUDES TOWARD MANAGERIAL FUNCTIONS

A few firms are management-conscious, but primarily on an intuitive rather than a planned basis. Even in these cases, they tend to emphasize one rather than all of the management functions, without fully recognizing the implications which these actions may have for the over-all efficiency and profitability of their firms. The general lack of management awareness has not halted the growth of these firms, but it has made their growth painful and costly. In almost all cases, the awareness of the need for the management functions has developed slowly through experience and perception rather than through the adoption of a positive approach to recognizing the specific tasks of management.

The failure of small businesses to utilize fully the tools of management has been due, in a large degree, to a tendency for management theorists to couch their applications and examples in terms of the large firm. Thus, we find the anomaly of a group of theorists arguing for the universality of their principles but niggardly in their attention to a significant area of management problems. However, even if the principles of management were made more applicable to brokerage operations, there are other factors in this business which tend to complicate managerial functions.

LIMITATIONS ON THE APPLICABILITY OF MANAGEMENT PRINCIPLES

The majority of brokerage firms will probably always remain relatively small and never be faced with really significant managerial problems because of the nature of the product with which they deal and the highly local nature of the markets in which they operate. Furthermore, the ease of entry into and exit from the business, and the relatively minor capital requirements for beginning operations, encourage the continuing formation of numerous small businesses. For these reasons, small firms probably will continue to dominate the real estate business for the foreseeable future, but the increasing complexity of brokerage operations in the emerging large-scale firms will direct more and more attention to management problems. Those factors which have led to continuing small operations in the past will lose their impact as firms become more knowledgeable regarding real estate markets and brokerage operations.

Failure to Anticipate the Future

One of the most important factors in the creation of numerous small brokerage offices which operated on an "opportunistic" rather than a planned long-range basis was the expectation that the huge demand for housing generated in the decades after World War II was temporary. This has not been the case; instead, housing construction and home sales have been maintained at high levels and have become key factors in our national economic health. For this reason, an increasing number of real estate brokerage firms have realized that they can anticipate a future of reasonably active markets. Previous goals of immediate, short-run profits and short-lived business experience now tend to be modified in favor of seeking levels of profit consistent with longer-run, continuous operations.

Consistently Keen Competition

The persistently keen competition in real estate marketing forces brokerage offices to search constantly for more effective means of meeting it. For this reason, any brokerage operation must be organized around a competitively minded, aggressive sales force. The efforts required in creating and maintaining such a sales force leave the owner with little time to think about general managerial problems. Until the manager who wants to expand his operations finds at least one sales manager or partner to whom he can delegate the sales-management functions or the general-management functions, he cannot give thought to any other facets of his operations.

The realities of business competition usually force the owner to search for a good sales manager rather than a management-inclined partner. An effective sales manager can have an immediate impact on the firm's sales and income, whereas general-management changes will normally produce only long-range results. It is also possible that the management-minded partner might require some interested assistance and cooperation from the sales-inclined senior partner, and these might not be forthcoming for some time. Thus, the contributions which good management could make are delayed and the managerial talents remain unused, producing expenses rather than income for the firm.

Increasing Complexity of the Sales Function

The levels of current real estate construction and the increasing emphasis on all types of apartment and nonresidential buildings have not only maintained sales at high levels but have also introduced a variety of new sales problems not previously faced. Formerly, sales were concentrated on single-family homes that sold easily because of unmet demand and liberal financing. Currently the demand is less insistent, and financial terms are much stricter, so that selling efforts must be more intensive and of longer duration. In addition, an increasing proportion of sales involve investment properties and commercial and industrial developments that require better-organized and more knowledgeable sales efforts. For these reasons, sales personnel must not only meet stiffer competition but also be competent at selling more complex types of properties. These needs, in turn, complicate the problems of selecting and training sales personnel.

The complexity of selling in today's real estate markets means that the requirements of each selling job must be studied carefully so that they can be matched with a person who has the proper experience, character, and education. Extensive programs must be developed for locating, interviewing, and selecting sales personnel. Compensation policies must be revised so that they will attract and hold the higher caliber of persons needed. Finally, more attention has to be devoted to the human-relations aspects of sales management so that sales personnel will identify themselves more closely with the firm, maintain their productivity, and not be inclined to leave when faced with minor disappointments in or obstacles to their sales production.

The manner in which sales personnel are being trained in the larger, successful offices also suggests that the selling function must be redefined to include larger elements of buyer and seller counseling. Today's buyers or sellers face numerous decisions relating to selling and financing, their personal, financial, and tax position, and similar matters. Under such conditions, the salesperson must be ready with a variety of suggestions for handling each particular sale. Such counseling usually requires the firm to provide such services as insurance, property management, appraising, financing, building and remodeling, and investment counseling.

MANAGEMENT THEORY AND BROKERAGE OPERATIONS

The relative lack of guidance which the owner of a small business receives from management theorists means that he must develop the capacity for adapting general-management principles to his problems. The difficulty of such a process can be appreciated from a review of the use of all of the basic management functions—planning, organizing, directing, and controlling—in a typical evolving brokerage office.

Planning

The importance of competency in planning can be appreciated merely by a recital of areas in which some planning has to be done, whether or not the manager believes in it. For example, business success depends on the creation of a productive sales force. If this force is to be used most effectively, some thought must be given to forecasting sales needs, establishing sales quotas, and planning advertising campaigns. From these analyses must be developed operating cost budgets and estimates of clerical and stenographic needs, printing outlays, telephone services, and business report needs.

If sales operations are to be on any significant scale, the firm will have to decide which markets it wishes to serve: the new or used single-family home market, the low- or high-priced property market, the home or apartment or commercial-property market, and the nearby area or more distant localities where branch operations become necessary. The fact that opportunities constantly arise in all of these markets means that a decision must be reached as to where the emphasis is to be placed in the firm's activities, and this is possible only through planning.

Planning needs can be summarized in these terms:

1. How large should the operations be? What sales volume is desirable?
2. How many types of activities shall be used to supplement the sales efforts? Are property management, appraising, and insurance financing needed, and on what scale?
3. How many salesmen will be needed, and how much staff support will they require?
4. Shall operations be concentrated in a single office or dispersed among branch offices?
5. Shall operations be limited to particular neighborhoods, to particular types of properties, or to properties in a particular price range?

6. What general and specific sales policies or guiding rules of action must be formulated for the benefit of the sales force, the public, and the firm?

Organizing

Diversified sales activities, large numbers of selling and nonselling personnel, and the creation of service departments and branch offices require that some form of organization be developed so that a major portion of the activities generated by these items can be handled in a fairly routine manner. Moreover, these diverse functions cannot be welded into a smooth operation until the authority and responsibilities of each are clearly outlined. Failure to anticipate these needs and provide for them gives rise to situations which are found so frequently in the medium-size, low-income offices. The owner-manager is constantly harassed by interruptions from the sales manager, and the sales staff is constantly asking assistance in a variety of sales situations. Often the owner is assisting in almost every sale closed by his firm. He is also busy preparing correspondence, contacting mortgage-fund sources, preparing advertising and arranging for its insertion in various media, attending various meetings relating to his professional activities, and probably also developing new sales contacts.

In such a situation, neither the business nor the sales staff receives the proper assistance or attention from the owner. The most common complaint in such offices is that the owner is never available or, when he is available, he fails to pay attention to what is being discussed and often gives advice which is neither pertinent nor helpful. The harassed owner becomes increasingly perplexed by the complaints of his staff because he finds himself working 50, 60, and more hours per week. The answer to these conditions is, of course, organization.

Management theory, for instance, tells us that a manager can extend himself only so far before he must use organizational help. The more competent managers can work constantly with upward of 15 persons and be effective; others cannot work with more than one or two. In any case, regardless of the manager's competence, the assignment of some responsibilities and authority to other persons in the firm by means of organization frees the manager from constant harassment, gives him opportunities for personal as well as professional development, and permits him to concentrate his activities in his special area of competence.

A first step in organizing is, therefore, to train subordinates who can make a maximum number of decisions for themselves. A second step is to limit the manager's duties to those of major policy decision making in one or more of the functional areas, such as selling, advertising, and property management. For instance, the owner-manager can decide that 15 homes with an average sales price of $15,000 must be sold each month. The sales manager can be given the responsibility for deciding which of the homes offered for sale by the firm shall be selected for sales emphasis, on what terms they should be offered, how much advertising should be done, and so on. Once these objectives have been crystallized, the sales personnel can then be informed of them, standards of performance can be announced, and the staff organized to accomplish them.

The manner in which a real estate firm might be organized is indicated in Figure 1–1. Three major assistants report to the owner of the firm: the sales

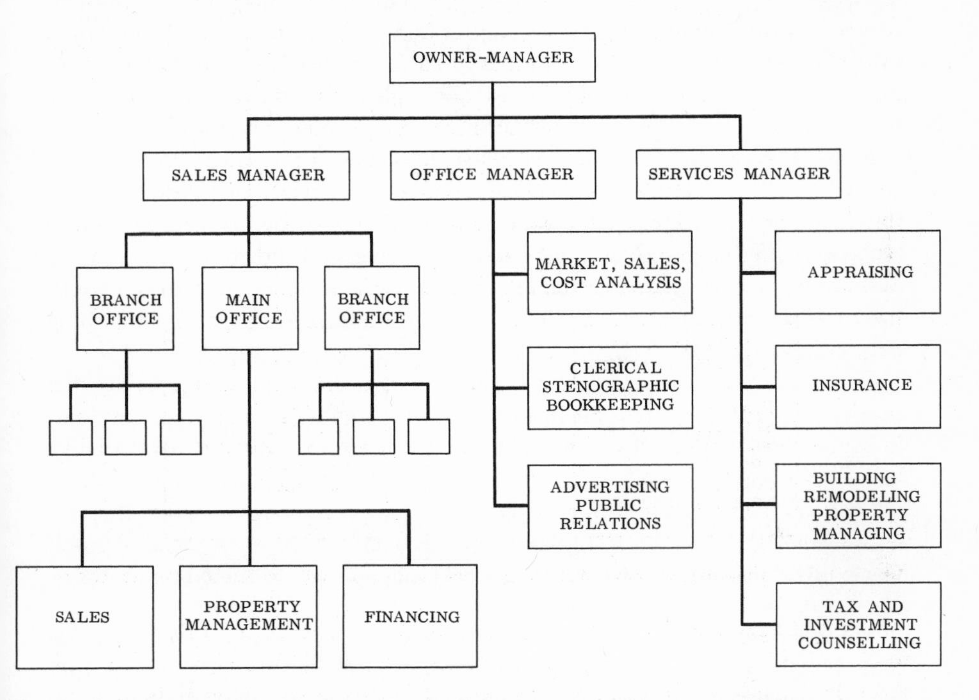

Figure 1-1. Proposed Organization, Medium Size Brokerage Office

manager, the service department manager for miscellaneous nonselling departments, and the office manager. Each of these persons has full responsibility and authority for his department and equal responsibility and authority with the other department managers in the operations of the business. This means that no one of the department managers can override the decisions of the other, and that all conflicts must be referred to the owner of the firm.

The types of activities performed in each of the three major departments are indicated in small boxes. One person would not necessarily be needed for each box indicated, but the duties suggested by the box title will have to be performed by someone. In the smaller firms, the department managers might be required to attend to these activities themselves. None of these activities can be eliminated without impairing the over-all performance of the firm. Each of the activities requires a slightly different set of talents, so that, in any reasonably-sized brokerage office, each department would have to be under the control of a different individual. In many cases, the office-management function has been very capably filled by an executive secretary.

The types of function which would be associated with each of the activities are indicated in Figure 1–2. From this chart we see that the owner of the firm has the important responsibilities of planning, organizing, and leading his firm. The sales manager is concerned principally with staffing or per-

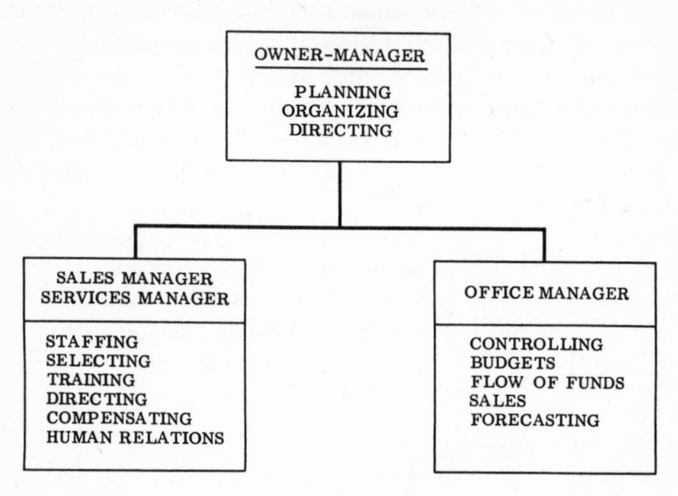

Figure 1-2. Assignment of Basic Managerial Functions in a Medium Size Brokerage Office

sonnel management. In fact, the personnel function is sufficiently pervasive to be found in all executive positions but would be the principal concern of the sales manager. Controlling is found in both the department manager's and the office manager's positions but is more important in the latter. If the size of the operation permits, each needs the support of secretarial-clerical staff help, although this need can often be met through the creation of a secretarial pool.

Directing

The problems of directing sales efforts in the real estate business are complicated because the majority of businesses treat their sales personnel as independent contractors. The reasons for this stem from federal income tax and Social Security laws and the business tradition that a salesman should be held accountable only for sales results. If all salesmen were equally experienced and competent, and if all offices were operated in the same manner, the concept of salesmen as independent contractors might be valid as a policy, but, as we have seen, this is not the case. Each owner has his own set of objectives, business policies, and interpretations of business ethics. Owners' ideas about sales-personnel performance are alike generally, but they differ in important details, so that a salesman who works for one owner under one set of operating policies may find himself working under a completely different set in a new position.

Furthermore, the large numbers of inexperienced and poorly trained persons entering real estate selling every year indicate the need for owners to provide some direction to those whom they hire. Direction need not involve rigid adherence to a set of fixed rules and may mean nothing more than a loosely developed set of policies to guide salesmen when they are in doubt as to how they should perform in a given situation. Often this doubt can be dispelled with a few minutes' conversation with the owner; but, more often than not, the owner either is not present or is not available, and the salesman must decide for himself.

An increasing number of real estate sales offices are solving the problem of providing at least minimum direction through the creation of a sales policy manual which contains the guiding rules of action for the majority of situations in which a salesman might need guidance. A typical list of areas in which policies are needed are discussed in later chapters.

Controlling

The most needed form of control in the typical real estate brokerage office is financial, particularly in the small and medium-size offices. Many of these offices employ bookkeepers who have little responsibility except to record receipts and payments and to summarize the accounts periodically, chiefly for income taxes. Larger offices, however, usually employ the services of an experienced accountant who prepares not only tax reports but also detailed reports on sources of income, types and nature of expenses, and sources of greatest profits and greatest losses.

The flow of funds in a typical real estate brokerage office, regardless of size, is indicated in Figure 1–3. Income is derived from three major sources: sales, nonsales fees such as for appraising or insurance, and deposits as evidences of good faith in sales under negotiation. These are typically channeled into a checking account. A journal may also be used to record income received and due and accounts paid and payable. Deposits in trust accounts are converted to income receipts when a transaction is completed. Payments are made for the expense of operating the office and for the making of sales, and any remainder is counted as profit to the owner and used by him as income or placed in a capital account for investment pur-

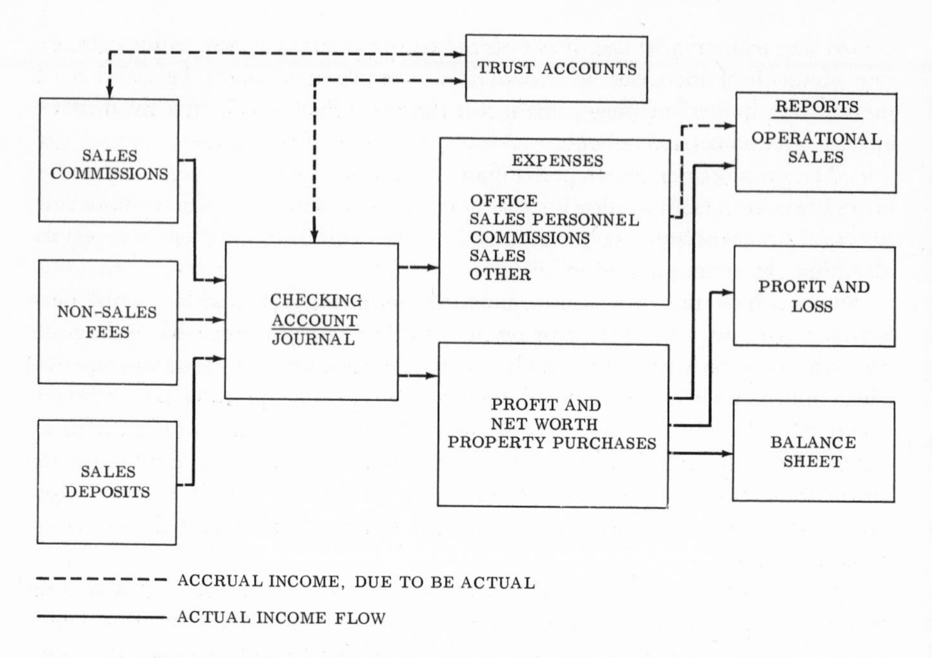

Figure 1-3. Flow of Funds in a Typical Real Estate Brokerage Office

poses. The profits and/or capital accounts are used to purchase assets—usually, real estate.

Records of performance are then prepared from the trust, expense, profit, net worth, and assets and liabilities accounts, and any weaknesses in operations sought out and corrected. The most important control report will be that which shows how many sales were made, the average income derived from each sale, and the costs of making the sale. From such analyses the owners can discover whether they are paying too high commission rates to the salesmen, the costs of advertising per property sold, which salesmen are producing the most income and which the most expenses, and other similar types of financial progress information. The profit and loss statement becomes important only as a general, over-all statement of net income receipts. The balance sheet reflects the degree to which other assets may be available for operations in case the firm should run into financial difficulties because of low sales or high expenses, or the degree to which assets are available for unexpected or planned investment opportunities.

THE ROLE OF MANAGEMENT

The importance of personality and technical ability in the success of the majority of real estate brokerage offices is indisputable; however, this situation is due primarily to the smallness of the operations of these offices. As the size of the firm increases, and with it the requirement for coordination of increasing numbers of personnel and activities, the need for improved managerial functions becomes more critical.

The emphasis on selling, as opposed to the management function, grows out of the keen competition in the real estate business, which consumes so much of an owner-manager's time and energies that he has little interest in attending to other phases of his business. The few management functions which he might perform can be neglected or attended to in a perfunctory manner without seriously injuring his profits. In addition, the feeling of uncertainty as to his future, which is pervasive throughout the industry, is so great that he feels little need to devote his resources to building his organizational structure at the risk of neglecting immediate income-earning opportunities. Finally, the lack of training or education in managerial functions and a failure to appreciate what attention to these functions might do for him leads to his almost complete neglect of his basic managerial responsibilities.

The more intelligent and experienced owners of the small and medium-size businesses do recognize in some degree that they might improve their earnings and reduce their daily routine burdens if they spent more time managing their businesses. However, they are reluctant or unable to perform this function themselves, and unpredictable business volume and erratic earnings make it difficult for them to guarantee salaries for the managerial talent which might give them the management counsel they need.

Instead of searching for this managerial talent exclusively, the owner will seek constantly to find sales managers who can perform in the dual capacity of selling and some managing. Unfortunately, his search is rarely rewarded, because of the dearth of effective sales managers in the real estate business. Even when a good sales manager is found, he is rarely kept for any period of time before he seeks to open his own business or, if he stays, he fails to improve net profits because his pay is based on gross sales volume rather than net income. Furthermore, he rarely relieves the owner of his more pressing and time-consuming management functions except those related to staffing.

Although the urge is strong to expand operations and increase net earnings, few firms are able to achieve stability at a medium or large size because the typical owner is unable to cope effectively with the complex nonselling managerial problems which are a direct function of size. If size could be achieved merely through increasing the sales function, more real estate firms would grow to a larger size; but, unfortunately, greater size produces more difficult problems, more diversification of activities, and, usually, the addition of branch offices, and these introduce the whole gamut of nonselling managerial problems.

The owner of a small firm who is content with the status of his firm could do a great deal to stabilize his earnings and reduce his expense if he paid more attention to the personnel and human-relations needs of his business. However, even here it may be good business for him to ignore this possibility and simply exploit the talents of the constant stream of sales personnel who will pass through his office. Traditionally, real estate salesmen do not respond well to attempts to channel or direct their activities to any great degree. They cherish and protect their status as "independent contractors" and will not give up even a small portion of their independence unless they can see immediate benefits to themselves. On the other hand, their average sales production indicates clearly the need for better definition of their duties, better training, and more attention to means of motivation in order to secure consistent and high levels of sales results.

The need for effective personnel programs, as well as more properly defined organization structure and closer control, looms larger as a firm reaches medium size. This is the critical size at which the decision of the owner to pay more attention to his managerial as opposed to sales functions determines whether the firm will survive. If the owner decides in favor of his managerial duties, then inevitably the economies of larger-scale operations will eventually force him into large-size organization.

Attention to the full range of management functions becomes of paramount importance in a large organization, typically a firm with 25 or more selling and nonselling personnel. The minimum planning and reliance on tomorrow being better than today, which are characteristic of medium-size operations, are no longer possible, and a positive approach to planning becomes a necessary first step. The several kinds of markets in which the large firm must operate, and its diversity of activities, require more intricate systems of organization and the development of a constant flow of operational information so that progress may be charted and controlled to conform with objectives. The assignment of both responsibility and authority and accountability for results become necessary in order to relieve the owner-manager of the need for solving the incessant and recurring technical problems of selling.

WHAT OF THE FUTURE?

The rapid increase in the size and complexity of business operations in the early part of the twentieth century forced consideration of management principles which could cope with this growth. The need for management principles was most critical in the large organizations. It was therefore natural that management principles should be designed for their needs. However, the growth of small business suggests that the application of management principles to their problems is also necessary.

Fewer managerial skills may be needed in a small firm and the emphasis on managerial functions may be different. Nevertheless, the managerial principles needed in a small firm must be understood and skillfully used if these firms are to develop and maintain stability of operations and profits. Recognition of this fact would produce more efficient and effective operations. The talents of owner-managers would not be wasted in ineffective routine, and their sources would not be used in unproductive ways which result in the present typically low levels of profit and in operational instability. The manner in which management principles have been and can be used in successful real estate brokerage offices is discussed in the remaining chapters.

Principles of Management for Evolving Real Estate Offices

1. *Growth.* The dynamic nature of real estate markets requires that real estate brokerage offices plan for a continuous process of growth.
2. *Continuity of operations and profits.* The real estate brokerage firm that seeks a high level of continuous profits and operations must be managed by an executive who delegates the selling function to others.
3. *Survival.* Survival in current real estate markets requires that real estate brokerage offices provide increasingly better services to clients and improve their "professional" reputation through more effective use of basic management principles.
4. *Planning.* Planning must be the first step in developing higher levels of profits, because it provides the goals that maximize the resources of the firm.
5. *Organizing.* In order that each planned task may be completed successfully, it must be assigned to the person most capable of completing it.
6. *Span of control.* Ordinarily, a sales manager should not be asked to supervise more than 15 sales personnel.
7. *Authority.* Authority to make decisions should be placed at the lowest possible level in a real estate brokerage office in order that sales and operating personnel may maintain maximum independence and initiative in their daily tasks.
8. *Direction.* A set of guiding rules of action, or policies, are needed as a means of minimizing the need for constant supervision of sales personnel by the chief executive of the firm.
9. *Control.* Sales and financial budgets must be used to check on the progress of the firm toward its profit goals and desired sales levels.
10. *Management.* The successful evolution of a real estate brokerage office depends upon its ability to secure an executive who can plan, organize, control, and direct the personnel and resources of the firm toward attainable goals of continuous operations and high, consistent profits.

CASE STUDIES

Each of the brokerage firms in the following case studies is large, well-established, and earning an excellent net income. Each firm has many good points and some weaknesses. Read the first study and notice how the analyst has written his conclusions. Use the materials in the second study and prepare a one-paragraph analysis and recommendation for each of the following items: organization, staffing (top management and sales staff separately), planning, directing, controlling, and finances.

CASE 13-E: SUMMARY AND ANALYSIS

I. *Identification*

Classification: Large brokerage firm.
Size: Corporation with one president, a sales manager, 30 brokers and salesmen, 37 engaged in nonbrokerage activities, and seven clerical people.
Income: Estimated at $520,000 gross and $50,000 net; N/G is 10 per cent. (No more detailed breakdown available.)
Location: There are two offices, the principal office being located at an intersection of two principal thoroughfares in a high-income suburb of a large city .

II. *Organization*

A comprehensive analysis of this firm is difficult, because it has been in business for some time and the information supplied—particularly financial—is incomplete.

Thirteen-E is organized as a corporation under the direction of a single individual. The activity of the 75 personnel is distributed as follows: 45 per cent are engaged in real estate brokerage, 5 per cent in leasing, 10 per cent in property management, 5 per cent in appraising, 5 per cent in land development, 20 per cent in loan negotiation, and 10 per cent in insurance.

One of the most striking observations about this firm is its extensive departmentalization. The owner decided to departmentalize his operation during the depression, when he observed that successful firms had established property-management and insurance departments to hedge the falling-off brokerage business.

Diversification has been effective. The firm underwrites the loss incurred by a new department until it is able to sustain itself.

Since the decision made during the depression, management has organized property management, insurance, accounting, mortgage lending and brokerage, and subdivisions as separate departments, each headed by a manager or vice-president reporting directly to the owner.

The firm represents a major insurance company as its largest loan correspondent. Through this connection the loan department secures information which the sales department would like to have; however, the owner prohibits this sort of communication. If this policy is enforced, then this firm maintains enviable internal standards.

Questionnaires completed by the sales force indicated that the better members tended to spend shorter hours engaged in selling activities and depended to a lesser extent on the firm's services than did poorer salesmen. The latter group spent a significantly greater amount of time in selling and leaned heavily on the firm for reinforcement.

Observations indicated that the physical plant was not of sufficient size for optimum operating efficiency. However, expansion of the main office may be difficult because of surrounding land uses.

III. *Staffing*

Because of the attitude of this firm toward decentralization of authority into departments, department heads are allowed to act independently, even to the extent of hiring their own staff. The owner is only occasionally approached for his opinion about an applicant. He delegates authority and responsibility in order that his time may be devoted to the functions of top manager.

The policy seems to have worked well. Relying on observations of the property-management department, departments appear to be headed by thoroughly competent personnel.

The owner has properly delegated authority to qualified people. The staff work together harmoniously. The only qualification would be the tendency of the employer to hire "refined" people, who may be more attractive than productive. There is, however, no doubt that this distinguished staff represents the firm well and contributes a good appearance to the office. Most of the salesmen are not only well experienced but often specialists who know well the merchandise they handle.

To maintain their desk, salesmen are expected to return $3,000 minimum per annum. However, management calculates that a $5,000 income per desk is required before the firm profits from its investment. The owner, by enforcing these rather high standards, attempts to prevent unproductive personnel from being carried by good producers.

The owner further requires that every applicant for a sales position be financially able to carry himself for some time in order to minimize pressure on the client; he must also live in this high-rent area. If these two requirements are invariably enforced, employment policy serves to narrow down the group of prospective applicants relatively to a few who are economically sound and self-sufficient.

According to the owner, the chief problem of the firm is acquiring good salespeople. Possible remedies will be suggested in "Conclusions."

IV. *Direction*

Thirteen-E accepts only signed, exclusive listings that have been examined and approved by the sales manager and two salespeople. Consequently, the sales force devotes its effort to salable listings and recognizes its correct marketing responsibility.

The owner very properly recognizes his function as coordinator and in no way competes with his salespeople. He is aware of the various management functions and attempts to follow accepted principles of good management. It is this progressive attitude, together with his high personal qualifications, that is principally responsible for his success.

Observation indicates that some of the employees may not be adequately supervised. For example, the clerical staff did not appear to really work effectively and wasted time.

Results of questionnaires submitted by salesmen indicate that the training program is lacking. Even though the owner tries to hire experienced salespeople, management must still engage in some sort of training, if only to orient these experienced new employees in the policies, programs, and procedures of the office. Furthermore, with only one exception, the salesmen unanimously agreed that sales meetings were valueless.

V. *Planning*

Because 13-E weathered the depression of the 1930's, there is no reason to believe that they are riding a tide of prosperous business conditions at present. It may be implied that the age of this firm suggests hardening of the arteries. This does not seem justifiable; in fact, there is every evidence that it will prosper in the future and continue to produce at its present very satisfactory level. The owner appears eager to leave a prosperous firm to his son and grandson. He mentions a firm in another part of the country which has been in business for more than 80 years. Thus, he is not merely concerned with current income, but is notably farsighted in his approach to planning.

As another example of his foresightedness, he spoke of a goal that had recently been reached and of new goals that had been set for the future.

The firm establishes over-all quotas, and many of the salespeople have individual quotas based upon past performance. Questionnaires completed by the salesmen reveal a striking contrast between good and poor salesmen regarding attitudes about goals. Good salesmen had invariably set reasonable sales goals; the poor producer gave no indication of having thought about a goal.

As a part of the diversification program, the business will underwrite the losses of a new department until it has proven its success. This nursing of such departments is indicative of foresight.

In every respect, the manager seems capable of handling all types of situations and has an excellent knowledge of records and accounting methods. These records and systems are adequate and comprehensive for their purpose.

VI. *Control*

Control is probably more difficult, yet more important, in a departmentalized firm than in a simply organized business. As described, the firm under analysis is characterized as a departmentalized operation; yet, control could be stronger.

Thirteen-E maintains no advertising budgets. The owner explained that they advertise more when business declines. This is contrary to the practice of most brokers interviewed and indicates that this firm properly recognizes the correct purpose of advertising. Salesmen write their own ads and submit them to the sales manager, who rewrites them into acceptable form for publication.

There are statistical means by which departments check themselves to prevent overextension of credit to clients. This was only one control method of several. The owner is informed of his company's current workings through a series of periodic reports and balance sheets.

VII. *Conclusions*

A. Extensive departmentalization has proceeded in a well-planned manner and has proved effective in relieving the executive of many duties.

B. Standards of the firm are consistently high in every department, at every echelon of management within the firm, and in their apparently wide variety of business dealings.

C. Owner seems to be farsighted in his approach to real estate brokerage, constantly aiming to improve his business and to plan for progress.

D. Success of the firm may be attributed to:

1. Personality of the owner.

2. Effective delegation of authority.
3. Enviable reputation in community.

E. The principal problem, according to the owner, is in acquiring "good" salespeople. Analysis suggests the following solutions:

1. The 50–50 commission split may be competitively unfavorable in this area; consider, for example, a 60–40 split in favor of the salesman, or a sliding scale depending on tenure and production, or giving more information to the sales force.
2. The economic requirements that applicants must meet are high and undoubtedly discourage many. To provide the necessary security, this firm could underwrite new salesmen for a certain period until they became productive. This would have the desirable effect of attracting young people, who often find the need for security to be more important than high income, particularly in early years. Underwriting could be in the form of advances on commissions to be earned or merely a salary continuing for a fixed period. New salesmen could start out in property management, as is done in certain other firms.
3. Lack of a good sales training program discourages the entrance of people from non-real estate fields. Hence, the firm probably relies on obtaining personnel "experienced" with other firms.
4. Finally, the criteria that applicants must meet may need re-evaluation.

F. Other recommendations:

1. Make an inventory of materials and subjects discussed at sales meetings, with the purpose of eliminating those subjects which are of apparently little interest or value to the sales staff.
2. Institute a more disciplined advertising budget. This is vital in a departmentalized firm for control and for measures of effectiveness.
3. Establish a training program. If the sales manager is competent and willing, he is probably the obvious choice for coordinator. Instruction can be carried out by several staff members.
4. Re-study methods of setting sales goals for each salesman.
5. Evidence indicates that the sales policy may be weak or just ineffective. Better producers may be allowed to continue operating in a fairly independent manner, but the questionnaire suggests that poor salesmen need better guidance to improve their production records.

CASE 51-C: SUMMARY OF FACTS

I-S. *Identification*

A. Classification: Large brokerage firm.
B. Start of operations: 1905.
C. Personnel size: Five owners, one general manager (the person interviewed), 20 salespeople, four nonbrokerage personnel, and seven clerical and administrative workers.
D. Income: See attached statements for 1953–1956.
E. Location: In 100-percent area of a large metropolis.
F. Recommendations:

1. That management take under advisement:
   (a) Re-establishing the insurance department to its previous level.
   (b) Reorganizing lines of authority and responsibility among top management.

(c) Updating the policy book.
(d) Installing machine accounting systems.
2. That sources of new blood be sought after, as well as new avenues of approach to selection and a revised set of employment criteria.
3. That every effort be made in formulating the Five-Year Plan (a commendable idea) to make it palatable to the established members of the firm.

G. N. B. The person interviewed in this firm was the assistant general manager, who in some cases was unable to answer questions or who refrained from doing so to avoid possible policy conflicts.

N. B. 2. Because of the firm's size and diversification, it is impossible to get a sufficiently intensive interview to gain a true insight into the affairs of the firm. It is for this reason that recommendations and analyses may seem somewhat superficial and often inferential.

II-S. *Operation*

A. Organization of the firm:
1. 51–C organized in 1905 and incorporated in 1921 simultaneously with its move to its present location. It is incorporated into distinct companies:
   (a) The mortgage-bond company, which was originally formed to sell real estate through the issuance of bonds. This corporation is headed by the two senior partners (see below). This corporation now holds real estate, serving merely as a holding company. 51–C is now considering liquidating the corporation but retaining its "shell" to perform other activities, such as land development.
   (b) The brokerage company, headed by the three principal stockholders, sons of the two owners of the bond company (above). Upon the death of the company's founder, his interests were acquired by the above-mentioned two and in 1947 sold to their four sons, one of whom has since relinquished his interest. Although the two seniors enjoy no rights of ownership, they still play semiactive roles in corporate affairs and are regarded for all intents and purposes as "owners." Their duties are to assist in certain larger transactions (as well as to perform their duties in the mortgage bond company). "Their position is informal."
   (c) The insurance company was incorporated in order to make the insurance manager a "partner" (see part B below).
   (d) Reasons for incorporation:
      Avoidance of personal liability.
      Continuity and growth of the organization.
      Tax savings.
      Opportunity for personnel to participate in the company.
2. There are two offices with activities functionally divided between them: One handles property management; the other, brokerage.
3. Owners of the firm:
   (a) Position: President; age: 76. Although president, he does not in reality participate, merely assisting the sons. Formerly president of the chamber of commerce and an invaluable asset for contacts and public relations.
   (b) Position: Senior vice-president; age: about same as Owner *A*. Spends the majority of his time helping in property management and handling mortgage bond accounts; also assists members of the sales staff. A former realty board president who has a wealth of contacts.

(c) Position: Executive vice-president, acts as head of the company and sales manager. Prime duties are to set over-all plans and objectives; liaison with Connecticut General; is son of Owner *A*.
(d) Position: Vice-president; primary function is to develop mortgage loan department, which he has succeeded in doing; is son of Owner *B*.
(e) Position: Secretary-treasurer; handles legal aspects and property management, drawing up leases, and so forth; son of Owner *B*.

B. Activities of the firm:
1. Residential sales: Firm handles no residential properties and thus does not belong to any multiple-listing service. Only exception to this rule would be when a property would become available through property-management activity.
2. Business opportunities: Are handled by a subsidiary corporation. Provide private financing internally; two men service these.
3. Industrial and commercial properties account for the bulk of sales and leases; they are channeled through the brokerage corporation.
4. Property-management activities embrace 400–425 properties; their fee is five per cent. Attracts insurance, leasing, and mortgage-loan business; has managed properties since the 1920's, but the department has never expanded.
5. Appraising was discontinued when their appraiser left the firm.
6. Insurance: The firm represents Connecticut General Life Insurance and receives 1/8 to 3/8 of a point service charge on the consummation of a deal.
7. Mortgage loan department is an area where the office is relatively inexperienced. They represent no source of money but principally review loan applications for Connecticut General; at the time of the interview, they were looking for additional sources of money.
8. Nonbrokerage services were not considered important sources of buyers.
9. Activity was divided approximately as follows: Brokerage, 35 per cent; leasing, 30 per cent; loan negotiation, 25 per cent; property management and insurance, each 5 per cent.

C. Community and business relations:
1. The company makes conscious efforts to promote its good name by:
   (a) Working with the Industrial Department of the Chamber of Commerce.
   (b) Maintaining relations with railroads.
   (c) Making speeches. If one of the firm's executives cannot make speeches, the interviewee will do so.
   (d) Community participation of the officers: President of Chamber of Commerce; member of local realty board, Lions Club, and Merchants and Manufacturers' Association. They sit on the boards of the Better Business Bureau, National Safety Council, Bankers Association, and many other organizations.
2. Relations with other brokers:
   (a) They have had some unhappy experiences with competing brokers but retain cooperative relations with all of them. They have had 10 commission disputes with other brokers and sellers during the year—usually the result of a lack of understanding by lessor or seller that he must pay the firm a commission.
   (b) Most troubles are caused because no interoffice agreements exist in writing. They have prepared a form which stipulates the working agreement with other brokers, but the salesmen have been lax in getting the form signed by cooperating offices, although this is policy.

3. Public relations:
   (a) Most deals fell through because of contingent escrows, and very rarely for reasons of unclear title. The firm always tries to iron out all contingencies before going into escrow. Most troubles arise from a lack of understanding at the beginning of the deal (at the offer) or are due to the changing complexity of the deal.
   (b) An example: The deal involved building a market for party *A,* who would hold title and lease to party *B.* 51's commission was to be based on the size of the lease. When party *A,* the owner, decided to run the market himself, 51 was left in a tricky position. Fortunately, the contractor saw to it that they were reimbursed.
   (c) Chief competition (for salesmen as well as customers) in industrial real estate are the smaller industrial offices; in commercial real estate, a large, well-established form with many branch offices.

D. Planning:
1. At the time of the interview, the firm had suspended hiring new salespeople in order to formulate a five-year program for the future. They were in the process of setting new objectives and "redefining the business." One facet of the plan is to develop and assign fixed areas to individual salesmen: the salesman would have to work to develop his own territory, otherwise, he would fall by the wayside. To the interviewee's knowledge, the firm had never undertaken a plan of this type, or, for that matter, a formal plan, before. They have come to realize that they must set definite goals and objectives, in contrast to the past, where their directions were uncertain.
2. Over the long period of time the firm has been doing business, they have tried a variety of ideas and gimmicks to get salespeople on the job, to spread the company's fame, and so forth; most of these ideas have been discarded because they did not work. Why they did not is not known.

E. Records:
1. Financial records are not departmentalized; thus, cost accounting is impossible. However, the company arbitrarily charges against departments those expenses which they believe apply. From this rather elementary system, they are able to recognize sharp fluctuations in the brokerage activity, whereas income from property management and insurance is much more stable. They employ a bookkeeper and a consulting accountant, who prepare monthly profit and loss statements, quarterly balance sheets, and budgets. Only recently have property management records been typed; entries were formerly made in pencil.
2. Nonfinancial records:
   (a) Keep records of calls received as a check on advertising effectiveness. For example, the best drawing card is the property sign. They ask of customers where they heard of the firm or property, and if it was through the property sign, they note the location of the sign. The same applies to classified ads. These records are kept only for calls, not for drop-ins (of which they have very few).
   (b) In the past they have kept records of each salesman's activities but found them not too helpful, in that they could not relate activities to production record.
   (c) A variety of forms are used: those relating to legal aspects are handled by Owner *E*; Owner *D* takes care of forms that pertain to productivity.

III-S. *Sales management*

A. Personnel:

1. Owners (see II-S, A-3).
2. Sales manager.
   Together with an executive vice-president (Owner *C,* see II-S, A-3), the sales manager handles sales management. A third party, the interviewee, is responsible for public relations, advertising, sales promotion, and some of the sales-management duties.
3. Sales personnel.
   Twenty, classified as follows: Ten specializing in industrial sales, five in commercial, and five in miscellaneous.

B. Policy:

1. When a buyer calls in to the office, a notation is made and given to the salesman who is most qualified to assist; this depends on the area in which he works, the type of property in which he deals, and the compatibility of the salesperson to the client. The interviewee does not feel that any serious problems have ever arisen from this policy.
2. Because of the firm's varied activities, floor days do not work. For example, an inquiry may come to the mortgage-loan man on the floor about an industrial property of which he knows nothing. Furthermore, the salesmen like to work by area, to develop their own leads and deals.
3. No methods are used to control salesmen's activities and production, for example, sales quotas, listing quotas, floor days, and so forth. Their responsibilities (other than returning income) are limited to dictating their correspondence and filling out personal forms.
4. The firm does not make extensive checks on the activities of the sales force; the general attitude is that each salesman is in business for himself, and they will not pressure him. It is estimated that to keep each man costs $500–$600 per month; nevertheless, if he is not returning this figure, he is still not pressured; "if the salesman isn't making a living, he will leave on his own."
5. It is a policy to keep a man until he leaves voluntarily. Only one man has been fired.
6. Many of the salesmen have been with the firm for a number of years, some longer than the present owners. Consequently, they have their own habits and eccentricities, which often conflict with policy, but *laissez faire* still reigns and little is done.
7. The policy book was formulated in 1936 and few revisions have been made since. Labeled "Standard Practice," it deals with handling listings, preparing leases, use of options, handling telephone inquiries, developing prospects, handling deposits on deals, correspondence, use of exclusive-agency contracts, and advantages of our service.
8. Occasionally the firm will buy a property for speculative reasons; usually, when this is done, it is done by a member of the firm.
9. Individual salesmen are encouraged to own property, but the deal must be transacted through the office. If a salesman consummated a deal outside the office (which is possible) and it was discovered, it would not be taken lightly. This would most likely be discovered by reference to the "ownership service" to which the office subscribes.
10. Chief recurring problems are of a management nature. As an example, the

problem constantly arises of salesmen finding it more profitable to focus their attention on deals outside of the business, rather than directing their efforts toward building the business. Creative selling has been subordinated.

11. The salespeople make suggestions about the firm's operation. These are considered, but probably not so much as in a smaller industrial firm.
12. The interviewer recalls that, while copying records for another study, he heard a salesman talking loudly and continually for some time, obviously disturbing the rest of the sales staff.

C. Staffing:

1. Selection:
   (a) Criteria: According to the executive vice-president-sales manager, it is close to impossible to predict the success of a job applicant. One of the outstanding features is the will to sell. The salesman must be able to associate with business people and industrialists. Most of the younger people are college-educated. Two members of the staff are former managers of manufacturing firms. Most of the people who have entered the firm recently had experience in selling, although not in real estate.
   (b) Hiring is the responsibility of Owner *C,* who is currently training the man interviewed in this area.
2. Training:
   (a) New men are not placed under one of the older men, and they are not given weekly lessons. Rather, the executive vice-president-sales manager, Owner *C,* reviews the firm's objectives. Thus, their future supervisor discusses with them the types of deals they will handle, their territory, how to develop prospects and put deals together, how to negotiate, and generally, how to merchandise properties. Then Owner *E* goes over legal aspects with them. Then the trainee goes into the field, where he studies properties and talks to owners. There is no set training method—the man is merely shifted from department to department for a month, then goes into the field.
   (b) The firm does not expect immediate production, particularly because they deal primarily in industrial properties, and this takes a special knack. Usually a man will not be making a living before he has passed a year in their employ.
   (c) Earnings are extremely irregular. Take the case of *A* and *B*. *A* did very well in the first year, netting $8,000; *B* earned $3,000. The second year, *A* slackened off and *B* made $12,000, one deal alone returning $10,000. This inconsistency continues from year to year, even among the older members of the firm.
   (d) Sales meetings are directed by the executive vice-president-sales manager. Sales, listings, and prospects are foremost in the subjects of discussion. Next in importance are matters affecting the salespeople: announcements, legal forms, and so forth. Often outside speakers are brought in to talk with the staff.
3. Turnover:
   (a) The main problem in meeting competition is training and holding good career men. The reasons: Salespeople prefer to work for smaller organizations, where they can assume more responsibility and more directly influence company policy; they prefer to work for themselves.
   (b) Characteristically, once the man has made the grade in selling, he feels that he can get along without the firm. In the last two years, 15 men have

left because they could not make a go of it, or have retired, or have joined smaller organizations. A lot of the men think that when they make $25,000 a year, they should be vice-presidents.

D. Listing:

1. Sources of listing, in order of importance, are: Phone calls to office, responses to newspaper ads, direct mail, former clients, and public relations activities.
2. Each man has five exclusives and 20 opens. "Different men can handle different numbers of exclusives." One man who has been with the firm for 30 years refused exclusives because he did not want to assume the responsibility inherent in this type of relationship.
3. Ninety per cent of active listings are open, but only 50 per cent of selling time is devoted to opens. Interviewee believes the firm loses commissions from open listings quite often but does not know *how* often. Perhaps once a year, a suit is filed to collect a commission from an open listing. Policy, however, is to avoid suits whenever possible. Policy is also to get a written, signed exclusive, because the firm deals in investment-type (or "user") properties. It is difficult to get accurate information on the subject property unless the listing is exclusive; the listing thus becomes a record. With opens, they try to protect themselves with a letter of authority from both parties. Opens are advertised but without addresses; they are considering revising this policy.
4. The firm takes 80 per cent of its listings at too high a price, assuming that the price can be trimmed later. Only when owner is cooperative will they bother to make an appraisal. When they have a specific user for a specific property, they will then talk about fair price.

E. Selling:

1. The principal sources of buyers, listed in order of preference, are: property signs, direct mail, firm contacts outside the real estate business, former clients, classified ads, and phone calls. They have no data on the amount of business resulting from referrals.
2. Salesmen complete a qualification form for each prospect which lists the type of property and business desired, area of the city desired, size needed, and all other needs in detail, including a diagram of the need.
3. Intracooperative sales are split 50–50 between the lister and the salesman who brings the buyer. There has been some confusion in applying this rule. It was made for exclusive listings only but seems to apply now to all listings; however, this is not disadvantageous. For example, a salesperson makes a contact in a section of town with which he is unfamiliar; he arranges with the salesman within the firm who specializes in this area for a 50–50 split. Because this is not (exactly) company policy, there have been a few misunderstandings, particularly among new men. But once it is straightened out, it seems to work to advantage, particularly among those who specialize area-wise.

IV-S. *Advertising*

A. Media:

1. Chief media are: Classified ads, personal letters, and lot signs. Nonclassified ads, form letters, publications, brochures, and souvenirs are occasionally used, but never radio or television. A variety of advertising gimmicks have been tried.
2. Classified ads are usually individually run because each salesman carries his name on the ad, and the owners further like to individualize the properties.

INCOME AND EXPENSE STATEMENTS

	Year 48 19	Year 49 19	Year 50 19		Year 51 19	
	Amount as % of total gross	*Amount as % of total gross*	*Amount*	*As % of total gross*	*Amount*	*As % of total gross*
Income:						
From Brokerage	75.0%	65.0%	$ 350,000	100.0% (?)	$ 370,000	100.0% (?)
From Nonbrokerage	25.0	35.0	—	—	—	—
Total Income	100.0%	100.0%	$ 350,000	100.0%	$ 370,000	100.0%
Expenses:						
Salaries	20.0%	20.0%	?	?	?	?
Occupancy	4.0	4.0	$ 136,000	38.9%	$ 142,000	38.4%
Other Business	10.0	10.0				
Commissions	50.0	50.0	200,000	57.0	200,000	54.0
Advertising	6.0	6.0	18,000	5.0	25,000	7.0
Total Expenses	90.0%	90.0%	$ 354,000	100.9%	$ 367,000	92.0%
Net Profit Before Taxes	10.0%	10.0%	($ 4,000)	(0.9%)	$ 3,000	8.0%

The firm has no idea how productive block or display ads are in comparison to classifieds.

3. Advertising is carried regularly in the two largest metropolitan papers and less often in most other newspapers. Other advertising is carried in industrial journals and *The Wall Street Journal*. The firm has made no analysis of which paper is most productive, but tries them all.
4. The firm tries to keep in contact with all kinds of organizations that may refer clients to them.
5. Occasionally management sets up a "merchandising program." This includes signs, classified and display ads, direct-mail advertising (which will include cards, personal letters, or brochures), general publicity through the newspapers, and data sheets on the subject property. Thus, they marshal all the firm's efforts for the program. The average cost of such a program is $250. They decide to "merchandise" when the firm has control of the property, size of the transaction, and interest of the participant. The idea is too new to know whether it is effective.

B. Budgeting:

1. Although there are financial budgets, there is no advertising budget. The firm tries to allocate advertising expenditures by the property rather than by any sum amounts. There is, in other words, an individual budget for each property.
2. It is the opinion of the interviewee that advertising expenses are running rather high (six per cent of gross) and should be trimmed. The firm tries to keep advertising expenditures within 10 per cent of gross volume.

C. Control:

1. Advertising copy is written by the interviewee, using data and suggestions provided by the salesmen. Occasionally he writes it on his own without their assistance.
2. Advertising was most important in the earlier days of business—much more important than now because of the increasing numbers attracted by the firm's reputation.

Chapter 2

CAUSES OF THE SUCCESS AND FAILURE OF REAL ESTATE FIRMS

One of the easiest things that a real estate salesperson can do is to open his own real estate brokerage office. One of the most difficult things in his entire business life will be to keep the office open and earning continuous profits at reasonably high levels. Hundreds of new real estate brokerage offices are opened each year and almost as many fail. Failures are due to lack of ordinary business competence, undercapitalization, failure to control fraud and incompetence on the part of employees, and, primarily, the lack of managerial and technical competence on the part of the owner-manager of the firm. As the real estate brokerage office grows, the lack of managerial competence becomes a greater factor in the lack of success than does a lack of knowledge about the technical aspects of real estate brokerage. The managerial techniques of successful offices and the causes of failure of unsuccessful brokerage offices are reviewed in this chapter.

FACTORS INFLUENCING SUCCESS OR FAILURE

In many cases, the owner-managers of real estate brokerage offices assume that, if they can expand and diversify their operations, they can reduce their chances of failure while increasing their net profits. This has not proven to be true. In the majority of cases where this was tried, the expanded operations have been abandoned rather quickly because they presented too great financial risks and too many complex managerial problems. Even medium-size firms of only 10 to 25 persons were converted to smaller firms of only three to five persons when the chief executives of these firms found that they could cope with their real estate sales problems but not their managerial problems. Among the technical and managerial factors that contribute to the continuing success and growth of real estate brokerage firms are the size, age, and location of the office, the financial and organizational structure of the firm, the business and managerial experience of the owners of the firm, and the firm's personnel policies and training programs.

Size of the Office

Real estate brokerage offices come in many sizes, and each size has its special business problems (Table 2–1). Small firms, of three to five persons, are primarily sales organizations, can offer few other services except brokerage, and are always faced with high sales personnel turnovers. Medium-size firms, of five to 25 persons, represent an awkward-size business in which a firm must concentrate on selling to produce income but must also begin to branch out in other kinds of related services in order to diversify and to stabilize income. The large firms, of 25 or more persons, suffer from a constant shortage of good managerial talent and the need for financing rather high, continuing service overhead costs.

The differences in the average numbers of personnel in the various-size firms is much greater than the differences in the gross incomes earned by them. This fact is a reflection of the degree to which the costs of operating larger firms absorb more of the gross income than is true in the smaller firms. Small firms are usually new, flexible in their organizational and operational policies, and able to capitalize quickly on new sales opportunities. The larger firms are usually well established in their sales areas and offer more and more services, such as financing, appraising, constructing, insurance, and related items as they increase in size. The larger firms have much greater difficulty in changing the direction and scope of their operations. Size, therefore, is the best single indicator of the types of technical and managerial problems that a real estate brokerage office will face.

Date of Starting Business

A typical real estate brokerage office must expect to spend three to five years becoming established and accepted in a community. During these formative years, all members of the firm must make strenuous efforts to keep the firm name and services before the public. These will often be lean financial years, but, if properly utilized, they will insure the continued future success of the firm.

Table 2-1

INCOME AND PERSONNEL CHARACTERISTICS OF REAL ESTATE BROKERAGE OFFICES

Type of Firm	*Income Status*				*Average number of sales personnel*
	Gross income	*Gross income from brokerage*	*Net Income**		
			Amount	*As percentage of gross*	
All firms	$ 98,854	$ 77,873	$ 20,388	25%	6.0
Small firms:					
All small firms	$ 47,943	$ 39,618	$ 16,734	35%	4.0
Low-income firms	42,281	35,513	10,645	25	3.0
High-income firms	51,483	40,561	20,682	40	4.0
Medium-size firms:					
All medium firms	$ 76,272	$ 69,397	$ 17,369	23%	7.0
Low-income firms	73,063	69,658	13,468	18	7.0
High-income firms	78,081	69,144	19,708	25	7.0
Large firms:					
All large firms	$ 226,804	$ 187,670	$ 33,897	15%	18.0

*Net income is the amount of spendable income remaining for the owner of the firm after all expenses of the firm have been paid. This amount does not include the commissions that the owner or owners of the firm may have earned.

SOURCE: Based on records furnished by 80 brokerage offices over a period of five years

The more successful real estate brokerage offices are usually those with the longer business experience. For example, more than 58 per cent of the high-income small brokerage offices have been operating between seven and 20 years, as compared with only 45 per cent of the low-income small firms. The same was true with the medium-size firms but more so, because almost two-thirds of the high-income firms had been in business at least seven years. The very long business lives that are typical of many other industries are not found in the real estate brokerage business. The large brokerage offices are almost the only type of brokerage offices with reasonably long business histories, and among these only about one-fourth have been operating for 15 or more years.

The Appearance of the Office

The type of office that a real estate brokerage firm occupies is a direct function of its size but not of its income status. The small and medium-size firms have offices that are often drab in appearance and furnished chiefly with ordered rows of desks, usually one or two more desks than the normal number of sales personnel, with two chairs per desk, and little else. The office of the small firm is almost always empty except for that occasional salesman who is between calls or who is arranging additional appointments by phone. The medium-size firm will usually have an office with a receptionist and at least one salesperson stationed in the office to handle the needs of prospective buyers and sellers. The appearance of the office and the absence of any but a minimum number of personnel are due largely to the fact that the majority of selling takes place away from the office. The office is used chiefly for the fleeting moments when a contract is being signed, a sales meeting is being held, or sales activity is momentarily slack.

The large firm reflects its greater maturity and stability in the extensiveness of its furnishings and the size of its quarters. In fact, some of the better-established firms will be housed in their own buildings. A staff of receptionists, secretaries, and bookkeepers, the department heads, and several salesmen are always on hand to meet the needs of clients. In general appearance, it resembles any typical administrative office of a busy concern.

Location of the Office

Real estate offices, regardless of size, are usually found grouped together in the same general business area in a city. The small and medium offices, however, are most often located in the suburban areas, in the fringe areas of the central business district in large cities, and in the central business district of small cities. Large offices are found almost exclusively in the central business districts of the larger cities although, if they have branch offices, their branches will be found in many of the same areas as the small and medium offices.

The choice of location is an important determinant of success, because inspection of sales records of the offices indicate that the bulk of the sales will be completed within a three- to five-mile radius of the office. The choice of a particular site is apparently much less important, because the bulk of the contacts with buyers and sellers is made by telephone or away from the office. Few of the firms, for example, report any significant percentage of business from persons stopping in at the office.

Mobility apparently has a significant impact on earnings, because more than two-thirds of the high-income, small, and medium-size firms and three-fourths of the large firms have had more than one location for their principal office. For example, 11 per cent of the small firms and 7 per cent of the medium-size firms in the high-income category and 14 per cent of the large firms had been in three or more locations. In the case of the large firms, mobility was more often a characteristic of the early years.

Financial Structure

Instability of net income is a characteristic of all real estate brokerage firms (Table 2–1). Low-income small firms, for example, showed fluctuations in gross income in a five-year period of from $16,000 to $53,000, and high-income small firms showed fluctuations between $28,000 and $57,000. Medium-size firms reported fluctuations during the five-year period of between $23,000 and $77,000, whereas large firms had gross incomes that ranged from $126,000 to $267,000.

The high-income firms consistently showed an ability to produce a much higher net income from their gross incomes than did the low-income firms. Few of the owners of small firms seemed to realize how much of the total sales efforts of their offices were wasted as earnings were squandered in uncontrolled expenditures (Table 2–2). Effective executives were able to reduce expenses to 60 per cent of gross income, while the less efficient had expenses that equaled 75 per cent or more of gross income. The small percentage of gross income that was earned as net income by large firms gives an appearance of inefficiency that is misleading. These firms produced their profit from many other sources than brokerage but used brokerage income to pay all costs of operating their offices.

The greatest expenses for all types of firms were sales commissions. Typically, low-income firms paid 40 to 45 per cent of their gross income as commissions, as compared with 30 to 35 per cent paid by high-income firms. Because brokerage activities dominated the activities of small and medium-size firms, other expenses related to selling were also high percentages of gross incomes.

Table 2–2

EXPENSES AS PERCENTAGE OF GROSS INCOME

Item	*Type of Firm*					
	All firms	*Low-income*	*High-income*	*Small*	*Medium*	*Large*
Gross Income:						
From brokerage activities	94%	98%	93%	98%	96%	88%
From nonbrokerage activities	6	2	7	2	4	12
Total	100%	100%	100%	100%	100%	100%
Expenses as percentage of gross income:						
Commissions	38%	41%	34%	28%	45%	45%
Advertising expenses	11	10	10	9	10	8
Office occupancy expenses	6	7	5	7	5	5
Salaries	6	6	7	6	6	14
Other business expenses	9	7	8	9	7	9
Miscellaneous	0	3	1	2	1	3
Net profit as percentage of gross income	30%	26%	35%	39%	26%	18%
Total	100%	100%	100%	100%	100%	100%

Explanation of Income and Expense Constituents. Income from brokerage activity includes only that income directly attributable to the sale of real estate properties, not to rentals or leases. Income from nonbrokerage activity includes income from sources such as property management, insurance sales, building, contracting or subdividing, rentals and leases, appraising, and so forth.

"Commissions" expense includes both commissions paid to salesmen within the office and those split with other offices in cooperative sales. "Advertising expenses" embrace all advertising and public relations media, from classified ads to souvenirs and gifts. Expenses of occupancy are rent, heat, light, other utilities, janitor, depreciation, property taxes, and any other expense directly attributable to occupancy. "Salaries" include salaries paid to clerical and administrative workers but not salaries paid to owners. "Other business expenses" include telephone, supplies, entertainment, travel, and automobile expense. "Miscellaneous" expenses are those which are either classifiable into one of the above groups or the imbalance when total expenses are deducted from total income (thus, a compensating expense item).

Advertising expenditures are the most crucial item among all of the office expenses. All firms tend to spend an amount related to their gross earnings, usually between eight and 10 per cent, but not all of the firms capitalize on the sales produced by their advertising. For example, low-income firms typically are unable to account for expenditures that amount to as much as three per cent of their gross income, whereas among the large firms this miscellaneous expenditure is always watched closely and used effectively. Some offices attempt to raise their profit levels by reducing their clerical and secretarial assistance, thus cutting salary costs. This is often a foolish saving, because the salesmen often have to spend valuable sales time preparing their own correspondence or doing other office chores that could be performed by less expensive clerical personnel. In addition, clerical personnel can be used to keep the office open, to answer phone calls and greet visitors, and in other ways take advantage of the attention that is directed to the office as a result of the advertising expenditures. Because selling is the primary activity of real estate brokerage offices, successful real estate firms evaluate each expenditure in terms of its ability to produce more sales at lower costs. They are not concerned with the amount of the expenditure, but with its ability to increase the percentage of gross income that can be retained as net profit.

Sales Activities

The higher gross incomes of the more successful firms are due primarily to their greater home-sales volume. The low-income small firms averaged 34 home sales per year, with a few—8 per cent—even selling between 100 and 124 homes. On the other hand, the high-income small firms averaged 44 home sales per year and 11 per cent of them sold 100 or more homes per year. Low-income medium firms averaged 86 home sales per year, with 47 per cent selling 100 or more homes per year, and the high-income firms averaged annually 99 home sales and 42 per cent sold 100 or more homes per year. Large firms averaged 222 home sales per year, with 36 per cent selling 300 or more homes per year, 27 per cent selling between 200 and 299, 27 per cent selling between 100 and 199, and the remainder less than 100 homes per year.

Owners and Organization

The personal background of the owner of the firm apparently had no ascertainable impact on the success of the firm. In general, 40 per cent of the owners had previous real estate sales experience, 25 per cent had been in businesses allied to real estate—for example, insurance investments, building, mortgage financing, and appraising—and the remainder, 35 per cent, in miscellaneous business activities. Experience in real estate apparently preceded their assumption of managerial functions in their own firms, because the typical owners had been in the real estate business 9 years but had been heads of their firms only 6 years. Familiarity with the local community has also played a role in their business lives, because the typical owners had resided in their communities at least 12 years. Longer years with the firm and in real estate activities are more widespread in large firms than in small or medium-size firms, because the typical owner of a small or medium-size firm has been with his firm between 4 and 4.5 years while he has been with the large firm an average of 12.5 years. Owners of small and medium-size firms have averaged between 8 and 9 years in the real estate business, and owners of large firms, 13 years. Perhaps the most significant fact is that owners of small firms have been in their communities 12 years, owners of medium-size firms 9.5 years, but owners of large firms, on the average, 43 years.

There is less difference between owners in age or education, although, as might be expected, owners of large firms are older and somewhat better educated. The average owner has had 2 years of college, whereas the owner of the larger firms has usually had 4 years. The majority of the owners have taken at least one course in real estate, usually in some type of university extension program. The average age of all owners is 46 years; for owners of small firms, it is 40 years, and for owners of medium-size and large firms it is 48 years.

Real estate firms are usually assumed to be the elongated shadow of a single man, and this picture is generally true except that the incidence of single proprietorships decreases as the firm gets larger (Table 2–3). Multiple management apparently has minimal effect on the income structure, how-

Table 2-3

FORM OF OWNERSHIP OF SELECTED REAL ESTATE BROKERAGE OFFICES

Type of Firm	Per Cent in Each Category				
	Sole proprietor	*Partnership*	*Corporation*	*Total*	*Controlled by another firm*
Small:					
Low-income	90.0	10.0	0.0	100.0	10.0
High-income	79.0	16.0	5.0	100.0	6.0
All firms	85.0	13.0	2.0	100.0	8.0
Medium-size:					
Low-income	50.0	50.0	0.0	100.0	0.0
High-income	73.0	20.0	7.0	100.0	29.0
All firms	67.0	29.0	4.0	100.0	20.0
Large	44.0	9.0	47.0	100.0	20.0
Total, all offices	69.0	16.0	15.0	100.0	19.0

ever, because the number of partnerships or corporations among high-income small firms was double that of low-income small firms but equal to or only slightly more than half the number of single proprietorships among high-income as compared with low-income medium-size firms. Among large firms, 48 per cent were organized as corporations, 9 per cent as partnerships, and 43 per cent as sole proprietorships. However, among all firms, two-thirds were single proprietorships.

In a few instances, the real estate firm was actually controlled or owned by another firm. Most often this occurred when the parent organization was engaged in construction and had organized a brokerage office to handle sales. In some cases, the parent organization had become relatively inactive. In the older, larger firms, the parent organization was usually an investment company which was using the brokerage office to maintain market contacts and to handle the legal and mechanical details of acquiring, selling, and managing their investment properties. Control of brokerage offices by parent organizations was present in 8 per cent of the small offices, 28 per cent of the high-income medium-size offices, none of the low-income medium-size, and 35 per cent of the large offices.

Personnel Policies

The most important and recurring problem among all real estate brokerage firms is that of finding and keeping competent sales personnel. Among small real estate offices, annual turnover rates of 76 to 100 per cent are not uncommon, and smaller but significant rates are found in the medium-size and larger firms. The source of these and other personnel problems lies in the lack of knowledge or understanding among owners of basic modern personnel principles. The problem will not be solved until the owners develop well-rounded personnel programs which give proper consideration to selecting, hiring, training, and compensating their sales personnel.

Perhaps the most interesting aspect of the personnel practices of small real estate firms is their general unwillingness to pursue an active and aggressive program for securing good salesmen, even though this is their principal personnel problem. Over 50 per cent of the small firms obtain sales personnel from unsolicited applications received in the office. Another 20 per cent have salesmen referred to them, but only 29 per cent search out and invite promising prospects to join their sales forces. That such procedures are not particularly successful is indicated by the 63 per cent of the firms who had sales personnel leaving regularly before completing a full year of employment.

Hiring is rarely carried out as part of a long-range plan for expansion or in response to an orderly program of personnel replacement; rather, the most frequent reason given for choosing a particular person was that he "looked good." The owner usually reasons that the new man can occupy one of the extra desks, that phones are already in, and that the advertising program will not change; that therefore hiring the man costs nothing and he might turn out to be a very successful person. Variations of this type of reasoning were the bases for hiring in 75 per cent of the small firms; the remaining cases were the hiring of replacements for persons who had left.

Small firms showed considerable uncertainty as to whether some real estate experience was desirable for a new man. In fact, 46 per cent of the firms had refused employment to men with real estate business experience, usually because the men gave indications of having developed sales habits which would not fit in with a firm's methods of selling. However, the reasons cited most often for accepting a particular person were that he did have some sort of business experience and he "looked good."

Medium-size firms are even less active than the small firms in seeking out personnel, as is indicated by the fact that 70 per cent secure their personnel from persons who apply on their own. Two interpretations might be placed on this practice. Either these firms are less aggressive in their hiring practices, or they attract such a large number of applicants that they do not need an aggressive program. The indications were that the latter was more often the case. This is confirmed to some degree by the fact that 45 of the medium-size firms hired personnel who applied on their own initiative and were deemed qualified for employment.

The weakness of the sales personnel program in medium-size firms is underlined by the fact that 55 per cent of the personnel in the typical office left after one year or less of employment. Weakness in the sales training program rather than lack of selectivity in hiring appeared to be the real reason for the higher turnover, because the medium firms regularly refused two or three out of every four applicants. Thus, the attempt by the medium-size firm to give more attention to the sales personnel problem through the hiring of a sales manager is offset to a considerable degree by their failure to develop adequate sales training programs and effective personnel policies.

The personnel programs of large firms usually include at least parts of all of the important elements of a complete personnel program. The completeness of their programs is more often due to the effectiveness of the sales manager than to the efforts of the owner of the firm. However, unless the owner recognizes the need for such a program and supports the sales manager in its development, an effective program is not likely to be achieved. Unfortunately, even the best of these programs is usually rather rudimentary when compared with those used in other types of business.

Large firms do not follow aggressive programs of recruitment because their reputation and size are usually such that they receive a constant stream of applicants coming to the office. The pressures generated by this flow do not, however, stampede these firms into hiring anyone who applies and is qualified. In 91 per cent of the firms, salesmen are hired only after careful screening and only because of expansion or replacement needs.

Unfortunately, the large firms are no more accomplished than their small compatriots in their skill in keeping their experienced personnel. Forty-one per cent of personnel who leave have been with the firm only one year or more, and 59 per cent have been with the firm for less than one year. Large firms also show the same preferences for hiring experienced salesmen as are shown by the medium-size and small firms.

Training Sales Personnel. The training of real estate sales personnel assumes a variety of forms, ranging from occasional informal conversations between the salesman and the owner of the firm to carefully structured classes lasting for several weeks. Training is the one personnel function practiced by almost all offices. Usually, however, this training has little long-range effect on sales performance because of the degree to which attention is focused on sales techniques or gimmicks rather than on selling principles. The frequency and character of sales training programs are directly related to the size of the firms.

The management of real estate sales personnel is complicated by the fact that, for tax and other legal reasons, salesmen are treated as independent contractors. Many sales managers and owners of firms interpret this to mean that sales personnel can be held responsible only for meeting sales volume quotas, and that salesmen cannot be given close supervision or direction while doing this. Thus, their participation in sales training programs and their attendance at sales meetings cannot be required. Some firms attempt to overcome this situation by asking sales personnel to sign an employment contract which outlines, in a general way, what is expected of the personnel. However, the legal status of such arrangements has never been tested, and many owners feel that such a contract would not be enforceable. Other firms prepare sales policy manuals and ask new salesmen to read the manuals and sign a statement that they have read and do understand the sales policies of the firm. All but a small minority of firms use some variation of these two practices, and very few are content to leave the sales personnel free to follow their own selling methods.

Few small real estate firms care to assume the burden of training inexperienced sales personnel. Many do use sales meetings in lieu of training programs. Slightly more than one-half of the small firms usually have weekly meetings devoted to discussing the most urgent current sales problems and, occasionally, to reviewing basic selling techniques and procedures. A few of the firms which do not have sales meetings will ask newly hired persons to work with an older man, or the owner will "sit in" with these salespersons when they are ready to close a sale.

The policies of the sales meetings for small firms are designed primarily to meet the immediate needs of the sales staff. For example, 91 per cent of the firms use the meetings to discuss problems of listing and selling real estate, and 80 per cent of the firms sometimes discuss such topics as economic conditions and market trends. Almost three-fourths of the firms supplement their sales meetings with periodic "caravans" to newly listed properties. The firms defend their use of minimal training programs by citing the minimal interest of their sales personnel in any training topic that does not relate directly to current sales activities.

The practice by medium-size firms of hiring experienced sales personnel almost exclusively is reflected in their policies of minimal training for either newly hired or long-time sales personnel. Training programs rarely include formal training sessions. Instead, new personnel are usually required to study written company policies, to observe other sales personnel, and to work under the guidance of experienced and successful personnel. Approximately one-half of the firms feel that any type of sales training can be incorporated into regular sales meetings.

The firms that conduct training programs expect sales personnel to become productive very soon after the training program is completed. Almost one-half of the firms that give one month or less of sales training expect the trainees to be productive in six months. Firms with longer sales training programs expect the trainees to be productive in about one-half of this time.

Large firms are more insistent than small or medium-size firms that new men be given special training, usually for a period of three months, but in most cases they are willing to wait at least six months for the new men to become productive. Large firms evidently feel that training is good not only for the new salesman but also for the experienced men, because 76 per cent of them have training programs in which all salesmen must participate. The types of training used most frequently by these firms include not only formal training sessions, but also the regular sales meeting and apprenticeships under the more experienced and successful salespersons in the office.

Controlling Sales Personnel. The role of the salesperson as an independent contractor complicates the problems for all employing brokers, because, if more than very minimal controls are used, the employer has numerous legal and financial responsibilities to these persons. Employing brokers solve this problem in ways that reflect the size of their operations.

In the smallest firms, the salespersons receive little if any supervision and only minimal sales assistance; they are left reasonably free to set their own sales quotas. On the other hand, these persons receive little clerical or secretarial assistance and are usually expected to plan and prepare their own advertising copy. In the medium-size office, the salesmen are usually given sales quotas and are expected to conform to some general sales policies. They are not required to do any appreciable amount of clerical work or advertising copy preparation. In addition, they are usually required to spend certain days at the office in meeting and servicing clients.

Sales personnel are often closely controlled in large offices, but not sufficiently so as to threaten their status as independent contractors. However, almost every large firm has an extensive policy manual with which the sales personnel are expected to be intimately familiar. In addition, salesmen are expected to attend sales meetings regularly. Sales contests and bonus incentives are used frequently in place of sales quotas.

The threat of dismissal is often used in business as a control device; however, it is rarely mentioned and even less frequently used by real estate firms of any size. Flagrant misconduct will cause instant dismissal, but poor sales production rarely will. Apparently, these practices are followed because the majority of firms do not have a clear picture of what they expect from a salesperson. For example, sales managers agree that a top-producing salesman would normally be retained. They would usually dismiss him only if he proved to be a continuing disruptive influence on the remainder of the sales staff. Other managers would not dismiss a man of low sales productivity if he was dependable, if he showed a willingness to work hard, or if he had a wide acquaintance in the local community. Typically, a salesperson reaches his own decision about leaving the firm.

Compensating Sales Personnel. All real estate firms follow the practice of paying sales personnel on a commission basis. A few have experimented with salaries but have found them unsuccessful. Some firms pay department heads fixed salaries or, in the case of sales managers, a guaranteed amount plus a percentage of all commissions earned by the office. Theoretically, the commission arrangement should inspire salesmen to attempt to get higher prices for the properties they sell, and also to sell more properties. The simple-commission arrangement, however, has not been universally acceptable as an incentive device, and numerous variations have been developed by real estate offices.

The typical commission arrangement calls for payment to the salesman of 50 per cent of the total sales commission paid to the real estate office, plus an additional 10 per cent if the property he sold was listed by him. One of the striking differences between low-income firms of all sizes and high-income firms is the consistently higher commission percentages paid by the low-income firms. Apparently, these firms have found that these rates are the most effective means of retaining sales personnel, but their lower net incomes reflect the financial impact of this policy.

Low-income small firms have reported paying the sales personnel as high as 70 per cent of the total commissions collected by the office, whereas the highest rate reported by high-income firms was 65 per cent. Such pay scales, however, are unusual and normally represent rates paid only after a salesperson has produced a given volume of sales in a single year. Typical commission rates for all sizes of offices range between 50 and 60 per cent of the commission collected by the office.

The most common variation of the commission arrangement is to relate total percentage received by the sales force to total volume of sales. Under such arrangements, the salesperson would receive higher commission percentages as his annual volume increased. In the small firms, sales personnel may have to pay the company for unusual advertising incurred as a result of his activities. Many offices supplement commission arrangements with bonus payments, although there is no standard pattern for determining the amounts to be paid. Most often the amounts paid are related to the salesperson's total annual volume but are determined arbitrarily by the owner.

A few firms have been experimenting with compensation devices related to a salesperson's sales volume and his tenure with the firm. Very few of these firms have found that they can keep good sales personnel merely by increasing the commission percentage as the salesperson continues to stay with the firm. Many firms have been experimenting with some form of profit sharing, sometimes including distribution of stock shares tied in with annual sales quotas.

A principal reason why an adequate compensation formula has not been developed by the majority of the firms is the poor quality of their financial records. Very few are able to estimate accurately what they can afford to pay and, as a result, they pay what they think they need to pay to attract and retain quality sales personnel. Thereafter they continue to bargain on payments with the sales force, with the constant disruptions in sales activity which attend such bargaining sessions. The assumption that the commission rate is almost the only device that will solve their sales personnel problems is so prevalent among real estate offices that other phases of good personnel practice are regularly neglected. That this assumption is a shaky one is indicated by the number of firms with high commission-rate schedules and high turnover.

SELLING AND SUCCESSFUL REAL ESTATE BROKERAGE OPERATIONS

The distinction between selling ability and managerial ability is as important in real estate brokerage as it is in any other form of business operation. Either or both of these abilities will contribute to success in real estate brokerage but in different ways. The person with only sales ability and no interest in management should plan his activities so that he can concentrate on selling. If he starts his own office, he should keep it small so that he will avoid the managerial problems associated with the operations of a large office. If he wishes to increase the size of his business, he should be sure to secure effective managerial talent. If he does not wish to own his own firm, he will find good opportunities in almost any type of real estate organization.

A person with both sales and managerial ability can use both abilities effectively in any size of real estate organization. If he chooses to open his own office and increase its scale of operations, he must be prepared to spend less of his time on selling and more on managing. He can use his sales experience to excellent advantage in training his own sales managers. He cannot afford to do any but a very limited amount of selling. If he finds that he likes to manage and would prefer to do this rather than selling, he can find full room for his talents either in running his own firm or in working for a large real estate office.

Principles of Organization and Operation of Successful Firms

1. *Size.* The number of personnel in a real estate brokerage office is the most important determinant of the types of technical and managerial problems that the firm will face.
2. *Smallness.* A small firm has the advantages of flexibility in organization and operation and of the ability to capitalize quickly on new sales opportunities. It has the disadvantage of having to limit its activities primarily to selling.
3. *Largeness.* A large firm can offer more diversified services to its clients, engage in a variety of sales, financing, construction, and other related activities, and develop the capital needed to support new ventures. It cannot change the direction or scope of its activities easily and must carry a relatively heavy burden of overhead costs.
4. *Age.* A successful real estate brokerage firm must expect to spend from three to five years in becoming established and accepted in a community.
5. *Office appearance.* A successful, mature real estate brokerage office is characterized by the excellence of the location and the extensiveness and quality of the furnishings in its sales offices.

6. *Location.* The most successful real estate brokerage offices are usually located near other brokerage offices and adjacent to mortgage-lending institutions.
7. *Sales area.* The majority of property sales will be made at a distance not to exceed five miles from the sales office.
8. *Financial structure.* As a firm increases in size, more of its earnings will be derived from activities other than brokerage. Smaller firms achieve high levels of profits by giving equal attention to sales efforts and control of expenses.
9. *Expenses.* Sales commissions will be the largest expenses, but advertising will incur the most crucial expenses in all sizes of brokerage firms. The levels of these expenses will be determined by the level of these items in the local, competitive firms.
10. *Ownership.* The most successful firms are usually managed by owners who have had a strong background in real estate selling or fields related to it and who have lived for at least 10 years in the community in which they operate.
11. *Personnel.* Applying basic, modern personnel principles to the finding and retaining of sales personnel is the most crucial activity the owner of a real estate brokerage can perform.
12. *Hiring.* Each firm must create its own criteria against which it should evaluate each person who is being added to the sales personnel staff.
13. *Training.* A continuous program of training is needed for both new and experienced sales personnel.
14. *Independent contractor.* Although each salesperson should be free to develop his own selling methods, he should be required to meet general levels of sales performance and to conform to the selling policies of the office.
15. *Dismissal.* Threat of dismissal is the least effective and least used method of securing maximum sales performance.
16. *Compensation.* Sales personnel respond most enthusiastically to compensation in the form of commissions. Higher financial rewards are also the most effective means of encouraging increased sales efforts. Higher commission rates are not effective when the office is poorly managed.

CASE STUDIES

Each of the firms in the following case studies is new. One has had a very fine earning record but the other is on the brink of failure. After studying the researcher's reports, see if you can determine why one firm has done so well and the other so poorly. You do not have to accept the researcher's conclusions—in fact, they may be incorrect. Do you think that anything can be done to save the failing firm? If so, what would you recommend?

CASE 37-H: SUMMARY AND ANALYSIS

I. *Identification*

Age: 1½ years.
Classification: Small, High-Income.
Income: Net, approximately $3,500 in first year and $5,000 in the first six

months of second year. Ratio of net to gross, approximately .50 and .35, respectively.

Size: Owner and four salespeople. Daughter does some clerical work.

Owner: Has extensive selling background in real estate and insurance.

Location: In suburb of large city.

II. *Organization*

The firm is primarily engaged in residential brokerage, with hopes of expanding into commercial and industrial sales and leases. Owner has definite policies and is able to check the activities of the sales personnel, but realizes that they have a lot of experience and gives them a reasonable amount of freedom of movement. Communication within the firm is excellent, as the owner talks over matters of policy that affect salesmen and constantly solicits opinion of a broker who has 24 years of experience. Policies of firm are not too general, but more particular and specific.

III. *Staffing*

The primary weakness of this firm lies here. Turnover has been as high as 13 or 14 in a single year. Owner does not show foresight or ability in analyzing the potential of future salesmen. He states that he likes people who have need for work. Although this is O.K., he should not let it dominate his selection. He also makes the statement that inexperienced people are a luxury he cannot afford. What is needed in this firm is for the owner to analyze the qualifications of a salesman for his office and then look for these qualifications in applicants. He has hired people and then became dissatisfied with them in a short time and fired them. None of the salesmen left of their own accord. In matters dealing with commissions, the firm is very generous, with a 15 per cent listing commission and a 66 per cent maximum, and an incentive program favored by the salesmen which encourages sales and listings.

IV. *Direction*

Owner has a surprisingly enlightened view in that he purposely limits his activities of selling in favor of supervising the staff. He consciously tries to turn over deals to his staff and not to compete with them. When salesmen are not producing, he will sit down with one and try to analyze every aspect of the salesman's performance to find out what is wrong. Just how effective this is in view of his high turnover is hard to say, but, because this is a very young firm, the owner is probably learning a lot from this which should be of great help in the future. Also, the owner is a top salesman himself, and thus he may well be able to help others, but how good he is as a teacher is difficult to say because he admitted that he let one man go because he could not be trained properly. (This outcome may be due to the fact that the experienced brokers and salesmen that he hires are too set in their ways.) Other aspects of direction are good—sales meetings are held once or twice a week, with diversified subjects being discussed and the staff taking part in the presentation.

V. *Planning*

One important aspect of the owner is his ability to look ahead to the future and not think in terms of present gains. In the first year, the owner improved his position by moving to a central location where he could serve four areas instead of his previous one. He has plans for doubling his sales staff, and looks at his advertising in terms of the future by spending from 10 to 11 per cent of anticipated future sales. He knows how important it is to build recognition, and his advertising program is aimed in this direction and shows a great deal of imagination and flexibility. His expenses for advertising are closely controlled and budgeted one month in advance, and he keeps a tight control over all his expenditures, mainly because of his lack of beginning capital. Owner is also active in the community in his program of consciously building identification. On the debit side is the fact that he jumped into business with neither planning nor capital.

VI. *Control*

Control of personnel is also excellent and planned in this office. The firm uses the "board" system in a very effective manner, thus solving the problem of inequality of prospects and deals among the staff. The staff is encouraged to spend time out of the office, but they are always in the office when their name comes "up" on board. Control over activities is also insured by requiring a listing salesman to keep an up-to-date folder on each property. Also, the firm has had no commission disputes. Owner lets salesmen close deals, but he must approve every deal before it goes to escrow. It is believed that, even if salesmen close deals, owner is completely informed and aware of all aspects. Records in this firm are also good—owner keeps a printed, simplified bookkeeping system that requires him to keep up to date with expenditures but does not take a lot of his time. Over-all records of this firm are excellent and better than those of many older and larger firms. Another method that owner uses to control salesmen's activities is the standard that every salesman should make around $5,000 a year. Owner shows tendency to make salesmen stick closely to this requirement—probably because of his shaky financial condition; the extent to which this expectation has affected his turnover is difficult to say.

VII. *Strengths*

A. Great emphasis by firm upon service.
B. Unwillingness to take a property unless they are positive they can serve.
C. Imagination and initiative of owner. (Especially in advertising and telephone service.)
D. Direction, planning, and control function.

VIII. *Weaknesses*

A. Inability of owner to select personnel.
B. High turnover.
C. Lack of beginning capital.

CASE 56-K: SUMMARY AND ANALYSIS

I. *Identification*

Classification: Small, Low-Income.
Age: 2 years.
Income: (See income and expense statement).

Size: Owner and four salesmen, plus wife of owner doing part-time clerical work.
Owner: Thirty-two years of age, 10 years in real estate, one year of college, no real estate education.
Location: Good for area, but poor for drop-ins.

II. *Organization*

This firm can be rated about average in organization. Activity is divided between brokerage (80 per cent) and insurance (18 per cent). Firm appears to be too specialized in brokerage, devoting 90 per cent of its time to residential resales. Owner feels this is their best market because other firms in the area are devoting attention to new homes. Communication within firm is good, and firm has a policy book that spells out relationships and authority in an average manner.

III. *Planning*

Management should be rated weak in this function. Owner has no future changes planned and is highly concerned with present stabilization. Advertising is not planned in advance, is not planned to build the name of the firm, is just concerned with the present sale of properties, and is not checked for productivity. There are no budgets (advertising depends on the decision of salesmen solely). The present size of the firm was not planned. Owner does not seem aware of this function and of its importance, and, although it is important that the firm build up its present business, it should not overly emphasize this to the detriment of long-run growth. The answer may be due to the owner's emphasis on security and his lack of formal education. The interviewer mentions that the owner did not understand what he was driving at when he questioned him about proper allocation of time and expenditures. Where this firm does show some planning, is in its community relations and in its choice of location. Owner, probably because of his past experience, recognizes the value of referral business and is very active, along with his staff, in community activities. Whether the owner realizes the long-run value of these activities is not clear, but the 25 per cent referral figure attests to their present value. The owner also appeared to have chosen his present location carefully and consciously for the future aspects of the area, but nevertheless is not too happy with the present physical location because it is hard to see from the road.

IV. *Staffing*

The staffing problem seems to have been solved fairly well, as the salesmen appear to be very professional and ethical and the firm has had a relatively low turnover. However, the salesmen and the owner are not hustlers and do not go out after business actively in their effort to be professional, and, thus, they have not made much money. If this keeps up for very long, the turnover problem might reverse itself. Otherwise, the firm has a fairly typical commission schedule supplemented by a more imaginative bonus plan (undoubtedly copied). The owner seems to make a conscious effort to hire experienced and ethical salesmen and so far has been fairly successful, but it is worth mentioning that one man he took on recently was a known poor producer elsewhere and has been a poor producer with him.

V. *Direction*

Because this firm hires experienced salesmen primarily, there is no formal or informal training program, although the owner has given some personal unplanned training to one man who was experienced in insurance but not in real estate. He mentions in the interview that he looks upon himself as a sales manager: what he means by this is not too clear, as the interview ended before this was delved into. It is believed that 56-K does assist his salespeople now and then, but it must be remembered that he does some selling and plans to increase this activity. The firm does have a policy book and sales meetings twice a week, but it is important to note that neither are devoted to much training and are more concerned with defining situations and discussing present listings and sales. Interviewer mentions that owner is a former Air Force officer who has a strong personality and likes to be the boss.

VI. *Control*

This firm is very mediocre in controlling salesmen's activities, merchandise, and expenses. Prospects are distributed through the floor schedule and to those who listed properties, thus making for some inequality (not that $6,000 of the salesmen's commissions of $7,700 went to one man). Also, the owner does not keep a close check on the salesmen or know much about their activity (no analysis is made when they are not producing). He also does not know how much a salesman should bring in to pay his expenses. Advertising expenses are uncontrolled and it is left more or less to the salesmen to decide when they should advertise a specific property. Advertising material is not controlled either, because the salesmen write their own ads. The firm also has no sales kits, brochures, or records to show listing clients and customers, and no record of each property is kept. Otherwise, the firm's records are average, and some control is maintained over the staff by requiring them to be ethical, to join the real estate board, and to be professional;

INCOME AND EXPENSE STATEMENTS

	Year 1 19		Year 2 19	
	Amount	*As % of total gross*	*Amount*	*As % of Total gross*
Gross Income:				
Brokerage Commissions	$ 17,569	93.8%	$ 23,927	95.2%
Insurance Commissions	1,152	6.2	1,200	4.8
Total Gross Income	$ 18,721	100.0%	$ 25,127	100.0%
Expenses:				
Commissions	$ 7,750	41.0%	$ 14,214	57.0%
Advertising	1,771	9.5	1,871	7.5
Occupancy	2,460	13.1	1,744	6.9
Other	1,560	8.3	3,196	12.7
Total Expenses	$ 13,540	71.9%	$ 21,025	84.1%
Net Income Before Taxes	$ 5,181	28.1%	$ 4,102	15.9%

thus, there have been no cuts in the five per cent commission and no disputes with buyers or sellers. Owner realizes that, as a young firm, they should judge salesmen not on production only, but also on whether they are making an effort.

VII. *Strengths*

A. Emphasis on ethics—high business and professional standards.
B. Location in area where the firm has a good-sized market.
C. Emphasis on community activities.

VIII. *Weaknesses*

A. Lack of education of owner in management function and management ability.
B. Lack of diversification of firm in brokerage.
C. Lack of drive and enterprise on the part of owner and staff.
D. Extremely poor planning due to overemphasis on present and security.

Chapter 3

PLANNING FOR BROKERAGE OPERATIONS

Planning is probably the least understood and most poorly performed of all the managerial functions in typical real estate brokerage operations, if we accept *planning* as the function of "selecting the enterprise objectives and the policies, programs, and procedures for achieving them."[1] The lack of planning in the brokerage offices can be revealed by a simple enumeration of the various activities included under planning which these offices do not perform or which they perform inadequately: (1) long-range selection of objectives, (2) establishment of uniform business procedures, (3) creation of consistent business policies, (4) the use of budgeting—financial and other kinds, (5) the use of programs and interpretive planning in response to the actions of competitors, and (6) some minimal work in forecasting. The lack of planning in brokerage offices is particularly surprising in view of the great attention which has been paid in recent years to forecasting housing market trends. The tremendous real estate business potential which has been anticipated as a result of the expected economic and population growth has apparently not excited the interest of real estate brokerage executives sufficiently to encourage them to plan to realize the potentials of this growth.

THE PURPOSE OF PLANNING

The failure of brokerage-office management to plan in a comprehensive manner is due in a large measure to the typical manager's concept of his

---

[1] Harold Koontz and Cyril O'Donnell, *Principles of Management* (New York: McGraw-Hill Book Company, Inc., 1959), p. 35.

firm's place in the real estate market. For example, many feel that real estate brokerage offices are so numerous, the resulting competition so keen, and the housing-market movements so capricious that it is folly to attempt to anticipate business for more than one year ahead. They feel that, because they must respond to any significant efforts on the part of their competitors, and because the actions of competitors cannot be anticipated, any planning which they might do would quickly prove to be useless. Furthermore, they have observed the sudden and apparently unexplainable changes of fortunes which brokerage offices have undergone, and they feel that planning is rarely likely to affect the future course of their operations but may, indeed, take valuable time away from the consideration of necessary current programs and operations.

The failure of brokerage-office managers to use any but the most simple, short-range type of informal planning is also due to their feeling that any other type of planning is basically an exercise in "futility." In support of this contention, they point to the fact that all salespersons are basically independent contractors who cannot be required to meet any but the most general objectives of the firm. This means that salesmen can be given general sales quotas or objectives but cannot be told how to function in order to meet these quotas; that they cannot be disciplined if they fail to meet their quotas; and that they are free to leave if they do not subscribe to the manager's view on what are proper objectives or proper means of reaching these objectives. Managers tend to feel that the real estate markets' instability, particularly at the level with which they are most directly concerned, makes it impossible to cope with current market changes sufficiently, let alone to see future objectives, which would probably be unattainable.

Successful planning must, in a large measure, grow out of past performance, and, because real estate brokerage offices rarely know "where they have been," they do not know "where they want to go." It is a regrettable fact that few of the offices take advantage of basic market data which are available in almost all localities and which tell them whether construction permits and deed recordings are increasing or decreasing, whether there is a shift in price or a shift in the types of units being sold, and so forth. Instead, they are content to accept the idea that people create markets, and, as long as people are increasing in number, as has been true in parts of the country since 1946, then markets will continue to be good and probably not much different from what they have been in the past. The facts that there may be different kinds of persons and families coming into their markets now than was true in the past, that their offices may not have been selling in markets which take maximum advantage of this new "population" market, and that they may not be organized in ways which maximize their exploitation of these markets, apparently do not disturb their complacency with respect to successful planning.

Another reason for real estate managers' failure to engage in proper planning can be traced in large measure to the feeling that they cannot afford to take time for anything so nebulous when their immediate problems are so demanding. This attitude stems usually from their feeling that they must attend personally to all of the details of operating their offices. For example, they can see little reason or opportunity for planning when salesmen bring to them daily numerous problems of how to "write advertisements," "close deals," and "secure financing." They see several good properties that have been listed for sale in their offices remaining unsold, so they feel a personal responsibility to maximize on these profitable sales opportunities. They see new kinds of properties which might be sold if someone took only a "little time" to analyze them and present them to the "right" clients. It is not surprising, therefore, that, because they have never engaged in any serious planning, they can see no significant advantage to be gained from doing it now while immediate problems are so pressing.

EVIDENCES OF LACK OF PLANNING

Books on management argue that all firms engage in some form of planning, although much of it may be informal and so not easily identified as what it is.[2] They cite as an example the fact that a firm will sign a long-term lease for the premises which it occupies and yet deny that it is engaged in long-range planning. Certainly the willingness to agree to pay for the use of space over a long period of time suggests that someone in the firm is anticipating continued operations for at least the term of the lease. For this reason, minimal or no formal planning in real estate offices could mean that much of their planning is of the less easily recognized but perhaps equally important informal variety.

The first indication that some planning, even if it is ill-conceived, is being done by real estate brokerage offices is the answer given when the managers were asked where they intended to be in terms of sales and personnel in another three years. In almost all cases, they had a general notion of what they wanted even though the achievement of the projected goals would have meant a drastic change in their operations as compared with the levels at which they had been operating over the previous five years (Figure 3-1). Gross earnings from brokerage activities would have had to be increased sharply and be maintained at a constant high rate of year-to-year increases well in excess of anything achieved historically. In addition, the gross income from all sources, including brokerage, would have had to be increased. Meanwhile, net income would have been increasing at a rate much more compatible with previous trends. Obviously, the gross income figures repre-

---

[2] Koontz and O'Donnell, *op. cit.*, pp. 453–63.

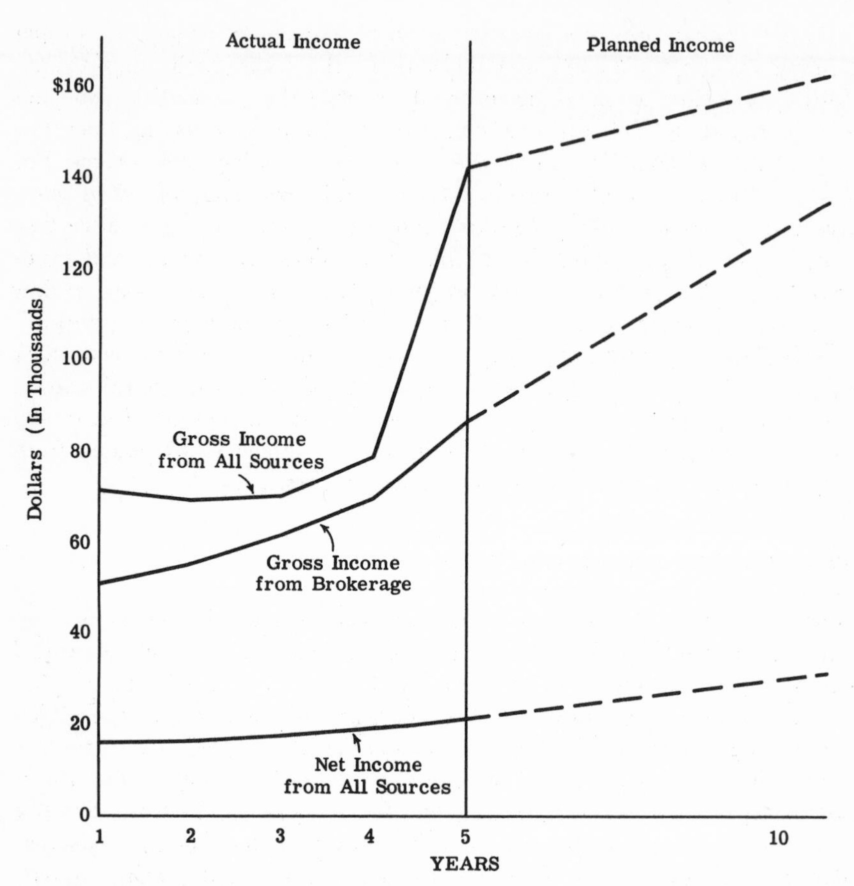

Figure 3-1. Actual and Planned Average Income and Net Profits, 80 Real Estate Brokerage Offices.

sented primarily "guesses," but the net income estimates were reasonably realistic. If the patterns they estimated were to be achieved, then the very large differences between gross and net income would suggest anticipation of sharply rising expenses and a much greater risk in operations. In any case, the estimates cannot be accepted as the kind which would be associated with knowledgeable, careful long-range planning.

The general lack of planning is evidenced further in contradictions which were shown in the manager's thinking about future operations. Almost 70 per cent of the managers said that the present size of their firm was satisfactory, but 43 per cent said they contemplated changing the firm's size, 25 per cent were contemplating changing the number of offices, 17 per cent expected to change their location, and 55 per cent were looking forward to changing the scope of activities included in their operations. Obviously, some difficulty would be experienced in reconciling these varying attitudes toward the future even if we can assume that satisfaction with the present is compatible with future changes in the present arrangements.

FIRST STEPS IN PLANNING

When planning is being carried on properly, it is necessary for the manager to translate planning objectives into operational policy. In many cases, particularly in small firms, the major part of this policy can be transmitted orally, although this may lead to some inconsistencies in applying the policies through misinterpretation and failure to remember exactly what previous policies had been. Normally, much of the manager's time can be freed from the oral transmission of policy, and the weaknesses of such a method can be overcome by preparing written policy statements. Written policy statements are particularly necessary in real estate brokerage because of the high turnover of personnel, the absorption of the manager in a variety of miscellaneous activities, and the number of constant public contacts made by the firm's members. Furthermore, the majority of executives agree that a written policy book is a very necessary business tool. Yet we find that only a small percentage of real estate brokerage firms have even this most important and easily prepared planning device.

This over-all lack of planning in the typical real estate brokerage offices stands in contrast to the conduct of successful firms which recognize that planning will not only help them overcome existing problems but also put them in a position to capitalize on future opportunities. If their assumptions are true and if planning is so effective in handling some of the most difficult problems which executives face, why is it avoided? In addition to the reasons which have already been given, we must also recognize that planning is difficult because it deals with intangibles. The real estate executive who is accustomed to dealing with the everyday realities of deposits, contracts, and commissions finds great difficulty in visualizing a future that he can forecast only inexactly and with great difficulty. Rather than engage in this disagreeable task, he avoids or minimizes it.

THE NEED FOR PLANNING

There can be no question about the fact that successful firms are those which anticipate problems and are prepared to solve them, and that many less successful firms have survived only because growth provided them with unusual opportunities to compensate for their mistakes. However, the keenness of competition has now reached the point where future growth will not permit any but the best-managed real estate brokerage offices to survive successfully—particularly when the current rates of licensing in real estate, as compared with the rate of population increase, suggest that in the foreseeable future the number of persons selling real estate will increase faster than the numbers of persons needing their services.

The future is exciting, but it will not support such a high proportion of licensed persons. In the next 40 years the population of the United States can be expected to increase at least 20 to 25 per cent, while average annual family income will double. Although it is difficult to forecast how many of these families will move into the cities, it seems reasonable to expect that at least 80 per cent of the entire population will be located in urban areas. In addition, the federal government has clearly committed itself to extensive programs of urban redevelopment, housing for the aged and low-income families, and continuation of some form of Federal Housing Administration loan insurance program. Basic trends in the mortgage markets indicate that mortage loans on reasonable interest terms will continue to be available. All in all, the picture is one of continued opportunities for a well-managed brokerage office which plans now to take advantage of this growth.

The poorly managed firm will have difficulty in surviving even though these prospects are bright because of current trends which are in marked contrast to those mentioned and which will gain in momentum over the next few years. Ever since real estate licensing was introduced, the license legislatures have been tightening licensing requirements. More restrictive entrance requirements will be developed and will include stiffer educational standards, more comprehensive and difficult examinations, and periodic renewal of licenses with requirements for evidences of maintenance of business proficiency. In addition, there is the likelihood that not only will entry conditions be more restrictive, but that better-educated personnel will continue to enter the business, particularly in the house-sales segment. Personal competition with the rising multiple-listing agencies will favor the creation and maintenance of many relatively small but well-managed brokerage offices.

The efforts of trade associations and individual realtors to improve the quality of services offered by real estate offices are also going to result in increasing stature for the real estate business and growing public recognition of its contributions to community growth. As a result, well-managed firms will seek to improve their competitive positions by offering the services of qualified experts in the fields of appraising, finance and investing, property management, community planning, development and redevelopment, property exchanges, and income tax law. At the present time, there are few real business giants in real estate, but the emergence of these firms suggests that there will be real estate firms in the near future which will offer under one roof the entire range of services needed in connection with the purchase, sale, and exchange of properties from the smallest to the largest.

IMPACT OF PLANNING ON REAL ESTATE BROKERAGE OPERATIONS

The rapidity with which change is occurring in real estate brokerage operations and the rate at which change is going to increase in the future suggest that success in real estate brokerage operations is going to occur only to those persons and firms that face up to the real choices of the future. Again it is important to emphasize that these future choices must be anticipated only by those who wish to be successful, that there is no reason to believe a policy of drifting and exploiting current opportunities will not permit the continued survival of too many unsuccessful firms. The chief difference between the future and the present will be that an increasingly smaller proportion of the total brokerage business will be done by these marginal firms.

The first type of future opportunity has already been hinted at in previous paragraphs: it is the chance to plan for a large-scale, integrated real estate business operation. In such a large firm, a high degree of effective executive ability will be needed and only a minimal amount of "technical" real estate ability. However, the most successful executives will undoubtedly be those who have served an apprenticeship in real estate brokerage. Executive ability will be a paramount requirement because of the range of specialists who will have to be assembled, trained and organized into an effective business unit. Because of the size of the operation there will be a need for substantial capital to pay for the kinds of business quarters, equipment and staff which will be needed to support the large scale of the operations. The value of such an organization will lie in its ability to capitalize on the most lucrative types of real estate transactions which the market warrants because such an organization can move easily from single-family home to apartment to office building to industrial property sales while offering the necessary supporting financing, appraising and property management services. The increased need for executive talent and capital will produce greater potential for loss if they are not secured but these businesses will also have greater potential for stability of earnings at higher levels.

The second type of future opportunity will probably be attractive to the majority of real estate brokers because it will consist of intense specialization in sales. This type of operations will appeal to the persons who like to focus on selling and who do not want to be burdened to any degree with other types of business problems. These persons will continue to form the smaller types of sales offices that direct their sales efforts to those segments of the single-family home market where a high volume of sales can be made with a minimum of sales effort. The most successful of these will consist of persons who have proven consistently that they can maintain regular sales efforts.

The home-sales type of brokerage office will face constant problems of maintaining a satisfactory sales force, so that the principal management problem will be that of finding, training, and compensating sales personnel in such a way that continuous sales results will be insured. The capital requirements of such business firms will be very modest compared with those of the larger organization mentioned, but the competition will be more severe because of the ease with which such firms can be created. Furthermore, because mortgage financing plays such a large role in the sale of the majority of homes, such a firm will have either to organize its own mortgage financing department or to develop reliable sources of funds to finance its sales.

SPECIALIZATION

A final potential for future real estate firms will be to specialize in various forms of business services needed in a specialized segment of the business. For example, such a firm might specialize in selling, financing, and managing industrial or commercial properties or other types of income-producing properties. Such a possibility would be attractive because it would require only slightly more capital than the home-sales firm, the competition would not be so keen because of the high degree of specialized technical knowledge required, and it would have more stature in the business community.

The latter two potentials might also be attractive to someone just entering the real estate field because it could be used as a means of getting a foothold in real estate and then building to the larger type of operation discussed as the first potential. There is also the very real possibility that some combination of these three potentials could be worked out and result in the emergence of a new type of real estate business operation which cannot now be envisioned. However, whatever potential there may be cannot be realized unless one of the potentials is selected as an objective and careful planning undertaken to reach that objective.

PLANNING PRINCIPLES AND PROCEDURES

If a future of successful real estate brokerage operations can be achieved only by planning, we must then ask if there are principles or procedures which can guide such planning. Unfortunately there is little, if anything, in current real estate business operations which can be used for this purpose; rather, we must turn to the general field of management. Fortunately, management theorists have already established that their work is generally applicable to any type of business operation, and specific applications can be easily made.

Planning, in its general sense, is a process of creating a basis for future business action which first determines what alternative lines of action are available and then selects the most favorable alternative among these lines of action. For example, the typical successful real estate brokerage office sets as its planning goal the achievement of a carefully defined level of profit and operational stability, and then it develops a balance between those factors which will help it reach this goal (Figure 3-2). In developing its plans, it

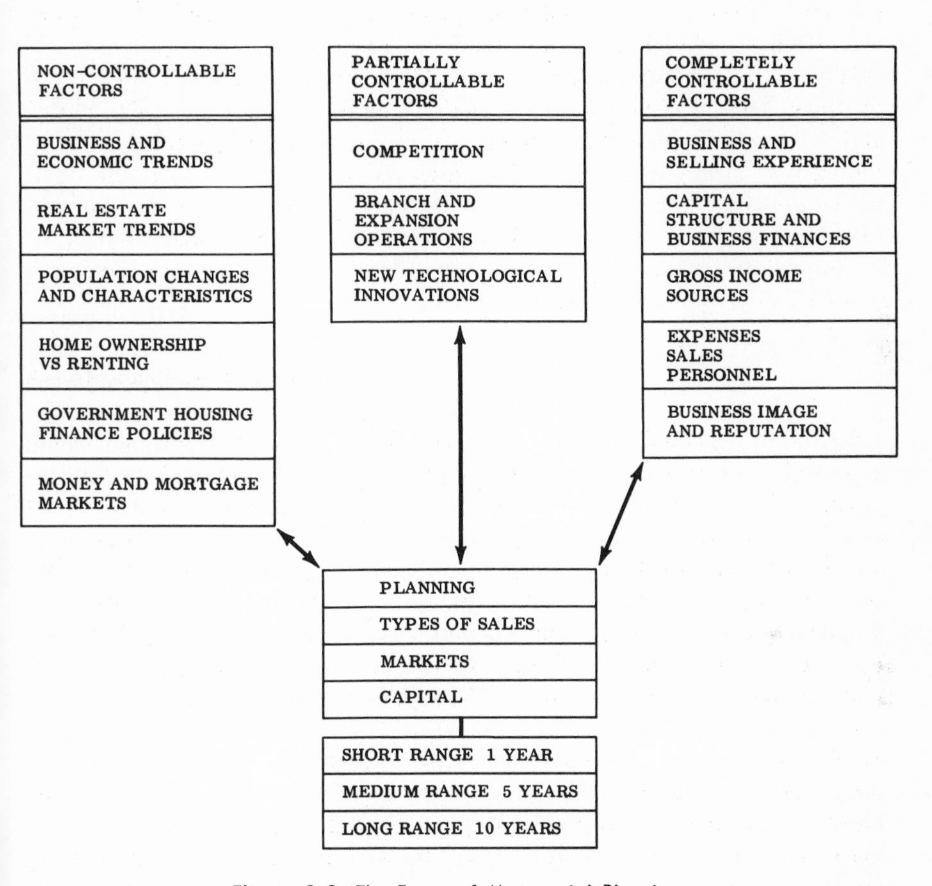

Figure 3-2. The Focus of Managerial Planning

considers those lines of action which must be undertaken in the immediate future—usually the next year—and those in the long-range future—usually in five to ten years. After doing this, it must then assess those factors—noncontrollable, partially controllable, and completely controllable—which affect its ability to accomplish its plan.

The pervasive attitude that little can be done by a real estate office to shape its future has a considerable amount of truth in it because there are many factors affecting the future development of a real estate business over which the executives in these businesses have little control.

Noncontrollable Factors

The noncontrollable factors include business and economic trends, real estate market movements, population changes in both numbers and composition, percentage of population preferring home ownership to renting, federal government housing and home-financing policies and progress, and changes in the rates of money—particularly, mortgage money. Information on these items is obtainable from many sources and can be easily charted and followed. Because these factors are noncontrollable, planning must be sufficiently comprehensive to include alternative courses of action and alternative policies, depending upon what happens to these factors. Fortunately, these factors generally do not have an immediate and direct impact on brokerage operations, so that there is usually a lead time before action must be taken in response to changes in them.

Partially Controllable Factors

Partially controllable factors include actions by competitors, new technological innovations, and expansion plans for the business. A method of "living with" competitors is to join with them in various types of trade association and professional organization activities. In every instance, all members of the successful firms are members of organized real estate groups. By coincidence or otherwise, the number of persons and firms that are financially the most successful is approximately equal to the number associated with organized real estate groups. This, of course, does not prove that joining organized real estate associations automatically guarantees success; however, an important advantage of associating with organized real estate groups is that, through their conferences, conventions, educational programs, and publications, these groups keep members informed on the latest technological innovations likely to affect the operations of real estate businesses. The same information might be obtained in other ways, but there are some economies of time and money in securing it from the trade associations.

Perhaps the most difficult factor to deal with in planning is that of deciding whether to expand, either through enlarging the existing office or by adding branches. The evidence in this field is complex, somewhat contradictory, and not completely clear, but there is enough of it to warrant a full discussion of this problem in a later chapter. The histories of the firms included in this research suggest that a real estate firm can assure its future most easily if it will analyze the share of the local market it serves and then plan to maintain or increase this share. If it fails to do this in an expanding market, it will soon find that it can survive only with difficulty. A first step in planning what share of the market is to be captured in the future is to gain full control over those factors which can be controlled.

The controllable factors are so important to planning that they are also discussed in detail in succeeding chapters. At this point it must be emphasized that they cannot be controlled until good records are kept and historical patterns of operations are developed. There are three plans which a brokerage firm must concentrate on: the types of markets in which it wishes to sell, the costs and accomplishments of its sales program, and the type of financial backing it needs in order to make its sales.

The importance of market analysis cannot be overemphasized, although it is often overlooked, because the majority of successful firms were found to be making the majority of their sales at distances of a maximum of three miles from their sales office. Obviously, the office cannot specialize in nor produce much of a sales volume in high-priced homes if it is located in an area of low-priced or modest homes. One of the most successful firms once tried to open an office in an area of high-priced homes but planned to use the same sales force and selling methods which had proven successful in its low-priced home sales. In a period of six months following the opening of this new office, the owners of the office lost several thousands of dollars, and they were eventually forced to sell the office to another brokerage firm.

Table 3–1

SAMPLE MARKET ANALYSIS

Part A

Market Analysis

Total Families in Area (approximately 1½-mile radius)	8,000
Average Family Income	$ 5,400
Average Persons per Family	3.4
Average Value of Homes	$ 13,100
Average Number of New Families Moving in Annually	750
Number of Real Estate Offices	55
Total Licensed Sales Personnel	210
Average Annual Number of Homes Sales	2,200

Part B

Using Market and Ratio Analyses

	Ratio	*Planning Goals*
Desired Net Income to Owner		$ 15,000
Required Gross Earnings	(Expenses equal 40% of gross income)	$ 37,500
Required Gross Sales	(Gross Earnings × 20 [5% Commission])	$ 750,000
Required Advertising Outlay	(9% of gross)	$ 3,075
Number of Homes to be Sold	$\left(\frac{\$ 750,000}{13,100}\right)$	57
Number of Sales Personnel Required	$\left(\frac{57}{10}\right)$	6

MARKET PLANNING

The steps in market analysis are suggested in Table 3-1 in a hypothetical example. The average sale which can be anticipated is $13,100, because this is the value of the typical home in the area, and house prices are not likely to vary greatly from this if this is a typical city neighborhood. The maximum sales which can be expected in such an area are 750, because this is the average number of families who move in and out of the area each year and there are 2,200 homes sold each year. However, there are 55 real estate offices and 210 persons licensed to sell real estate in this neighborhood; thus, the competition is keen. If an office is to maintain its share of the market, it must sell not less than 40 homes per year (2,200 divided by 55 firms), each of its sales personnel must sell not less than 10 homes per year (2,200 homes divided by 210 persons), and the total volume of sales must be not less than $524,000 annually (40 homes multiplied by $13,100, average value). Such sales could produce approximately $26,000 in annual gross income to the firm.

SHARE OF THE MARKET

Extra care in planning would have to be exerted in cases where the owner wished to earn more than his share of the market. In Table 3-1B is an example of an owner who wishes to earn a net income of $15,000, and who must, therefore, produce gross income of $37,500 annually. This would mean that he must increase his share of the market by $11,500, and that total sales must rise to $750,000 annually. In order to sell the 57 homes which would produce this income, he must have a sales force of six persons who can sell the minimum average for salespersons in that market.

"The principle of management by objectives is well accepted and widely used by American businessmen. In brokerage operations, properly stated objectives should provide answers to such questions as: How much should the firm sell? Should emphasis be placed on residential or nonresidential selling? How much will the market permit us to sell? What impact will competition have on our sales efforts? What should be the average property sales price? What dollar and number volume of sales should be planned for? Should the firm include some nonbrokerage activities such as mortgage financing, insurance, appraising, property management, construction, etc.? How much and what kinds of mortgage or other kinds of financing will be needed to support the sales plan? Further discussion of the role of objectives in planning is included in the next paragraphs."

THINKING IN TERMS OF OBJECTIVES

Any type of successful business organization is expected to have a number of objectives, of which the most desirable are considered to be those of good service and merchandise for buyers and sellers, profits on sales, satisfactory wages to employees, salaries to management, and a reasonable return on capital furnished by the owners of the business. Perhaps another should be added for the real estate industry: acceptance of responsibility for aiding the local community in achieving its land-use objectives. These general objectives cannot become meaningful, however, until they have been translated into a series of specific goals under each of the major headings.

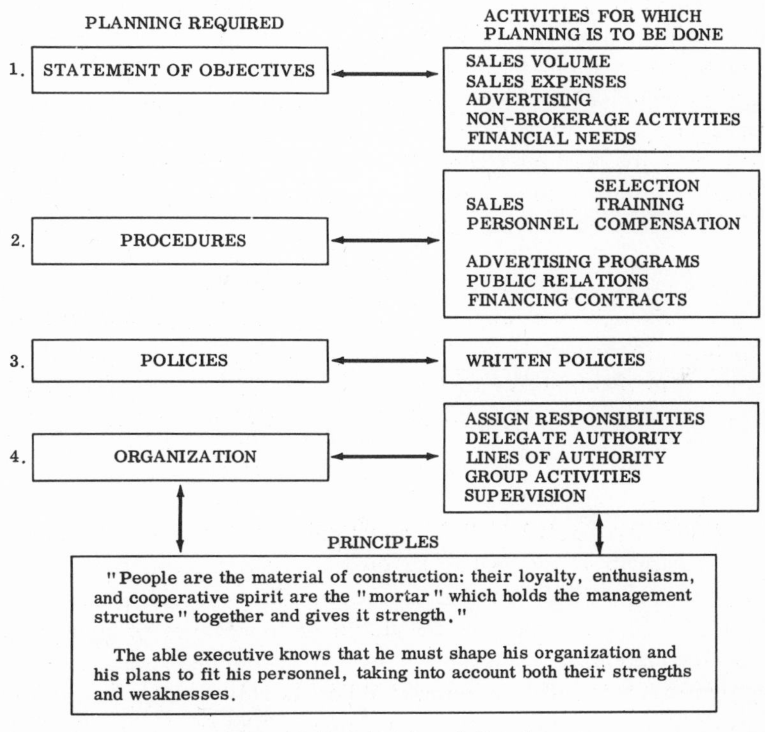

Figure 3-3. Principles of Planning

Good service and merchandise would require selectivity in listing, accompanied by a carefully planned advertising and sales program. Service would have to be given a major role in selling because of the very clear evidence that older, successful real estate brokerage offices have found that an increasing proportion of their business is derived from referrals from satisfied clients.

Specific Objectives

Planning objectives have little meaning until they are translated into specific terms that sales personnel can understand. To be most effective, these objectives should be based on past performance and modified to meet future goals. For example, Table 3-2 might be used to develop specific sales objectives if a firm did not have past-performance records on which to base its plans. The data in the table are derived from actual performance records of 89 brokerage offices and are averages. If the owner of a small office wanted his firm to produce $5,000 in net income, he might use the information in the table as a basis for his planning. If he did use it, he would plan for $19,000 gross income. Because this would probably be derived from home sales and his commission would probably average 5 per cent, he would have at least eight active, properly priced listings for each salesperson and would expect to have his sales force show 10 homes for each home they would sell. He should maintain a sales force of not less than four persons. The table reflects the differences in the selling problems of various types and sizes of firms. The more efficient firms can plan for more net income on a smaller volume of gross income than can the less efficient firms. Large firms need not depend exclusively on home sales to produce the net income they desire.

Table 3-3 lists some ratios that successful real estate brokerage firms have found useful in planning for specific sales goals. Not all of the ratios have to be used, but all of them should be experimented with until the most

Table 3–2

PLANNING GOALS FOR REAL ESTATE BROKERAGE FIRMS

Goals	Type of Firm				
	Small firm		*Medium firm*		*Large firm*
Net Income to the Firm (not including owner income)	$ 5,000	$15,000	$ 7,000	$20,000	$ 35,000
Gross Income	$19,000	$32,000	$35,000	$55,000	$190,000
Number of Homes to be Sold	34	44	86	99	122
Number of Homes to be Shown	340	220	430	287	240
Number of Active Listings per Salesperson	8	6	8	6	8
Number of Sales Personnel	4	3	6	6	15*

*A large firm has more sales personnel, but they would be selling homes and income properties, with homes representing only a portion of their total sales. In the smaller firms, the sales personnel would probably specialize in home sales.

SOURCE: Based on performances of 89 brokerage offices

effective are found. Table 3-2 will be useful in adapting these ratios to a particular firm, but all firms should base their goals on the ratios developed from their own operations. Table 3-2 is based on averages, and averages are usually applicable to only a portion of all real estate firms. The usefulness of the ratios in pinpointing weaknesses can be appreciated if they are used to solve the problem presented in Part B of Table 3-3. Once the weaknesses have been identified, see if you can then develop plans for overcoming these weaknesses.

The development of the ratios and the setting of the specific goals are clearly the responsibilities of the chief executive of each real estate office. These kinds of duties involving the setting of specific goals for all of the operations of the firm will become more numerous as the firm increases in size. Typically, such an executive will find that, as he diverts his attention away from personal selling efforts and into the field of specific planning, the net income of his firm will increase.

Table 3–3

RATIOS USED IN PLANNING SALES GOALS

Analysis for Planning

A. Important Ratios for Planning:
- (1) Number of listings obtained per sale made
- (2) Commissions paid as per cent of gross commissions earned
- (3) Commissions paid to other offices as per cent of commissions paid to own salesmen
- (4) Administrative expenses as per cent of total expenses
- (5) Advertising as per cent of sales expenses
- (6) Sales volume annually:
  - (a) Total dollar and number
  - (b) Total dollar and volume of own listings sold by other offices
  - (c) By each salesperson
  - (d) Average value of homes sold
- (7) Listings:
  - (a) Total obtained and number sold
  - (b) Obtained by each salesperson
  - (c) Per cent of listings sold to listings obtained for each salesperson

B. What is wrong with this firm?

Item of Analysis	YEAR 1	YEAR 2	YEAR 3
Number of listings per sale	5.2	12.1	19.6
Commissions paid as per cent of gross commissions earned	50%	55%	57%
Commissions paid to other offices as per cent of commissions paid to own salesmen	22%	16%	19%
Administrative expenses as per cent of total expenses	13.4%	11.7%	10%
Advertising as per cent of sales expenses	4.8%	8.5%	12.4%
Gross income	$ 100,980	$ 113,896	$ 131,928
Proprietor account	$ 20,052	$ 18,793	$ 18,112

Compensation Systems

The necessity for developing an adequate compensation system for employees, as well as for providing other forms of employee services, is one of the most evident but neglected needs in real estate brokerage offices. Again, the evidence is rather convincing that competent sales forces were developed in the majority of the successful real estate offices only after a careful development program extending over an average period of five years. This is true because there are few guidelines to be followed in developing workable sales policies, indoctrinating the sales force with these policies, and then training the salesmen so that they can carry out these policies. More importantly, too many real estate executives fail to see that sales management is a major executive responsibility and finally come to this realization only after numerous fumbling attempts to avoid it. Included in this responsibility is the necessity for knowing how much a salesman should be able to sell, how much he should be compensated, and what types of incentives will encourage him to maintain consistent sales efforts.

CAPITAL AND FINANCIAL PLANNING

One of the major attractions, and also one of the major pitfalls, of the real estate brokerage business is the apparent ease with which an office can be started with almost no capital. This assumption is an illusion which has led to an early demise of more new real estate firms than almost any other factor. The successful offices in the study found that at least three years were needed for establishing a firm business foothold in a community, and that five years were needed before really above-average sales and profit goals could be achieved. In any case, the first six to 12 months were usually ones in which the necessity for maintaining a high volume of advertising to attract business, the costs of training a sales force, office overhead, and numerous other expenses were sufficient to require substantial cash reserves of hundreds to thousands of dollars over any income which might be produced from any but the most unusual of sales records. Because the fees which an office can charge are set in the market place, it can produce profits needed for growth and expansion only by achieving a combination of high sales and careful control of expenses.

Capital is needed not only for office operations, but also for a variety of other purposes as the firm grows. One of the more lucrative activities of the larger firms is that of searching out sites with development potential, and then planning and executing the development. This type of activity requires large amounts of capital. The larger firms also often find it necessary to advance funds on a short-term basis in order to complete various types of transactions in which they are providing the brokerage services. Expansion by opening branch offices also creates a heavy capital drain for several months. There were at least two instances in which firms in the survey reported the costs of opening and sustaining branch offices until the offices could pay their way. In one instance, the estimate was that $9,000 was required; in the other, the amount was approximately $15,000.

The keenness of competition in real estate brokerage requires constant attention to means of differentiating the firm from its competitors. Perhaps the most effective means used by the most successful firms is that of setting as a basic objective to search constantly and to be always alert to providing services not currently being provided by their competitors, and to offer more effectively and efficiently the same services provided by competitors. In each case, the objective is to limit services to those which will provide the greatest competitive advantage while adding to the stature and business reputation of the firm. For example, some firms offer fast, correct escrow services, good secretarial services for sales follow-ups by the sales force, and accurate weekly records of financial and sales performance.

A BASIS FOR PLANNING

The many things which real estate offices fail to do in planning which cause them to be less successful can be summarized in a series of very pointed questions:

1. Do you really want to own and operate a business?

Too many offices are opened because of mistaken desires for prestige or because of unfounded ideas about easy profits, when the personal security needs of the persons would be better served if they were employees. Furthermore, there is very clear evidence that many very successful salesmen ruin their financial futures by attempting to become sales managers or the heads of brokerage offices. Some of the more important reasons given for wanting to own and operate a real estate brokerage office were: more income, independence of action, freedom to set personal time schedules, freedom from being "bossed" by others, more opportunities for following through on "personal" ideas, and dissatisfaction with present position and bosses. Some of these reasons are obviously very poor bases for deciding to open a new business.

2. Are you prepared to start a new business?

Do you have the capital for starting, or do you know how to borrow money wisely so that the repayment will not provide too heavy a burden for the new enterprise? Are you prepared to spend more time on management details, in working with people, in motivating them, and in directing them? Have you had sufficient training or experience in business to be able to handle all business details effectively? Do you know how to judge whether a business is being well run?

3. Have you picked a business location and decided what type of business fits that locations?

Because competition is such a major factor, a new business must be sure that it can survive in an area in the fact of the established competition. For this reason, a great deal of information needs to be accumulated about the area and the competition before a precise business location is selected. For example, some localities require that all business be transacted away from the office, whereas others require a large, attractive office equipped so that all activities can center in it.

4. Have you provided for business continuity?

Do you have a plan for developing the kinds of personnel who would be able to continue the business if you were forced to be away from the office for any period of time? One of the more successful businesses included in this study developed a $50,000 deficit because the owner-manager was forced to be away from the business a majority of one year. The owner had simply never taken the time to train his sales managers and staff to operate without his constant presence. One of the principal reasons given by many employees for leaving real estate offices is that they feel that the business would fail if the chief executive of the firm became ill or died. More importantly, giving attention to continuity provides the owner and his employees peace of mind in the knowledge that their future is reasonably assured if they become incapacitated. It also encourages well-qualified persons to work their way up in the firm and even, eventually, to become members of the firm instead of leaving to start their own businesses.

5. Have you anticipated what will be needed to survive and flourish in real estate brokerage, and have you prepared for it?

Successful management must be moving forward constantly to well-defined goals according to a thoughtfully designed plan which is sufficiently flexible to permit alternative lines of action as the realized future differs from the anticipated future.

6. What ratios should you develop as guides to future performance and as a means of judging present performance?

The tables and charts in this chapter will provide clues to the answers to this question.

7. What have you decided upon as short-, medium-, and long-term goals?

Are your goals compatible with the present performance of your firm and the capacities of your present staff? How much more capital will you need? What changes do you have to make now to reach those goals in the time allowed?

8. What is happening to business and real estate trends in the markets that you are serving that will affect your planning?

Principles of Planning

1. *Planning function.* In order to take maximum opportunity of real estate market trends, every real estate brokerage office must select its objectives, the policies needed to achieve these objectives, and the programs and procedures to be used to implement the policies.
2. *Planning basis.* The most successful planning grows out of continuing analyses of past performance and close attention to developing market trends.
3. *Planning for personnel.* The performance of independent salesmen is enhanced when they have been informed of and accept the long-range planning objectives of the firm.
4. *Planning flexibility.* Good planning permits a firm to take immediate advantage of unexpected changes in real estate markets while keeping the firm oriented toward its long-range potentials.
5. *Planning and policies.* Planning objectives are translated into operational policies by the development of a policy book that lists all policies that are to guide personnel in their daily activities.
6. *Planning need.* The full profit potential to be realized from population and economic trends in the next decades will be secured only by those firms who establish planning objectives that conform to these trends.
7. *Planning trends.* Future planning must provide for (a) large-scale operations; (b) integrated activities to include selling, appraising, financing, property management, construction, investment counseling, and insurance advising; (c) development of varieties of sales specialists; and (d) high degrees of specialization by selected firms as support to general real estate brokerage operations.
8. *Planning factors.* Planning must provide for changing operations to conform to uncontrollable factors, for joining with competitors in influencing partially controllable factors, and for developing good records as a basis for dominating controllable factors.
9. *Market planning.* A firm should base its sales objectives in the share of the market that it hopes to obtain in view of the competition it faces in that market.
10. *Competition.* A firm that intends to obtain more than its share of the local market must focus its planning on those objectives and policies that will

most effectively meet competition from adjacent firms by providing services that they do not or cannot provide.

11. *Planning goals.* After planning objectives have been determined, they must be translated into sales and financial goals for the personnel in the firm.
12. *Planning responsibility.* The statement of objectives and their translation into specific goals are the responsibility of the chief executive in the firm.
13. *Capital and financial planning.* The continued growth of a real estate brockerage office depends upon its ability to anticipate its needs for capital for expansion and for realizing profit opportunities in changing markets.

CASE STUDY

CASE 33-H: SUMMARY AND ANALYSIS

Identification

Classification: Small, High-Income.
Age: Started operations in 1946.
Type: Partnership, man and wife.

	1953	*1954*	*1955*	*1956*
Gross sales	$ 600,000	$ 800,000	$ 1.7 mil.	$ 1.7 mil
Gross income	$ 36,146	$ 48,000	$ 95,000	$ 95,000
Net income as a per cent of gross income	13%	21%	22%	21%

Organizational Size: One owner, two sales managers, ten full-time and three part-time salesmen.

The Problem

For many years the community in which this firm is located has been a small, rural community. The growth of the nearby metropolitan area, the extension of freeways, and the rapid increase in industrial activity have resulted in high rates of construction of both tract, or development, and custom-built homes. This office has always been one of the leading offices in the community and has had relatively little competition until recently. Now there are a number of offices offering effective competition. Four years ago, the owner attempted to expand operations and opened a branch office which failed. He then turned to property management and insurance sales as a means of increasing his income and of expanding his operations, and these have proven to be quite successful.

He has now outgrown his present office. Also, the downtown area on which he depends for business is shifting, so that he feels he must move. He cannot decide whether to secure another office of his present size, to secure a bigger office and expand in one office, or to open additional offices in the suburbs while retaining a central office either in his present or a new location.

Organization

The husband is a former company treasurer who was attracted to the real estate business after having had many dealings with local real estate offices in connection with his company's business. He was called to active duty in the army during World War II, and upon his return he opened this office in partnership with his wife. His wife was a practicing real estate broker at the time the office was opened.

The husband does all record-keeping, checks the paper work on all transactions before they are forwarded to the escrow company or the lender, prepares analyses of operations and reports for issuance to the sales force, and exercises some supervision over the sales force. His wife consults with him constantly on the goals the firm should achieve, engages in some selling, and assists in supervising the sales staff.

There are two sales manager, who do some selling, but not in direct competition with the sales force; handle all selection, training, and supervising of sales personnel, after first clearing all proposed actions with both partners; and prepare advertising copy, which is checked with the wife before being released to the newspapers.

There is one secretary-receptionist, who is supposed to furnish secretarial assistance to the sales force; however, the greater part of her time is taken up with handling the paper work in connection with the property-management department.

Activities

Total firm activity may be divided as follows: Brokerage (almost exclusively single-family homes), 80 per cent; leasing and property management, 10 per cent; insurance sales, 10 per cent. From time to time, the husband will do a limited amount of appraising.

The firm at present handles 100 properties for a fee of $5 each per month. These are almost all single-family homes, and the fee is essentially payment for rent collection, although the office will handle minor repairs. The partners justify the low fee on two bases: (1) these homes are good sources for listings and sales, (2) property management provides a continuing income which helps in paying office-occupancy expenses.

The insurance department has had an increasing amount of business from its inception. It deals chiefly with property insurance, although recently an increasing amount of business has been coming from the sale of mortgage insurance. A great deal of the business has also been derived from the property-management operations. The partners plan to build this business both as a source of continuing income and as a buffer or business hedge in periods of declining home sales.

The partners ascribe a large part of their brokerage sales to the reputation which they have built in the community of absolutely honest dealings. For instance, they will not take an overpriced listing; they refund deposits instantly (with the consent of the seller) if the buyer indicates some hesitancy after the signing of the deposit receipt; and they require each salesman to follow the code of ethics scrupulously. In analyzing their sales, they have found that a great majority of the firm's business has come from persons dropping in at the office; however, in the last two years, this has become increasingly less important as a source of business.

The present office is so small that only the secretary, the insurance man, the partners, and five salesmen can occupy the office at one time. When it is time to close a transaction, the owner lets the salesmen use his office.

Staffing

The owner has very definite attitudes and ideas on selecting and training salesmen. He will hire no one who has had tract sales experience, because he feels that these persons are either just order takers or accustomed to pressure selling. He is divided in his opinion as to the most successful kind of salesperson. He has hired older, experienced sales personnel, but says that most of them merely want to sit in the office and sell by phone.

The owner is now hiring promising young salesmen (25 years or older) who have had selling experience but not in real estate. They are hired for a six-months probationary period, during which they are given closely supervised training and opportunities to list and sell property. If they are not moderately successful at this, they are released at the end of the six months.

The partners have always been able to find both experienced and inexperienced salesmen to meet their needs. The salesmen invariably produce well, but only a few of them stay with the office for any period of time.

After training and indoctrination, each salesman is given a policy book which sets forth in detail his responsibilities and functions. The owner insists that salesmen follow this book closely, plan their time carefully, and keep themselves occupied in a productive way during their working day. Sales meetings from time to time are used to review the policy book and the way in which salesmen are using their time. Those not producing are asked to report their activities, and the others then make suggestions of ways in which the former might improve themselves in the coming weeks.

The commission split with the sales force is similar to that of all other offices in the area. The owner pays 50 per cent of the commission received by the office for a sale and an additional 10 per cent if the salesman sells his own listing. He does not pay if the listing is that of another salesman

All disputes among the staff are first referred to the policy book. If there is no policy to cover the situation, the salesmen are expected to settle the dispute among themselves: the owner will not arbitrate or appoint an arbitration committee.

The Competition

A large number of offices have entered the area to engage in tract sales and then have remained because of the rapid growth of the community. The area is now predominantly one of houses in the $11,000 to $13,000 price range, where formerly the majority of the homes were older, larger, and in the price range of $15,000 to $20,000.

The homeowners are typically industrial workers who work all over the metropolitan area but live in this community because of the attractive prices, the climate, and the network of nearby through roads leading to all of the principal areas of employment.

Many of the new real estate offices are large, offer extensive training programs, and engage in various types of mass selling, including some of the subtler forms of "pressure" selling. A real estate board was recently organized, but its membership and direction are essentially in the hands of the newcomers. Almost all of the offices have picked locations on principal business streets and have developed new, modern-looking quarters.

Planning and Direction

The man insists that he is a manager and not a salesman, and he is very conscientious about carrying out his full managerial responsibilities. Coupled with this, he has a very high standard of ethics with which he will brook no compromises. He repeats constantly that he "would forgo profits and have constantly done so rather than lower his ethical standards."

He has a very complete and thorough training program which is conducted by means of monthly meetings. The policy book and various texts are used and discussed. Office rules, proper conduct, and correct procedures are all included as part of the training.

The owner has engaged in little forward planning because he feels that this is not possible in the real estate business. For instance, he never plans his advertising in advance, but merely tries to anticipate the number of calls he should receive, considers how much he has spent previously on the same type of property, and then advertises accordingly. He feels that the amount and kind of advertising to be done should be tailored to the desires of the owner rather than to the market. He has used radio, television, giveaways, and classified ads. He feels that classified ads are a "necessary evil."

He has never analyzed his clients to determine where they come from, why they buy, and so forth. He feels that increased clientele come from improved economic conditions and high points in the real estate cycle.

He has not planned for the future, although he now feels that he should expand. He feels that real estate runs in cycles and that, by the time he would expand, the markets would collapse and he would be back where he started. He points to the declining business and slow growth he is now experiencing as an example. He is both pessimistic and conservative and would like to expand in such a way that he can have a depth of activities which will guarantee income in spite of poor market or business conditions.

Control

The records which the owner keeps are very much above average. He has detailed cost analyses of all phases of his operations except for advertising. He has a particularly elaborate set of records on his personnel and uses the records to check on performance constantly. He insists that all salesmen keep records of their activities and review them for places where they might spend their time more

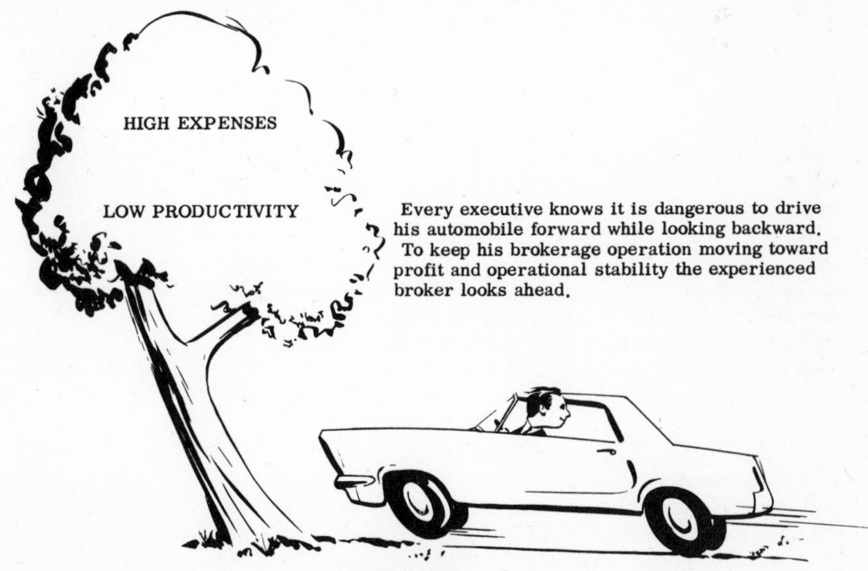

Figure 3-4.

profitably. He recommends that salesmen work on only a few properties at a time.

He requires all salesmen licensed as brokers to put their broker's license on "ice," and he will not permit them to buy or sell for their own account.

Currently the owner is worried about his listings because of the increasing difficulty of getting any at all. He insists that the men canvass their area constantly and report to him on their activities and problems.

Problem

In the light of the dicussion of planning in this chapter, evaluate the problems of the executive in this case and indicate what you would do if you were in his place.

Chapter 4

ORGANIZING BROKERAGE OPERATIONS

The organizing function is probably the least understood and most neglected managerial function in the typical real estate office. Real estate executives usually feel that their operations are on such a small scale and that so many of their sales personnel are "independent contractors" that only minimal, if any, consideration needs to be given to organizing their operations. These executives fail to realize that organizing must be undertaken whenever two or more persons are expected to work toward a common objective. "Organizing" is simply the process of insuring that all jobs that must be performed to keep the real estate brokerage office open and operating are assigned, and that the persons to whom they are assigned understand what is to be done and have the authority to complete the tasks.

Much of the waste in real estate brokerage operations can be traced to poor organization. The failure of many potentially effective salespersons can be traced to their early association with a poorly organized office. However, even though a brokerage office should be organized, it need not be organized in a particular manner or form. A small partnership type of office, for example, may be organized in an informal manner that is not possible in the large, impersonal type of brokerage office. This chapter explores the implications of different methods of organizing a real estate brokerage office.

THE IMPORTANCE OF ORGANIZATION CONTINUITY

The most common but least stable type of real estate brokerage organization is the one- or two-man partnership. These offices are sometimes organized for the administrative convenience of the partners. Any staff that is hired is given little training or supervision and is expected to produce only enough sales to pay the costs of operating the office. This type of office is exclusively a sales organization; all other functions are subordinated to the sales function, and each person is given maximum freedom in his selling activities. These offices are sufficiently flexible in their organization to permit them to move quickly to take advantage of any unusual profit opportunities.

The small partnership is attractive to many salespersons because it coincides with their assumption concerning freedom to sell with minimal supervision and no administrative duties. Such an office does have serious shortcomings, because the weak, the new, even the average salespersons have little chance to improve their sales abilities. The partners have little time for sales training and only minimal time to assist sales personnel in difficult selling situations. The best salesmen rarely stay with such an office, because they use it as an operating base while learning about the local real estate markets and building sufficient capital to open their own offices.

Even the partners may view their association as relatively tentative and may plan to move to another location or associate with different persons at a later date when market changes show that such a change is necessary.

Another important and often overlooked disadvantage of a small partnership is the degree to which the continuity of operations depends upon only one of the partners. Even when there are several partners in an office, one partner may have full responsibility for details of office-keeping and operating. If this key partner is absent for any reason, the sales force soon finds that it does not have proper support in advertising, securing loans, closing escrows, and similar tasks. Unfortunately few firms recognize this potential danger and make provision for continuity of operations if one or more of the partners is incapacitated.

On the other hand, the adventuresome spirit that characterizes many real estate salespersons leads them to conclude that they will trade the threat of operational instability for the freedom of a small office. New, inexperienced salespersons, those who specialize in certain types of selling, and those who expect strong escrow, financing, and other support in their selling typically gravitate to the larger offices.

The large office has two major advantages. It offers a continuous program of sales training so that all salespersons can improve their selling abilities. Second, it offers a variety of supporting services that improve the efficiency of even the best salespersons. The sales manager is available to assist in closing difficult or unusual sales transactions. Financing contacts are already established and a variety of financing plans can be offered to prospective clients. Investment counseling, income tax advice, property management, and a host of other expert services are usually available to assist prospective investors.

A large office presents an unusual opportunity to salespersons who wish to specialize. It is unfortunate but true that the majority of persons entering real estate selling are aware only of the opportunities for selling single-family homes. The specialized and lucrative sales opportunities that exist in industrial, office, store, and apartment property sales are never called to their attention, even though their temperaments. education, and background might have prepared them for these types of selling.

A final and very significant advantage of the large office is the continuity of its business life. The incapacitation or demise of key persons does little to its daily operations. This assurance of continuous life permits the firm to develop long-range profit goals which permit it to retain the best sales personnel by offering them profit-sharing opportunities.

The high quality of executive talent that is becoming increasingly available to large real estate offices is an important asset that is often minimized. These executives are able to free the salespersons so that they can concentrate on selling and not be burdened with excessive administrative duties. For example, the preparation of classified advertising is left to a specialist. Correspondence is prepared by competent secretarial assistance operating under the direction of an experienced office manager. New advertising media, such as television, are provided as soon as they are proven to be effective.

TYPES OF SALES OPPORTUNITIES IN BROKERAGE OFFICES

The majority of persons entering the real estate business wish to sell. Whether such a goal can be realized depends upon the type of firm with which the person associates. (Table 4–1.) Almost two-thirds of the small firms and over four-fifths of the medium-size firms engage in selling during between 76 and 100 per cent of their business time. Few of these firms devote less than 51 per cent of their time to nonselling activities. By contrast, large firms spend up to one-half of their time in nonselling activities.

Although all offices experiment from time to time with various kinds of nonbrokerage activities, few find these activities worth continuing for any length of time. A small office can sometimes develop some profit from leasing, property management, loan negotiation, and insurance sales. Medium-size firms sometimes also include escrow closing and real estate investing for their own accounts. Large offices show a different pattern, placing heavy emphasis on building, developing, private investing, and appraising.

Table 4–1

DISTRIBUTION OF BUSINESS ACTIVITIES
OF SELECTED REAL ESTATE BROKERAGE FIRMS

Activity	Percentage of Total Business Time Spent in Activity[a]														
	100—76%			75—51%			50—26%			25—1%			0%		
	Size of Firm and Per Cent in Category[b]														
	S	M	L	S	M	L	S	M	L	S	M	L	S	M	L
Brokerage	61	81	44	24	5	13	8	14	22	7		21			
Leasing							3		4	70	48	74	27	52	22
Property Management										46	62	65	54	38	35
Appraising										23	15	30	77	85	70
Land Development				3			3			15	10	22	79	90	78
Loan Negotiation							3			36	35	52	61	65	48
Insurance							3		13	38	60	61	59	40	26
Building				3						18	6	10	79	94	90
Operation for Own Account										18	24	22	82	76	78
Escrow										8	29	14	92	71	86
Other										11	10	9	89	90	91

[a]Percentage of time spent in the activity at some time during the operations of the firm
[b]S=small ; M=medium ; L=large

THE FORMAL AND INFORMAL ORGANIZATION

Perhaps the least stable but most challenging real estate brokerage office is one that is just beginning to grow. This firm can attract experienced, aggressive salespersons by offering them maximum personal profit opportunities associated with small offices and the supporting services of the larger, well-established offices. Unfortunately, this type of firm has the dimmest prospects for continuous business life. Because it is in a transitional stage from a small to a large size, its executives often fail to realize the necessity for their giving more attention to managing rather than selling problems. They can remedy this situation by taking an alert, capable salesperson and assigning to him the duties of a sales manager, personnel manager, sales trainer, or administrative executive.

Formal organization calls for the creation of job titles, written duty assignments, and job descriptions, among other things, but these are rarely found in real estate offices. Without these types of formal organizational tools, job applicants may be given widely divergent statements of their duties. Lack of organization can often produce an informal type of organization which leads to conflict and friction among associates in the firm. Particularly is this so if each person feels free to interpret his duties and responsibilities as he sees fit. Formal organization of a business firm may not improve its chances for success, but it does prevent the creation of an informal organization that will hasten its demise.

A method of creating job descriptions as a part of initiating a sales organization is discussed in the next chapter. The various ways in which the sales personnel may be organized are presented in the following paragraphs.

The preference among real estate offices for informal, loosely defined job responsibilities and authority does promote individual initiative and provide maximum freedom for individual operations. This type of organization, however, leaves the firm without properly defined goals and creates a constant state of "organizational crisis." Many small things that should be done may be overlooked. Correspondence may not be answered. Advertising may have to be prepared on a last-minute-rush basis. Phone calls may not be reported and clients may be ignored. As much time may be spent by all members of the firm in correcting administrative errors as is spent in moving ahead to new work.

Lack of organization is probably a chief explanation of the 50- to 60-hour workweeks that the majority of real estate salespersons find necessary. There is no necessary relationship between high income and long hours, but there is between organization and sales productivity. Proper delegation of duties relieves the sales personnel from all except minimal administrative duties so that they can focus on selling. In a well-organized firm, salespersons earn above-average commissions while limiting their activities to not more than 40 to 46 hours per week.

Effective, formal organization requires:

(1) A statement of business objectives
(2) A listing of jobs to be performed, in order that the objectives may be accomplished
(3) Creation of guiding rules of action
(4) Descriptions of the kinds of persons needed to fill the jobs
(5) Selecting and assigning persons to the jobs
(6) Providing a follow-up to test the effectiveness of the organization in meeting the objectives of the firm.

One type of formal organizational chart that is adaptable to almost any kind of real estate brokerage operation is show in Figure 4–1.

THE ORGANIZATIONAL CHART

Large business organizations use charts to indicate the types of jobs that must be performed and the persons who are to perform them. These charts are used only infrequently in small firms, because jobs and job responsibilities typically change as the personnel changes. Figure 4–1 can be useful to the owner of a brokerage firm that is in the process of growth. The chart indi-

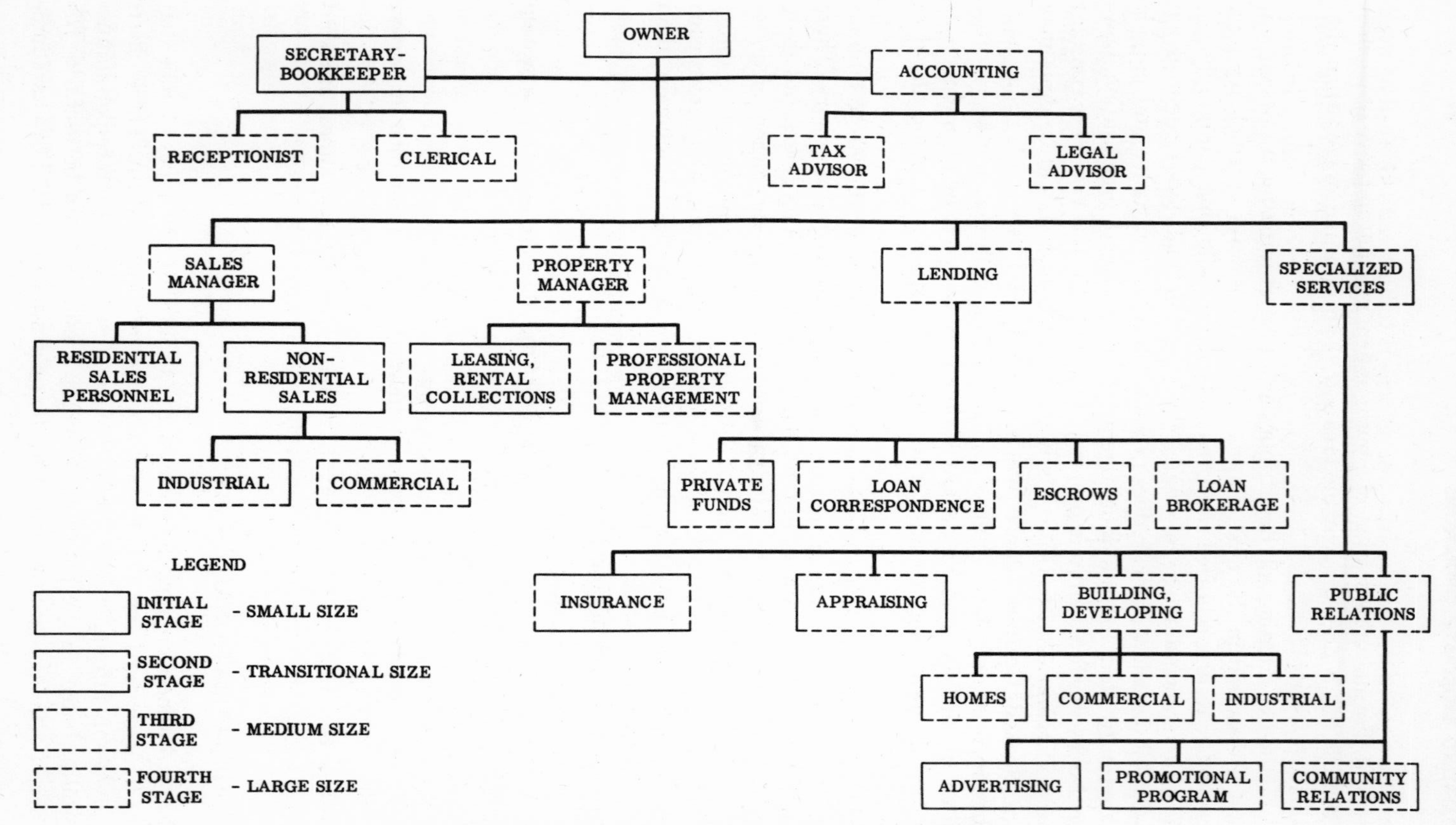

Figure 4-1. Expansion in a Typical Real Estate Brokerage Firm.

cates those positions that need to be provided for first and those that need not be added until the firm has reached a rather large scale of operations.

In the smallest firm, the owner needs salespersons, residential first and nonresidential as sales increase, and someone to prepare the advertising. In order to insure that the office is always open during business hours and that all business calls will be answered, the owner may add a secretary-bookkeeper who will also prepare the preliminary advertising copy. Some owners feel that an efficient secretary-bookkeeper is the most important employee in the organization and pay above-average salaries to secure such persons. Other owners are content to hire a clerical-type secretary who has no responsibilities except to prepare correspondence and answer the telephone. In the latter case, the owner keeps his own records and prepares all advertising copy.

As the firm grows, leasing and rental-collection services may be added, because fees from these services are sometimes sufficient to pay all costs of operating the office. More importantly, such services are an important adjunct to selling income properties to persons who do not wish to manage the properties, and managing properties often provides important leads to future home buyers. If insurance services are added, they are usually provided by an insurance agent who shares the use of the office and pays part of the office expenses. At this point, the owner of the firm will begin to give serious thought to increasing the size of his operations. For this reason, some owners add a salesperson who is also experienced in sales promotions, or they may hire the services of a sales promotional firm or expert to develop a continuous program of advertising in all types of media.

The third stage of growth is the most critical, because more emphasis must be placed on nonselling activities. For this reason, the owner may hire one or more sales managers, if he has not already done so. He should also add a mortgage-lending expert and allow him to organize a complete mortgage-lending and financial-counseling service. These activities can be supported later by legal and tax-advising services, because proper control of financing and taxes is the key to successful modern-day real estate investing.

Various types of specialized services may be added, depending upon the owner's interests and his ability to secure capable persons to perform the functions. In many successful firms, the owner of the firm will take full charge of the community relations program and devote a large part of his energies to developing a strong image for his firm in the local community. In this capacity, the owner will be spending large portions of his time attending conventions, educational meetings, service-club meetings, and similar kinds of gatherings.

The fourth stage is usually reached only after the firm has been in a community many years—usually, at least 10 or 15. If the firm is in a growth area, the purchase of raw land and the development of subdivisions or the building of custom homes will usually become an important activity. Specialization in the construction of particular types of properties may complement specialization in the sales department. By now the firm will be organized in departments, each headed by an experienced, competent specialist. Typically, the heads of the departments will form an executive committee that meets regularly with the president-owner of the firm to plan the firm's activities and to check on the progress of adopted plans.

A formal organizational chart is useful not only for plotting the growth of a firm, but also as a reminder of the jobs that must be performed. Sometimes one person may be occupying, or carrying out the responsibilities of, several positions.

THE SALES ORGANIZATION

Whatever the formal or informal organization of the firm, the sales staffs may be organized in a variety of ways, which tend to differ with the types of markets served and the preferences of the owners of the firm. Again, the typical salesperson may fail to realize that there is this variety and that he should try each of them until he finds the one in which he fits, because each has slightly different advantages. The key to selecting the proper organization lies in developing a specialty of some type.

Territorial

When the types of properties and land uses within a two- or three-mile radius (the usual limits of a firm's market area) of the firm's office are relatively homogeneous, each salesperson may be given a particular section within the market area as his exclusive jurisdiction. Within this jurisdiction, he is expected to be thoroughly familiar with all of the various properties and to have priority in all listing and selling activities. In some instances, it may even be necessary for other salespersons to clear all activities relating to that jurisdiction with him and to share with him any commission earned. In the usual case, he is merely expected to maintain a continuous canvass of the area to secure listings and buyers and to be ready to help the other sales personnel if they have problems relating to the jurisdiction.

In high-volume, modest-priced, homogeneous markets, the territorial-jurisdiction assignment is workable; however, it does keep a salesperson from building a wide clientele and from broadening his experience in a variety of sales situations. In time it also creates jurisdictional problems, because sales personnel will have a tendency to look to the other person's territory when his own territory is not producing the business it should. More importantly, a client tends to prefer to deal with a particular salesperson and is not pleased when he is referred to someone else because his property or problem lies in another salesperson's jurisdiction.

If the territorial method is used judiciously, it can be an important auxiliary source of business for a salesperson when he is not otherwise engaged. During his slack moments, he can make an effort to become thoroughly familiar with an area, develop firm friendships with key persons in the area, and, by consistent canvassing of the area, pick up a variety of sales and listing leads which would not come to him unless he pursued them. Even though he may not be given exclusive rights to the area, he will soon find the rest of the sales staff deferring to him as an expert when they have clients in the area and want to produce quick results.

Property Specialists

In market areas in which a variety of property types and land uses exist, the sales staff may be assigned to dealing with only particular types of properties. In the case of industrial and commercial properties, this plan is particularly effective because these types of properties often require specialized technical knowledge on the part of the salesperson if he is to sell them efficiently. Load limits on floors, freight rates, lease provisions, and percentage shares to be charged to tenants are just a few of the many types of technical knowledge which are needed. On the other hand, persuasion is important even in this type of property transaction, and a persuasive salesman could join forces with the technical expert in making a sale. Unfortunately, too many salespersons do not recognize the technical pitfalls connected with such sales, and they try to override these considerations by persuasion, with the result that they have a miserable sales record at the end of the year.

The new salesperson, the person with limited business experience or education, and the person who cannot easily deal with mathematics and technical materials will do the best selling when he limits himself to selling residential properties. The single-family home, for instance, is often bought on emotion or amenity appeal, which an experienced but technically unprepared salesperson soon learns to identify and to focus on a particular home. Such a salesperson soon learns how to match properties and buyers carefully so that he has a constantly increasing body of satisfied clients to help him produce more sales. The ease with which an experienced salesperson sells a home is usually highly deceptive to the newcomer, so that when he tries the same sales methods without understanding how methods must be matched to the client, and fails, he immediately decides that he should try to sell some other type of property.

Office Calls and Referrals

Many offices use a mixed system of encouraging each salesperson to find his own clients while at the same time requiring him to spend a given number of hours each week acting as an office receptionist, with the incentive that he has first priority on any business arising from the office contacts he makes. Obviously, he cannot have this priority when an office visitor asks for another salesperson by name. This system encourages the sales staff to visit the office regularly, and, when it is supported by an advertising program which brings clients to the office, gives each salesperson an excellent opportunity to meet a variety of clients with a minimum of effort on his part.

This method does have a number of serious shortcomings from the view of both the firm and the salesperson when it is not handled properly. There are, for example, certain hours during which the majority of calls will be made, so that anyone assigned to these hours may have more than he can do and anyone assigned to the off-hours may have almost no opportunity to produce business. More important, the person on duty will be tempted to keep for himself those items of business which promise to produce the most commission even though he may not be competent nor have the time to handle the transaction properly. His ineptness in dealing with such business may not only lose a client for himself but may do damage to the reputation of his firm.

From the salesperson's viewpoint, the office-call method is effective only when the hours are rotated so that each person has an opportunity to be present during the best hours; when each salesperson is free to decide whether he will participate, although all should be expected to participate to a limited extent; when office policy requires that each sale be referred to the person on the staff best able to handle it, although the one who established the original contact may be given some share of the income produced; and when the office is doing sufficient advertising and is so located that clients will visit it regularly. The new salesperson particularly will find this method attractive, because it helps him develop some clientele rather easily and exposes him quickly to a variety of client types. The method is beneficial to all salespersons if they use the period in the office when they are not working with clients to catch up on their paper work, to plan their future sales activity, and to become acquainted with the listings which the office owns.

Free-For-All

In the Free-For-All system, the sales staff is not required to be present in the office, and, when they are to be present, they are free to select the hours best suited to their convenience. In such circumstances, a secretary-receptionist is usually present to receive all callers and to direct them to the salesperson whom she believes is most capable of handling the business, or else she may refer callers on the basis of a prepared list of sales personnel. Some confusion may result in the office if procedures for greeting office visitors are not worked out ahead of time and firmly enforced, because the entire sales force may be in the office on a dull day and engage in a disorganized scramble to greet anyone who enters.

This system does give maximum freedom to each salesperson, because he can search for clients and business wherever he chooses, and he has full rights to all clients whom he contacts. Occasionally there will be office disputes as to which person contacted a client first, but good office policies can solve this problem. This method also gives each salesperson maximum opportunity to develop an active body of loyal clients who will do business with him regardless of the firm for which he is working. In this way, the insecurity which a salesperson may feel about the continuity of business existence of the firm for which he is working is offset by the security which this loyal clientele produces. This is a difficult system for the new salesperson, because he must spend a considerable amount of time developing his clientele, which means that he may spend as much as 18 months simply laying the groundwork for an effective personal sales campaign and as much as three years in building to his maximum income potential.

ORGANIZATIONAL CONTROL OF SALES PERSONNEL

Although the salesperson is an independent contractor, the majority of offices do try to control his activities in a limited way. Under license laws of most states, the employing broker is responsible for the actions of the salesmen whose licenses he holds; under the law of agency, an employing broker is responsible for the actions of anyone whom he designates as his agent. In any case, an office does want to protect its public image and to secure the maximum return for every dollar it spends. Therefore, it will expect to be able to exercise some control over a salesperson. From the salesperson's viewpoint, some controls are welcome, because they help to define what he is expected to do and what he will be paid when he accomplishes certain things. In fact, if he views controls as the means for him to use most effectively the total resources of the firm for which he works, he will find his sales successes mounting.

Requirements for New Sales Staff

Approximately one-half of the small and medium-size and one-third of the large real estate offices of one state ask each new salesperson to sign an employment contract. (See Figures 4–2 and 4–3.) These contracts are of two types: an independent-contractor or an employee arrangement. The essential difference between them is that the independent contractor receives certain sales assistance from the employing broker, although he is free to use his time as he sees fit. The employee contract gives the employing

Broker-Salesman Contract

(Independent Contractor)

CALIFORNIA REAL ESTATE ASSOCIATION STANDARD FORM

THIS AGREEMENT, made this..day of ....19........ by and between .... hereinafter referred to as Broker and... ....hereinafter referred to as Salesman.

WITNESSETH:

WHEREAS, Broker is now and for many years last past has been engaged in business as a real estate broker in the City of........................ ....County of......................................California, and is duly licensed to sell, offer for sale, buy, offer to buy, list or solicit prospective purchasers, negotiate the purchase, sale or exchange of real estate, negotiate loans on real estate, lease or offer to lease, and negotiate the sale, purchase or exchange of leases, rent or place for rent, or to collect rent from real estate or improvements thereon for another or others, has and does enjoy the good will of, and a reputation for fair dealing with the public, and

WHEREAS, Broker maintains an office in said City and County, properly equipped for furnishings and other equipment necessary and incidental to the proper operation of said business, and staffed with employees suitable to serving the public as a real estate broker, and

WHEREAS, Salesman is now and for some time past has been engaged in business as a real estate salesman, duly licensed by the State of California, and has enjoyed and does enjoy a good reputation for fair and honest dealing with the public as such, and

NOW, THEREFORE, in consideration of the premises and the

This contract prepared by California Real Estate Association as a suggested guide for members and their attorneys.

Figure 4-2. Broker-Salesman Contract with an Independent Contractor. (Used by permission of the California Real Estate Association)

mutual agreements herein contained, it is understood and agreed as follows:

1 Broker agrees to make available to Salesman all current listings of the office, except such as Broker may find expedient to place exclusively in the temporary possession of some other salesman, and agrees to assist Salesman in his work by advice, information, and full cooperation in every way possible.

2 Broker agrees that Salesman may share with other salesmen all the facilities of the office now operated by Broker in connection with the subject matter of this contract, which office is now maintained at...

3 Salesman agrees to work diligently and with his best efforts to sell, lease or rent any and all real estate listed with Broker, to solicit additional listings and customers of Broker, and otherwise promote the business of serving the public in real estate transactions to the end that each of the parties hereto may derive the greatest profit possible.

4 Salesman shall read and be governed by the Code of Ethics of the National Association of Real Estate Boards, the real estate law of the State of California and the by-laws of the local real estate board, and any future modifications or additions thereto. Each party acknowledges receipt of a copy of the said Code of Ethics and of the Local Board By-Laws.

5 The usual and customary commissions shall be charged. Broker shall advise Salesman of any special contract relating to any particular transaction which he undertakes to handle. When Salesman shall perform any work hereunder whereby a commission is earned, said commission shall, when collected, be divided between Broker and Salesman, in which division Salesman shall receive a proportionate share as set out in the current commission schedule as set forth in the broker's Policy Book and Broker shall receive the balance. In the event of special arrangements with any client of Broker or Salesman on property listed with Broker or controlled by Salesman, a special division of commission may apply, such rate of division to be agreed upon before completion of the transaction by Broker and Salesman and outlined in writing.

Figure 4-2 continued.

6 In the event that two or more salesmen participate in such work, or claim to have done so, the amount of the commission over that accruing to Broker shall be divided between the participating salesmen according to agreement between them or by arbitration.

7 In no case shall Broker be personally liable to Salesman for any commission not collected, nor shall Salesman be personally liable for any commission not collected. When the commission shall have been collected from the party or parties for whom the service was performed, Broker shall hold the same in trust for Salesman and himself to be divided according to the terms of this agreement. Complying with Section 10138 Business and Professions Code, all compensation shall be delivered to Broker to be paid as per this agreement.

8 The division and distribution of the earned commissions as set out in Paragraphs 5, 6, and 7 hereof shall take place as soon as practicable after collection of such commissions.

9 Broker shall not be liable to Salesman for any expenses incurred by him or for any of his acts, nor shall Salesman be liable to Broker for office help or expense. Salesman shall have no authority to bind Broker by any promise of representation unless specifically authorized in writing in a particular transaction. Expenses which must by reason of some necessity be paid from the commission, or are incurred in the collection of, or in the attempt to collect the commission, shall be paid by the parties in the same proportion as provided for herein in the division of commissions.

10 This agreement does not constitute a hiring by either party. The parties hereto are and shall remain independent contractors bound by the provisions hereof. Salesman is under the control of Broker as to the result of Salesman's work only and not as to the means by which such result is accomplished. This agreement shall not be construed as a partnership and broker shall not be liable for any obligation incurred by Salesman.

11 Salesman agrees that any and all listings of property, and all employment in connection with the real estate business shall be taken in the name of Broker. Such listings shall be filed with Broker within twenty-four hours after receipt of same by Salesman. All listings shall be and remain the separate and exclusive property of Broker.

Figure 4-2 continued.

12 This contract and the association created hereby, may be terminated by either party hereto at any time upon written notice given to the other. The rights of the parties to any commission earned prior to said notice shall not be divested by the termination of this contract.

13 When this agreement has been terminated for any reason, the Salesman's regular proportionate share of commission on any deals Salesman has made that are not closed shall be considered his property, and upon closing of said deals, said proportionate share of the commission shall be paid to him; and Salesman shall receive agreed listing commissions on his listings if sold within the life of such listings, and commission received by Broker. This shall not apply to any extension of the said listings beyond the original listing period.

14 In the event Salesman leaves and has deals or listings pending that require further work normally rendered by Salesman, the Salesman and Broker, or Broker alone, shall make arrangements with another salesman in the organization to perform the required work, and the salesman assigned shall be compensated for taking care of pending deals or listings.

15 Arbitration—In the event of disagreement or dispute between salesman in the office or between Broker and Salesman arising out of or connected with this agreement which cannot be adjusted by and between the parties involved, such questions shall be submitted to the local real estate Board committee governing such disputes or if this is not agreed upon, the problem must be submitted to a temporary Board of Arbitration for final adjustment. Such board shall be selected in the following manner: Each of the parties to the disagreement or dispute shall select one member who shall be a licensed broker or licensed salesman. Such selection shall be made within five days from the time notice is given in writing by either party to the other, that arbitration is desired. The two arbitrators thus selected, in case they cannot reach a decision after a single conference, or adjustment thereof, shall name a third arbitrator who shall be a person not licensed by the Real Estate Commissioner. Such arbitration may follow the provisions of Sections 1280 through 1293 of the Code of Civil Procedure for the State of California. Broker and Salesman hereby

Figure 4-2 continued.

agree to be bound by the decision of the above described arbitration body.

16 Salesman shall not after the termination of this contract use to his own advantage, or the advantage of any other person or corporation, any information gained for or from the files or business of Broker.

WITNESS the signatures of the parties hereto the day and year first above written. In duplicate.

BROKER

SALESMAN as INDEPENDENT CONTRACTOR

For these forms address California Real Estate Association, 117 West Ninth St., Los Angeles 15.

Figure 4-2 continued.

Broker-Salesman Contract

(Employee)

CALIFORNIA REAL ESTATE ASSOCIATION STANDARD FORM

1 This agreement entered into this..day of
.... 19........ by and between
....hereinafter called Broker and
.... hereinafter called
Salesman, hereby agree, subject to termination at will by either party, to the following conditions and details of their relationship:

BROKER

2 Broker is defined as the operator of a real estate firm or business, licensed as a broker under the laws of the State of California by the Real Estate Commissioner, to sell or otherwise deal in real estate, and who employs one or more salesmen.

SALESMAN

3 Salesman is defined as: (a) A person duly licensed under the laws of the State of California by the Real Estate Commissioner as a salesman and employed by Broker. (b) A person duly licensed under the laws of the State of California by the Real Estate Commissioner as a broker and employed by Broker as a real estate salesman.

GENERAL CONDITIONS

4 Salesman shall read and be governed by the Code of Ethics of the National Association of Real Estate Boards, the real estate law of the State of California and the by-laws of the local real estate board, and any future modifications or additions thereto. A copy of the Code of Ethics and of the local Board by-laws are attached hereto.

This contract prepared by California Real Estate Association as a suggested guide for members and their attorneys.

Figure 4-3. Broker-Salesman Contract with an Employee. (Used by permission of the California Real Estate Association.)

BROKER OBLIGATIONS

5 Broker maintains offices adequately and properly equipped with furnishings, equipment and facilities reasonable and adequate for the proper operation of a general real estate brokerage business, staffed with trained employees engaged in serving the public as a real estate broker.

6 As a part of these facilities, Broker procures and maintains listings for sale, lease and rental of real estate as well as purchasers, lessees and renters thereof, and has for some time and does now enjoy the good will and reputation for fair dealing with the public generally.

7 Broker is duly and regularly licensed as a real estate broker under license issued by the Real Estate Commissioner of the State of California and maintains memberships in the local real estate board, the California Real Estate Association and the National Association of Real Estate Boards.

8 Broker agrees to make available to Salesman all current listings in the office except such as Broker may find expedient to place exclusively in the possession of some other salesman.

9 Salesman has no authority, either express or implied, to represent anything to a prospective purchaser unless it is in the listing agreement or unless he receives specific written instructions from Broker.

10 Broker shall provide, within limitations herein set forth, Salesman with advertising and with necessary office equipment, including space, desk, telephone, telegrams, signs, business cards, stationery, escrow assistance, legal advice and supervisory assistance and cooperation with salesman in connection with his work.

11 All advertising shall be approved and placed by Broker.

12 Broker must first approve the ordering of all title searches and the opening of all escrows.

13 In the event any transaction in which Salesman is involved results in a dispute, litigation or legal expense, Salesman shall

Figure 4-3 continued.

cooperate fully with Broker and Broker and Salesman shall share all expense connected therewith, in the same proportion as they would normally share the commission resulting from such transaction if there were no dispute or litigation. In any event, the Salesman shall not be financially responsible for any expenses that are in excess of the amount that he would have normally received as his share of the commission had there been no dispute or litigation. It is the policy to avoid litigation wherever possible and Broker reserves the right to determine whether or not any litigation or dispute shall be prosecuted, defended, compromised or settled, and the terms and conditions of any compromise or settlement or whether or not legal expense shall be incurred.

14 Salesman shall not make any long distance calls or send any telegrams without prior approval of Broker. All telephone calls and telegrams over $1.00, including tax, shall be paid one-half by Salesman for whose benefit the cost was incurred, and one-half by Broker.

15 All Salesmen shall receive an equal amount of floor time.

16 All Salesmen shall be allowed to purchase a home from among the firm's listings, providing the Broker is paid the normal share of commission due Broker as Broker's share of commission. Said purchase of a home shall be for the Salesman's own use and occupancy. If another Salesman is involved through having obtained the listing, said Salesman shall receive his normal listing fee in the same manner as if a sale had been made to someone not connected with the office.

17 No Salesman shall be required to work an average of more than six days a week.

18 Broker shall close his office and his open houses on the following legal holidays: Fourth of July, Thanksgiving Day, Christmas Day and Easter Sunday.

COMMISSIONS

19 Broker agrees to pay Salesman as and for Salesman's compensation for services rendered on a commission basis for all work done by Salesman in accordance with fee schedule adopted by Bro-

Figure 4-3 continued.

ker's office, a copy of which is attached and shall be considered a part of this agreement. No commission shall be considered earned or payable to Salesman until the transaction has been completed and the commission collected by the Broker. Commissions earned shall be payable twice each month, on the..............................and.............................. day of each month.

20 The schedule of commissions and divisions thereof as attached hereto shall be used in every transaction, and any variation therefrom shall first be approved by Broker. Any arrangement for division of commission with other brokers shall be first approved by Broker. In the event two or more salesmen employed by Broker participate in a commission on the same transaction, it shall be divided between the participating salesmen according to prior agreement or by arbitration.

21 Any expense incurred in negotiating the sale, including travel expense, hotels, meals, maps, special services employed, listing fees, multiple listing commissions, etc., shall first be deducted from the gross commission received.

SALESMEN'S OBLIGATIONS

22 Salesman agrees to conduct his activities and regulate his habits so as to increase, rather than diminish the good will and reputation of Broker.

23 Salesman shall furnish his own automobile and pay all expenses thereof and shall carry liability and property damage insurance satisfactory to the Broker, name Broker as co-insured and deliver copy of endorsement to Broker.

24 Salesman shall remain continuously licensed by the State of California to sell real estate and shall pay the required renewal fee.

25 Salesman shall not obligate Broker for materials or service or the purchase of real property or anything or in any other way, without first obtaining consent of Broker, verbally or in writing.

26 Salesman shall use only real estate forms approved by Broker.

Figure 4-3 continued.

27 Broker reserves the right to reject any exclusive listing deemed unsatisfactory, and to return said listing to the owner.

28 Salesman acknowledges that he is an employee of Broker and that he will abide by all written rules and regulations now in force or subsequently adopted by Broker. Broker agrees to carry compensation insurance for all employees.

29 All letters received, and a copy of all letters written by Salesman pertaining to the business of Broker shall be the property of Broker, and be turned over to Broker's records. All letters written by Salesman shall be approved by Broker before mailing or delivering.

30 All money, documents or property received by Salesman in connection with any transaction of Broker shall be delivered to Broker immediately. All checks or money orders shall be made payable to either Broker, to a title company or to another Broker-approved escrow holder. In the event that all or any portion of the deposit is forfeited, and the seller has received his share of the funds, a division of the remainder of such deposit shall be made between Broker and Salesman in the same proportion as though the amount received was a commission received in connection with the transaction.

31 In connection with any transaction, if it becomes necessary or desirable to receive all or part of the commission in property other than cash, then approval of Broker shall first be obtained. In such event, Broker and Salesman may agree as follows:

a. To divide such property between Broker and Salesman in kind, in the same proportion as their respective interests in the commission involved; or

b. Broker may pay Salesman his full share of the commission in cash, in which event Broker shall have the full ownership of the property so received; or

c. To retain such property in the names of Broker and Salesman and thereafter to dispose of the same at such time at such price and on such terms as Broker and Salesman shall agree. Any profit or loss or any carrying charges or other expenses with respect to such property, shall be shared between Broker and Salesman in the same proportion as their respective interests in the commission involved.

Figure 4-3 continued.

32 This agreement for division of commission shall not apply to subdivision sales or acreage for subdivisions or large or unusual transactions which require special time and services on the part of Broker. Commissions received and paid on such transactions will be subject to special written agreement.

ARBITRATION

33 In the event of disagreement or dispute between Salesmen in the office or between Broker and Salesman arising out of or connected with this agreement, which cannot be adjusted by and between the parties involved, such questions shall be submitted to the local real estate Board committee governing such disputes or if this is not agreed upon, the problem must be submitted to a temporary Board of Arbitration for final adjustment. Such board shall be selected in the following manner: Each of the parties to the disagreement or dispute shall select one member who shall be a licensed broker or licensed salesman. Such selection shall be made within five days from the time notice is given in writing by either party to the other, that arbitration is desired. The two arbitrators thus selected, in case they cannot reach a decision after a single conference or adjustment thereof, shall name a third arbitrator who shall be a person not licensed by the Real Estate Commissioner. Such arbitration may follow the provisions of Sections 1280 through 1293 of the Code of Civil Procedure for the State of California.

TERMINATION OF CONTRACT

34 This contract and the association created hereby may be terminated by either party hereto, at any time, upon notice to the other, said notice to be in writing; but the rights of the parties to any commission which accrued prior to said notice shall not be divested by the termination of the contract.

35 When this agreement has been terminated for any reason, any deals Salesman has made that are not closed shall be considered his property and upon closing of said deals, full Salesman's share of commission shall be paid to him; and Salesman shall receive agreed listing commissions on his listings if sold within the life of such listings, and commission received by Broker. This shall not apply to any extension of the said listings beyond the original listing period.

Figure 4-3 continued.

36 In the event Salesman leaves and has deals or listings pending that require further services normally rendered by Salesman, the Salesman and Broker, or Broker alone, shall make arrangements with another salesman in the organization to perform the required services, and the salesman assigned shall be compensated for taking care of pending deals or listings.

37 Broker and Salesman agree to all the foregoing terms and conditions and to use their skill, efforts and abilities in cooperating to carry out the terms of this agreement for the mutual benefit of Broker and Salesman.

38 In Witness Whereof, the parties hereto have set their hands this day and year first above written.

....

BROKER

....

SALESMAN

For these forms address California Real Estate Association, 117 West Ninth St., Los Angeles 15.

Figure 4-3 continued.

broker more control over the salesperson's time and the manner in which he conducts himself, and it also obligates the employer to pay Social Security and other legally required benefits for the salesperson.

Many salesmen prefer not to sign a sales contract, feeling that it places undue restrictions on their activities. On the other hand, a careful examination of the provisions of each of the different forms will show that the responsibilities and duties of the salesperson and the hiring broker are carefully set forth. In the employee form, for example, the broker lists the facilities he will provide, his commission schedules, and the salesman's obligations in furnishing an automobile, selling materials, and a variety of other items. On the other hand, the independent-contractor agreement is less burdensome to both the hiring broker and the prospective associate, and requires little from the broker in the way of facilities or services.

One of the principal pitfalls which a real estate salesperson will want to avoid is that which is created because he and the employing broker do not have a meeting of minds on how the sales job is to be done. An increasing number of firms are avoiding this problem by preparing a written policy book which outlines procedures in the principal areas of business operations. Only slightly more than one-third of the brokerage offices report that they have such a book; almost an equal percentage do have some minimal type of written statement, often only a page of instructions; and generally throughout the business, the use of such written statements is increasing. These policy books can cover a wide variety of topics, many of which grow out of local practices and customs; therefore, it is good practice for a salesperson to ask for and study carefully the policy book of the office in which he is interested.[1] For example, practice differs widely in many areas on the commission splits between salesmen and employing brokers and in the securing of open or exclusive listings.

A final requirement for offices in many states is that all persons selling real estate for a fee must be licensed. Seemingly, this should be the first and most important requirement, but often it is not. Many offices say that they are looking for a potentially good person, and if he does not have a real estate license, they are willing to invest time and money in seeing that he gets the license and the training which he needs in order to succeed. For this reason, if for no other, an otherwise well-qualified person should not hesitate to plan for a career in real estate selling if he finds that the terms under which he will be employed are satisfactory to him.

---

[1] The variety of practices in the United States is very well discussed in *Office Polices and Procedures* (Chicago: National Institute of Real Estate Brokers of the National Association of Real Estate Boards, March, 1959).

Office Responsibilities

The smallness of the typical real estate brokerage office usually prevents if from offering any but the most limited type of secretarial service. Usually, the majority of the offices will prepare a limited number of letters for the salesperson when these relate directly to the closing of a sale, and they usually offer rather complete phone-answering services. However, research shows that one in four offices require sales personnel to prepare their own letters and other correspondence; more than one in three require salesmen to prepare their own advertising and to prepare and address their own mail solicitations; and one in eight will expect the salesmen to answer the telephone and help keep the office in a tidy and clean condition.

The larger offices in centers of active markets will almost always have a full staff of clerical and secretarial assistants so that the salespersons can devote their full time to selling. In smaller communities, in offices in fringe areas where not many persons are expected to call at the office, and in new offices struggling to keep expenses down, there may be little or no secretarial or clerical support.

All offices expect the sales force to share cheerfully in the office work which has to be done. An alert, pleasant staff is one of the most effective means an office has for building good public relations. For this reason, if for no other, the sales force are expected to receive all clients with the utmost courtesy and with a sincere desire to be of service whether or not the clients are theirs or those of someone else in the office. Salespersons are also expected to share with each other any knowledge they have about the properties listed by the office and to assist others on the staff whose lack of experience or whose background might prevent them from closing a sale as successfully.

Principles of Organizing Brokerage Operations

1. *Legal organization.* The legal form of organization has little relationship to the business organization but does affect the continuity of the firm's operations. Partnerships provide the greatest organizational flexibility; corporations, the strongest guarantee of continuous operations.
2. *Size.* As a real estate firm grows, it must provide formal organization or it will fail.
3. *Executive talent.* The type of executive talent needed to guarantee the success of a growing real estate office cannot be secured if the firm does not have a formal organizational plan.
4. *Job duties.* Every function that must be performed to keep the firm operating

must be assigned to a particular person, who must also be given the authority and responsibility needed to perform the job successfully.

5. *Delegation.* As a firm grows, the chief executive must learn to delegate more of his duties to subordinates, so that he can focus on setting objectives and on creating operational policies.
6. *Change.* As a firm grows, it must change its organization to permit the inclusion of an increasing number of nonbrokerage activities.
7. *Specialization.* Proper organization permits those persons with special business talents to devote their time to using these talents to improve the profits of the firm.
8. *Objectives.* The manner in which a firm is organized is determined by the objectives that it has adopted.
9. *Sales organization.* The type of organization developed for selling should be determined by the types of markets to be served, the local customs among brokerage firms, and the preferences of the chief executives in the firm.
10. *Flexibility.* The form of organization adopted by a firm should permit it to take advantage of unusual market opportunities or fundamental changes in market trends.
11. *Initiative.* The form of organization should encourage and permit all sales employees to use maximum initiative in solving their sales problems.

CASE STUDY

Introduction

The interview of this firm was conducted at the request of the partners. They pointed out that, in their first year of operation, they suffered a net loss of $15,000, in the second year a net loss of $8,000, in the third year they broke even, and in the fourth year they earned a net profit of $18,000, of which $15,000 was commission from a commercial-property sale.

They are disturbed about this record and feel that by now they should be earning substantially more. Furthermore, they are not satisfied with their present sales staff nor with the progress being made in achieving operational stability.

In asking for the survey, they said, "Tell us what is wrong. What would you suggest as a program for achieving both operational and profit stability?"

CASE HISTORY OF REAL ESTATE FIRM: 100-B

Characteristics of the Firm

The firm is a partnership. Mr. *X* has been in the business since 1930, moving to his present location and opening his office there in April 1953. His experience in the Midwest was essentially in selling used cars. He turned to real estate when he arrived in this city because is was easy to enter and because he felt that there were good prospects of making a high income. Mr. Z, his partner, has been in the real estate business four and one-half years. Prior to this time he was the manager of a retail store.

The staff consists of six full-time salespeople and three part-time salespeople. They hope in time to eliminate the part-time salespeople, because they are having difficulty controlling them. In addition to the selling done by the six full-time people, both partners also sell occasionally. One-half of the sales force consists of middle-aged persons with considerable selling experience who rely on their real estate income for about one-half of the total family income. The other half of the sales force consists of people who have newly entered the business and have had no experience in selling and who must rely entirely on their sales commissions for their income.

There is one full-time secretary who handles all correspondence and record-keeping and phone-answering. During the times when the office is closed, a phone-answering service handles calls to the office.

Division of Work Among the Partners

Since coming to this city, Mr. *X* has had a varied experience in selling real estate, but he prefers to concentrate on commercial and industrial properties because of the higher returns found there. However, he also sells vacant land and the higher-priced residential properties.

Mr. *Z* writes the advertising, pays the bills, and handles the routine office functions. Occasionally he sells; he is also in charge of the property-management department, particularly in terms of setting rents and securing special tenants; he keeps the books for the insurance department and handles most of the insurance business; from time to time, he checks the records for real estate sales.

Both of the partners supervise salespeople and assume general responsibility for seeing that sales production is maintained.

Division of Work: the Sales Force

One salesperson handles the insurance completely. This is a new salesperson who has been trained in the insurance business. This person's record is reasonably good. The principal use of the insurance department, however, is to provide contacts for future real estate sales and to serve as a supplement for selling real estate.

One of the salespeople has been given full responsibility for handling rentals and in general acts in the capacity of a property manager. However, problems dealing with maintenance, repair, and similar activities are turned over to one of the partners for further handling. Usually this is Mr. Z.

Both of the partners work to some extent in property management. They have introduced this primarily at the urging of Mr. *X*, who feels that this is a good hedge against decline in real estate activity. He has said, "When real estate sales are low, property management can carry the overhead; and in addition when times are good, property management can provide contacts for real estate sales." In spite of this optimistic attitude toward property management, the firm at the present time handles only two properties, although they have handled up to 15 or 20 at times. They make no attempt to canvass for property-management business.

The remaining personnel are all engaged in selling residential properties. They are given no special assignments in terms of either quotas or territories. The partners believe it is best to deal with the sales personnel on an informal basis; therefore, they avoid using a formal organizational arrangement. Sales personnel are expected to "cooperate" with each other and ask for help from the partners only when an informal agreement cannot be reached.

Real Estate Competition in the City

Real estate activity in this city is dominated by two or three of the larger, older real estate firms. Each of these firms has been in business at least 30 years and as a result enjoys the respect of the entire community. Each of the firms has approximately 20 to 30 salespeople working for it; as a result, they provide stiff competition for the newer offices and the smaller offices in the community.

Competition is so keen that there is no multiple-listing agency, nor do the offices cooperate with each other except on a casual basis. On the other hand, the real estate board in this community is extremely active and is one of the largest in the metropolitan area. New firms entering the business in this community have found that it takes at least one year for them to get reasonably well established and two or three years before they are making any amount of money. For instance, new firms report that it takes an outlay of $9,000 to $12,000 in cash during the first year of operation merely to keep their office doors open without making any sales.

Salesmen and Sales Training

The partners feel that, because of the area in which they operate, they should select those salespeople who present a good personal appearance and who operate according to the highest standards of ethics. They have summarized their feelings by saying that they want to hire "nice" people. However, they have not defined what they mean by "nice." They have not yet decided whether it is better to hire experienced or inexperienced people. As a result, they are hiring both kinds.

When the partners were pressed to give a more specific statement as to what they would use as a criterion for selection, they said that they wanted a salesman who was reliable and honest, who could furnish references, and who had a reasonable production record. Although they would hire inexperienced people, they felt that at least six months' experience was the minimum before they would consider such persons. Partners stress the fact that they want the kind of salesperson who will bring repeat business to the office and who can through his attitude make good friends for the office.

When they hire an inexperienced person, they have a very informal personal type of training program which is not on an organized basis. The new persons are expected to get acquainted with the area, to study the listings, to show properties, and to serve as a receptionist in houses open for public showing (for open houses). In their first month of employment, they are expected to concentrate on getting listings and to obtain at least one listing. Beyond this, they are left pretty much on their own; however, the partners will help them at any time in closing, arranging for financing, or preparing for escrow, or with other items on which the person feels that help is necessary.

The experienced people are left entirely on their own. The partners feel that they must be careful not to direct their salesmen too much—particularly the more experienced ones—and as a result they give these people only the most casual type of instruction or guidance. This has proven very successful, because at the present time they do have two older persons selling who have produced for themselves $15,000 net income for the year.

The partners say that they encourage their salespersons to specialize in a certain area or price range or type of property, but that to date this has not proven to be too successful. They feel that specialization will make the salesmen more willing to share listings when they secure listings which are not their specialty. At the present time, the salespeople are expected to work out between themselves the basis on which a commission will be split if one salesperson sells the listing of another person.

At the suggestion of the salespeople, the owners drew up a policy book. This book was discussed at sales meetings and was finally voted upon by the salespeople. The owners refrained from voting and let this be the complete expression of what the salespeople wanted. They did reserve the right to approve or veto any provision in the book. They insisted that the policy book be brief, with the thought that the salesmen could in most cases set their own rules and work out their problems among themselves.

In the three years that this office has been operating, they have found it necessary to fire seven persons. The word "fire" was used by the partners, and they explained that it was necessary to do this because the salespeople had proven to be incompetent. They stressed the point that some of the people they had hired were much too sharp in their dealings and were engaging in practices which they felt were, if not unethical, bordering very close on the unethical. Some of the salespeople who were released were women. In these cases they said that the women were just simply too inexperienced and knew too little about real estate to reach a production level which would pay for the desks which they were occupying. Partners felt that, if these women had taken advantage of the opportunities offered to them in the firm, they would have learned to sell within the year which they were with the firm, but that on the whole these women showed no inclination to learn and did not produce the required number of either listings or sales to warrant their being kept.

Summary

The partners were asked whether they felt that they had made any mistakes in previous years which they had not yet rectified and which, if rectified, might help them in their progress. Their answer to this was an evasion of the question. Rather, they said that they were new to the locality and the people in it, and that they were facing some difficulties in becoming acclimated to the way business was conducted and to the manner in which other firms competed in selling real estate. They felt that perhaps one of the things that had been bothering them was that they had hired too many incompetent salespeople, and that if they had gotten rid of these sooner, they might have increased their profit operations. Among the mistakes which they said salespeople made which cost money were: too much advertising was done for particular property; listings were taken at too high a price; and listings were taken which were too distant, that is, areas 10 to 15 miles from the office. They now insist that sales be taken within the two- or three-mile radius of the office.

They also say that when they started operations in their present office, they bought out the real estate business owned by a previous business. They did this because they felt that they were buying the good will of this office, and accordingly they had paid a good price for this good will; but to date they have found that they have bought nothing.

They could find no evidence of good will having been built up by this firm in its operations.

When the partners were asked to give more specific examples of the scope of their operations, they pointed out that, in their first year of operations, they lost $7,600; that in their second year they netted $5,500; and that in 1956 they netted $18,200 from the sales of real estate. When they installed the insurance department during the second year of operation, they earned $3,000 from this, and in their third year of operation they earned $7,000 from insurance commissions. They felt that they should by now have been earning approximately twice this much, particularly from the real estate sales. And, in summarizing their feelings, they felt that their lack of success was due to their newness in the area, their lack of established reputation, and the bad name which had been created for real estate offices by the part-time salespeople and the unscrupulous brokers who were working throughout the area.

Chapter 5

SELECTING AND TRAINING REAL ESTATE SALES PERSONNEL

No one has settled satisfactorily the argument as to whether good salespersons are born or made, but research has established that a well-executed selecting and training process can improve the selling performance of even persons with minimal talent. The importance of being selective in hiring salesmen and of providing good training for those that are selected can be appreciated when we see that real estate salespersons of average ability may earn as little as $4,000 annually but a well-trained person placed in the right job may earn three or four times this amount. (Table 5–1.) Training impresses on the novice the fact that selling is hard work and requires an average of 40 to 50 hours per week initially while demanding all of the energies and abilities that he possesses. Both the owner of a firm and his experienced successful salespersons know that good, continuous sales training can double the annual sales volume for the firm and for the salesperson.

The real estate field does not lack for books, articles, pamphlets, and good advice on the subject of selecting and training salespersons. However, the mortality rate among salespersons and real estate brokerage offices remains high because little of this good advice is heeded. An important ingredient that is often overlooked is the necessity for developing and maintaining a total selection process such as is presented in Figure 5–1 and for following it up with a total incentive program such as is presented in Figure 5–2.

An equally important ingredient in developing successful salespersons is the offering of a complete sales training program such as is presented in Figure 5–3. Training, it now becomes clear from research, should consist of more than providing sales techniques and "gimmicks." The program should begin with selecting the right persons for the sales jobs, encouraging them with a sound incentive program, and maintaining their sales abilities with an all-around sales training program.

Table 5-1

COMPARISON OF INCOME AND WORK CHARACTERISTICS OF SUCCESSFUL AND AVERAGE REAL ESTATE SALESPERSONS

Characteristics	Type of Salesperson		
	Successful	*Average*	*All Salespersons*
Annual Net Earnings (Exclusive of Business Expenses)	*Per Cent of Total Reporting*		
$ 20,000 and over	5.6%	0	3.6%
15,000—19,999	19.4	0	12.7
10,000—14,999	36.1	0	23.6
8,000— 9,999	19.5	5.3%	14.5
5,000— 7,999	19.4	42.1	27.3
3,000— 4,999	0	42.1	14.6
0— 2,999	0	10.5	3.7
Median Annual Net Earnings	$ 13,500	$ 4,700	$ 9,400
Number of Hours Spent Selling	*Per Cent of Total Time*		
65—69	5.4%	0	3.5%
60—64	21.6	10.0%	17.5
55—59	10.8	0	7.0
50—54	29.7	15.0	24.6
45—49	19.0	30.0	22.8
40—44	13.5	30.0	19.3
0—39	0	15.0	5.3
Median Weekly Hours in Brokerage	53.0	46.0	50.0
Per Cent of Total Income From Selling	*Per Cent Total Reporting*		
100%	60.0%	58.8%	59.6%
80—99%	22.9	5.9	17.3
60—79	8.6	11.8	9.6
40—59	5.6	17.6	9.7
20—39	2.9	5.9	3.8
Median Number of Properties Sold Annually	33.0	12.0	21.0
Median Average Annual Sales Volume (In Thousands)	$ 385	$ 200	$ 300

Activity	*Procedures*
Recruit constantly	Search for sales personnel constantly, particularly in areas where good salesmanship is required—corporate salesmen, insurance, route salesmen for bakeries and milk companies. Always maintain a file of good prospects.
Interview constantly	Talk to prospective salespersons constantly and maintain a file from which applicants can be selected. Include in the file notes on personal appearance, impressions about personality, and experience.
Secure written applications and maintain a file of these	The most promising prospects should be asked to complete an application form that gives a complete picture of their education, business experience, related real estate experience, and work capacities.
Interview the best-qualified	Use a face-to-face interview to answer any doubts raised by answers in the application. Outline the job requirements and get the applicant's reaction to them. Use tests to reinforce initial decisions about applicants.
Check credit, character, and work references	These references are the most important clues to the real ability of the applicant and his future potential. This step should *never* be omitted.
Get reactions of the sales staff	Because the applicant must work harmoniously with the sales staff, let them meet the applicant and give their views of his potential.
Place the applicant on the job on a trial basis	At the end of one week, one month, and three months, again meet with the applicant and give him your assessment of his progress and give him the chance to discuss his reactions to the job and the problems he has faced.

Figure 5-1. Steps in Selecting Sales Personnel

Activity	*Procedure*
Match the right men to the right job	Review and constantly improve the selection process.
Maintain a complete personnel program	Support the selection process with a compensation program that includes a full explanation of what will be paid, when payments are made, and why the system has been designed as it is.

Figure 5-2. Securing Maximim Sales Production

Recognize superior performance	Use bonuses, profit-sharing, sales contests, prizes, and other rewards for above-average performances. Do this on a continuing basis.
Set minimal goals of performance	Give each salesperson a minimal goal to meet and check with him constantly when he fails to meet this goal. Provide a continuing counseling service to assist him in difficult sales situations and when he appears to be in a "slump."
Provide "mental" security and stimulation	Provide means by which each person can improve his financial situation on a permanent basis; if he shows managerial potential, increase his responsibilities in the firm. From time to time, select some of the firm's best salespersons for managerial and ownership roles in the firm.

Figure 5-2. Continued.

Activity	*Procedure*
Introduction to the job	Introduce the salesperson to the job by reviewing with him the job requirements and procedures.
Introduction to the firm and the other personnel	Show the new salesperson around the office. Introduce him to the other sales personnel and explain what each does. Let them know what the new person is to do. Introduce him to other persons outside the firm with whom the firm does business regularly.
Begin initial training	Review the firm's history and policies, the types of properties sold, the services offered to clients, the forms used in the selling process, and the basic selling techniques that have worked well for other salespersons in the firm.
Continue with advanced training	Continue to review basic selling techniques while introducing some of the more sophisticated, advanced methods. Review personal selling habits. Hold clinics and review recent successful and unsuccessful sales. Invite guest speakers to discuss property law, income taxes, financing methods, and similar items.
Encourage continuing education	Hold special meetings to discuss business, community, and industry trends. Encourage and pay for attendance at sales conferences, conventions, special training programs, courses at colleges and universities, night-school programs, and adult education courses, and for correspondence courses.

ENCOURAGE AN ATTITUDE OF LIFELONG LEARNING

Figure 5-3. The Training Process for Real Estate Sales Personnel

SUCCESSFUL AND UNSUCCESSFUL SALESPERSONS

Success is an indeterminate word when used in describing real estate salespersons, because each salesperson and each real estate brokerage office will usually have different standards for measuring success.

Lack of Definition of a Successful "Salesperson"

Judgments about how to measure successful real estate salesmanship vary with market conditions, the type of office, and the attitudes of the salespersons. The lack of a universally acceptable definition is due also to the conflict between the notion that there is a single set of characteristics that are found invariably in all successful salespersons and the assumption that each type of real estate selling requires a somewhat different set of characteristics. For example, many sales managers believe that a person who is successful in selling single-family homes would not do well in selling income properties because home selling depends upon emotional appeals and income property selling depends upon a rational, financial approach.

Research has shown that the size of an office and the market it serves have very definite effects on how a salesman's success is judged. A small office facing stiff competition will define success as the ability to maintain a high sales volume. A large office with strong financial reserves and an established leadership position will accept salespersons who work hard and who maintain a proportionate share of the total sales volume.

Confusion on the part of sales managers and owners between what they think they want in salespersons and what they really accept also adds to the difficulty of defining sales success. Many sales managers hire persons with one set of characteristics but release them because they do not measure up to a completely different set. For example, many offices say that they are looking for salespersons who are honest, hard-working, self-starting, and so forth. However, these same offices will release salespersons with these characteristics who fail to meet sales quotas, who spend too much time listing, who do not use the telephone properly, and so forth—all characteristics that were not mentioned during the initial selection process. Furthermore, there is a tendency among such offices to tell the salesperson that he is being released because of "poor personal habits" or "failure to maintain a consistent volume of sales" or other reasons, when the real reasons are personality conflicts or other factors that might have been corrected in an adequate sales training program.

MINIMUM ELEMENTS FOR SUCCESS

There are some criteria that salespersons must meet ordinarily if they are planning to sell real estate. Almost all states, for example, require a license and usually expect the person to be at least 21 years of age. Many firms have a policy of never hiring anyone below the age of 25 or even 30. Two-thirds of the firms researched also had a maximum hiring age of 63.

Lack of any type of business experience is no bar to employment and to a successful selling carrer, but many firms will not hire an inexperienced young man under 25 unless he shows exceptional promise. On the other hand, many of these firms would hire a man of 50 or 60 with little or no business experience. Typically, firms expect at least one year of real estate sales experience before they will hire a person who is qualified in all other respects.

Although employing brokers did not admit to it readily, extensive interviews with them indicated that a salesperson who had a pleasing personality which he was able to project would be hired whether he met other requirements or not. In many cases, real estate offices searched diligently for such persons and provided training for them so that they could qualify for the real estate license. In accepting such persons, brokers usually justified their actions by stressing their conclusions that these persons gave evidence of reliability, acceptance of responsibility, amiability, ambition, and punctuality. By contrast, they would often reject someone who met the age and experience qualifications because he had the appearance of not being self-starting, or of being easy-going but not sufficiently personable or inspirational.

It is important to note, however, that the lack of one or more of the "desired" characteristics in a prospective salesman is rarely the cause for rejecting an otherwise acceptable applicant. The man is hired if the over-all impression which he gives is favorable. Weaknesses in some characteristics are balanced against his age and experience ratings.

WOMEN AS SUCCESSFUL SALESPERSONS

The number of women who are licensed to sell real estate is increasing each year; however, there is still a general feeling in the industry that women are on trial and have yet to prove their effectiveness. Not many employing brokers are indifferent on this subject, being either strongly in favor of or strongly against hiring saleswomen. The reasons most often given for not wanting women sales personnel were that they were "undependable," used poor or even unethical sales tactics, or could not grasp the complexities of the majority of real estate financing problems. The feeling was almost overwhelming that it took rare managerial talent to maintain an effective sales force of both men and women.

On the other hand, the minority of offices who had all-women sales staffs were enthusiastic over their selling ability. In such cases, the women were usually rated as being most effective in the sales of single-family homes. For the great bulk of real estate offices, the hiring of women is still rated as an experiment, which means that they will often hire a personable sales candidate but with serious misgivings as to her length of stay and her ability to maintain consistent performance. On the whole, it seems clear that women are making a better spot for themselves in real estate sales, but the industry generally is still searching for a good answer as to their effectiveness.

DESIRABLE PERSONAL CHARACTERISTICS FOR SALESPERSONS

No one has yet developed an effective and reliable means of predicting success in real estate selling, but many firms feel that they can expect more success when a prospective employee measures up in certain areas. For example, 58 per cent expect the person to be "well-dressed," 66 per cent want him to be able to speak "convincingly," all of them want him to be honest, one-fourth look for the ability to "get along with people," and another one-fourth expect him to have "personality and character." Beyond these few subjective measures, there is little agreement as to what other characteristics of this type are necessary. For example, frequently mentioned characteristics, defined in a variety of ways, include reliability, ambition, moral courage, foresight and sales sense, independence, pleasantness, and perseverance. In fact, the list of such often-used adjectives when totaled would do justice to an unabridged dictionary.

The best offices do, however, have an impressive list of measurable characteristics which, they find, provide clues as to *future failures* in real estate selling, including:

1. A single man with no dependents or family responsibilities.
2. A mature man with no assets such as a home, real estate, securities, or life insurance.
3. A person who could not explain bond refusals or arrests.
4. A person with a record of continuous illness or who had been refused life insurance for health reasons.
5. A person seeking only part-time work or limited work hours.
6. A person with an employed wife who was earning a higher salary and had a position with more "prestige."
7. A person with a wife employed in an occupation which required no education, no training, and no assumption of responsibilities.
8. A man subject to call by the armed forces.
9. A man who had had several jobs in recent years and who said that he was not satisfied with the progress he had been making on the last three jobs.
10. A person who could not satisfactorily account for his last ten years of work experience.
11. A person who could not give a satisfactory reason for leaving his last job.
12. Persons who have lost jobs more than once because the business they were in failed, or who were released for no apparent cause.
13. Former sales personnel of closely competitive local real estate firms.
14. Men whose families were not strongly supportive of their desire to sell real estate.

15. Persons who could not give good reasons for wanting to sell real estate.
16. Persons with limited income goals and no interest in improving these goals over the future.
17. Men under 23 or over 65.
18. Men over 60 with no sales or real estate business experience.
19. Men with continuous records of domestic difficulties, divorces, separations, and so forth.
20. Persons without previous selling experience and who are not certain whether they will like real estate selling. For example, they are attracted to real estate selling because they "like people."
21. Persons who indicated that they were completely satisfied with all of the previous jobs they held.
22. Men who say they have reformed after previous records of financial difficulties, heavy drinking, and so forth, but whose records show they have not.

This list is, of course, not complete, nor is it representative of that used by any single office. It is a composite list which reflects the thinking of most of the employing brokers in the offices included in the research study.

The previous paragraph tends to emphasize the negative aspects of anticipating sales success; therefore, it is important to present a full discussion of some of the characteristics which tend to epitomize the successful salesman. These clues are based on the experiences of some of the most successful real estate offices in the country.

Previous Earnings

"Average previous earnings" is perhaps one of the most commonly and successfully used criteria for differentiating successful salesmen. For example, at the time the survey was made in 1960, the net annual earnings for effective sales personnel averaged $13,500, as compared with only $4,700 for the typical salesman. In addition, none of the average salesmen earned more than $10,000 net annually, but 62 per cent of the best salesmen had done so. In achieving these incomes, the effective salesmen did not use unique sales methods, nor did they have particularly outstanding personalities; but they did tend to specialize in residential sales, to follow a consistent program of contacting prospective buyers and sellers, and to limit their sales activities to a particular section of the city in which they were located.

Reasons for Leaving Previous Employment

More than one-half of the effective salesmen could give cogent reasons for leaving their previous employment, usually listing such things as the closing of the office in which they had worked, too severe limitations on their sales methods, or lack of interest in the business on the part of the owner.

Reasons for Entering Real Estate Selling

Although all real estate salesmen tend to mention high income as a major factor attracting them to real estate selling, the most effective persons were usually those who had been especially recruited for the business or those who had never planned to do anything but sell real estate. The average salesman, by contrast, had usually drifted into the business after holding other types of selling jobs and finding that his income was not what he had anticipated.

Working Wives

Successful salesmen tend to be less tolerant of working wives, but almost all of those with working wives had wives who were employed in selling or in some type of managerial or administrative employment which helped to develop her appreciation of her husband's occupational problems.

Use of Leisure Time

Successful salesmen almost consistently show a decided preference for leisure-time activities which require some form of direct physical participation. For these men, golf, tennis, gardening, woodworking, and similar types of activities are important. Perhaps the leisuretime preferences of these effective salesmen, when related to other traits already mentioned, reflect a more energetic type of disposition.

Job Satisfaction

Successful salesmen tend to show great satisfaction with their current position, feeling that there are many unexploited opportunities still present. By contrast, the average salesman blames his lack of success on external factors and rarely recognizes that his own activities, interests, and capacities are the real limitations. In fact, one-third of the average salesmen, but none of the successful men, stated that they felt that they could make more money elsewhere and it was only a matter of time until they would move on to "greener pastures."

PREDICTING SUCCESS WITH TESTS

Perhaps more time, effort, and money have been spent by all businesses in a search for a test which will effectively predict success in selling than has been spent on any other personnel function. Over the years, a variety of tests have been developed by business and industry for placing prospective employees in the proper jobs, but, unfortunately, none of these have been developed specifically for use in predicting success in selling real estate. Tests which are used singly or in groups for this purpose fall into the general classes of measuring: (a) vocational interests, (b) personal preferences, (c) personality, (d) value systems and social adjustments, (e) ability to think critically, and (f) intelligence.

Experience with these types of tests has shown consistently that a great deal more work must be done in defining the characteristics of successful salesmen and their job responsibilities before these tests or any others can be developed for use in the real estate selling field. At present, these tests are most useful in reinforcing judgments made on the basis of the factors already mentioned or in resolving doubts which might arise from examining these factors.

There is strong reason to believe that some very useful results could be obtained if tests could be developed especially for use by real estate brokerage offices. In the meantime, vocational interest, value judgment, and intelligence tests appear to offer the most promise in differentiating the potentially effective salesperson from the ineffective or average one. Much more study and testing will have to be done before a consistently useful testing instrument can be developed, but meanwhile the following list of some of the best known and most frequently used tests mentioned in connection with the selection of real estate personnel may be helpful:

1. Firms who wish to develop tests for specific purposes should contact:

   Psychological Testing Service
   522 Fifth Avenue
   New York 36, New York

   The Dartnell Corporation
   Chicago, Illinois

Tests which have already been prepared and which might be adapted to the needs of an individual firm can be secured from the following:

2. Cooperative General Culture Test, Revised Series

   Cooperative Testing Service
   2½ Chambers Street
   Princeton, New Jersey

This test attempts to measure the applicant's knowledge of current social problems, history, social studies, literature, science, mathematics, and fine arts. In and of itself, it is an insufficient indicator of cultural acclimation, but it may be useful for supplementary testing. It has been criticized to the effect that its ease of use may lead to improper administration and interpretation.

3. Sales Questionnaire for experienced sales applicants

   Management Service Company
   3136 North 24th Street
   Philadelphia, Pennsylvania

"This is one of the tests available for measuring sales background. It is a multiple-choice 25-item omnibus test which includes questions concerning judgment in sales situations, meanings of technical terms in advertising and business practice, and relations between salesmen and office. The items. . . are concerned with facts that experienced salesmen might reasonably be expected to know. The questionnaire is easily administered. No time is set and most men will finish it in 15 minutes."—Robert G. Bernreuter, New York.

4. Steward Selection System for sales applicants

   Verne Steward & Associates
   P. O. Box 225
   South Gate, California

The Steward Test is a multi-division test and hiring guide subdivided as follows:

A. Personal Inventory of Basic Factors, 3rd Edition; 4 subtests:
   (1) A personality inventory of 75 items
   (2) A selected series of 10 items from Part (1), for each of which the respondent writes a short, descriptive paragraph if his answer to an item is "yes"
   (3) A 55-item mental ability test
   (4) A vocational interests test of 44 items

B. Personal Inventory of Background Factors, 3rd Edition
   This section appears in the form of a booklet requiring information on physical condition, educational background, employment and military experience, financial status, membership and activities, family status, interest in product and opportunity, and references.

C. Guide to Hiring Decisions
   The "Guide" is a key to the interpretation of tests and other hiring aids.

5. Tests of Ability to Sell for adults

   Center for Psychological Service
   George Washington University
   Washington 6, D. C.

This test is designed to measure ability to sell regardless of product or service offered and contains six subtests on social consciousness, arithmetical ability, memory, and ability to follow directions.

6. Strong Vocational Interest Blank

   Stanford University Press
   Stanford University
   Stanford, California

"The chief purpose of the Strong Vocational Interest Tests is to show a person the extent to which his interests correspond to those of successful men or women in a variety of occupations. Strong classifies occupations into four broad categories: Literary, social service, business and scientific. The business category measures three types of salesmen, among them real estate salesmen, by instructing the applicant to indicate his preference, indifference or dislike for a series of 400 occupations, activities, abilities and other pertinent items. The test is one of the most 'tried and true.' The author engages in a continual program of research aimed at raising the validity of the results."

The following observations have been made regarding the Strong Tests:

A. The evidence derived from the use of inventories as measurements of interests indicates that, within a given occupation, the relation between interests and abilities is not very high; the absence of a close relationship emphasizes the necessity for evaluating both interests and abilities in guidance and placement.

B. The available evidence also indicates that occupational interest patterns do not change materially during a lifetime of experience in a given profession.

C. "College groups (tested) show a greater relation between intelligence and interests in scientific fields than is found among the salesmen." Salesmen showed a negative correlation of the three types of salesmen classified.

6. Kuder Preference Record

   Science Research Associates
   57 West Grand Avenue
   Chicago 10, Illinois

The Kuder Test also measures interests in a number of occupations. It differs from the Strong Tests in that it includes a larger number of vocations and it tends to measure interest in types of situations rather than occupations and activities. Results are graphed on a chart indicating relative strength in activities described as mechanical, computational, scientific, persuasive, artistic, literary, musical, social service, and outdoor. The profile of this chart may be compared with profiles for specific occupations and their similarity or dissimilarity used as a basis for vocational guidance.

PRECAUTIONS IN THE USE OF TESTS

It cannot be too strongly emphasized that tests cannot, by themselves, be used to predict success in real estate selling. They are most useful and valid when they are used to reinforce judgments already made from personal interviews with and examination of the application of the prospective salesman. Research already completed with tests also indicates that salesmen with a variety of experiences, skills, talents, and personal characteristics can succeed in selling real estate—that there is no "universal" real estate sales type. For example, tentative evidence suggests that men with a strong interest in selling, of average intelligence, and a lack of interest in other aspects of business, particularly administrative, were most effective in larger firms. Men ranking in the higher quartiles of intelligence, and with a variety of selling and nonselling business interests and experiences, showed a decided preference for and great success in working for smaller offices. These tentative findings suggest that further study should be done to differentiate between types of sales personnel and the sales personnel needs of various types of real estate offices. Other precautions to be remembered in using tests are:

1. Tests are used most effectively for evaluating intelligence, skills, achievement and quality of performance, personality, interests, and preferences.
2. Tests are most effective when they are used for preliminary screening, with other factors considered in the final judgments.
3. Tests cannot predict conclusively potential success in selling, particularly in the field of real estate.
4. Tests present only one aspect of the total individual, and they are not infallible or precise in what they do measure.
5. In all but a few instances, the tests must be given by and interpreted by experienced, trained personnel.

USING EMPLOYMENT INTERVIEWS EFFECTIVELY

In the majority of real estate brokerage offices, sales personnel are hired after the most casual interviews, which often leave both the prospective employee and his future employer misinformed. This happens so frequently because the scarcity of good salespersons tempts sales managers to try out anyone who seems even slightly acceptable. The most effective means of preventing interview failures is to plan an interview in detail so that all pertinent points are covered.

A sales manager should use an interview form as the basis for developing a sound interviewing procedure. (See Figure 5–4.) Not only will the interview form assist him in acquiring all of the information he needs and in having a record of the interview conversation, but it will also prevent him from being overimpressed by someone with nothing to offer but personality.

Additional items not covered by the form but which he may wish to discuss with the applicant include:

1. The size of the office, the kinds of business it does, the past history of the growth of the firm, and a brief description of the present organization and personnel of the firm. At this point it might be well to have the applicant meet the key persons in the firm so that they can add their assessments of his potential.
2. An outline of the functions and responsibilities of each of the salespersons now on the staff. The minimum level of acceptable sales performance. At this time, information should also be given about hours in the office, office conduct, the number of listings and sales to be produced, writing and preparing advertising copy, telephone facilities, desk space, and related items.

Whether or not an interview form is used, the sales manager should remember that the purpose of the interview is to aid the applicant in making a good impression while also indicating his strengths and interests. Notes made during the interview and reviewed later often reveal that the most attractive applicant at the time of the interview does not measure up to other standards against which the applicant may later be compared.

The processes of testing and interviewing may seem to be too much trouble to the owner or sales manager who feels that he can "intuitively" find the "right" salesperson. The failure of many offices to find the "right" person is underlined by the sales-turnover ratios of 125 to 200 per cent that are reported annually by these offices.

1. SPEAKING ABILITY				
Measure vocabulary, grammar, tone, clarity, fluency.	Convincing and clear speaker	Speaks well	Some speaking limitations	Poor, ineffective speaker
2. PERSONALITY				
Measure direct effect on *you;* friendliness, tact, enthusiasm, sincerity.	Immediately appealing	Good personality	Average personality	Unappealing
3. PERSEVERANCE, AMBITION				
How hard do you believe he will work?	Will be a consistent hard worker	Will work required number of hours	Relies on encouragement from others	Probably won't work very hard
4. AGGRESSIVENESS				
What part does he take in conversation—indicating whether he is aggressive?	Tends to take a leading part	Initiates small points of discussion	Fairly responsive	Seldom participates in conversation

Figure 5-4. Personal Interview Checklist

5. JUDGMENT How are you impressed with his ability to size up situations, fairmindedness, etc.	Unusually keen and sound	Good	Average	Poor judgment
6. COURTESY Judge politeness and manners.	Exceptionally polite and courteous	Courteous in most situations	Usually courteous	Discourteous
7. APPEARANCE How does appearance impress you, facial expressions, bearing, physique, carriage, taste in dress, neatness?	Creates exceptionally fine impression	Good appearance	Appearance satisfactory	Poor appearance
8. HONESTY, INTEGRITY What is your opinion of his character (also check references on application)?	Absolutely trustworthy; references indicate unquestionable integrity	Seems honest	Probably honest; references uncertain	Bad references
9. PREVIOUS EXPERIENCE How has previous experience, if any, been divided between managerial and sales?	Experience mostly managerial and administrative	Little managerial; mostly selling	Experience other than selling or managing	No experience
10. AGE	30–45			Under 23 or over 65
11. AUTOMOBILE How old is his car?	New–2 yrs.	3–4 yrs.	5–6 yrs.	over 6 yrs.
12. MARITAL AND FAMILY STATUS Consider number of dependents, closeness of relation and age	Family and several dependents	Few dependents including self	Wife only	No dependents
13. FINANCIAL STATUS Consider ability to finance self in view of expenses and other income.	Can carry self for 6 months	Ability to sustain self 3 months	Can carry self financially for one month	Little evidence of carrying ability
14. ACTIVITIES, CONTACTS Consider breadth of activities, extent of participation, and offices held.	Leader of many groups	Active in a number of groups	Little participation	Inactive

Figure 5-4 Continued.

15. SUMMARY

How closely does he resemble *my* qualities and characteristics?	Very close resemblance	Fairly similar	Not very closely	No resemblance

REMARKS: (Would you be willing to work with this applicant? State in your own words how well you believe he would fit into this office; comment further on his desirability.)

RECOMMENDATIONS: ( ) Recommend highly. ( ) Willing to recommend.
( ) Dubious. ( ) Will not recommend.

Figure 5-4 Continued.

A COMPLETE PERSONNEL PROGRAM

The place of interviewing and other procedures in a complete personnel program has been presented in Figure 5–1. All steps are important and minimal for those firms that wish to have a percentage of productive salespersons. An important support for proper interviewing is the organizational charts and job descriptions that grow out of the statement of the firm's objectives. One type of job description is shown in Figures 5–5 and 5–6.

Many offices have various types of sales jobs, and each should be fully described. Figures 5–5 and 5–6 give a typical description for an experienced, senior salesman and a junior salesman. There should also be descriptions for new salesmen, for salesmen who specialize in various types of properties, for salesmen with some but limited experience, and so forth. Such descriptions grow out of the actual job requirements, which will suggest what types of experience and education may be needed. The major elements of a good job description are indicated by underlined subheadings in Figures 5–5 and 5–6.

BASIC PREPARATION FOR REAL ESTATE SELLING

Perhaps the most puzzling characteristic of the real estate brokerage business is the high rate of failure in selling even though there are more varieties of sales training courses and programs in this business than in almost any other business. Research tends to suggest that one of the reasons for this happening is that too much sales training is carried on in the same manner and at the same level of content for all types of salespersons in all types of sales offices; instead, programs should be geared to a variety of levels and backgrounds and different kinds of offices. Because the sales manager or office owners rarely offer much help to the salesperson in selecting a program of education, he must expect to do it for himself. Some of the elements needed for successful real estate selling are presented in the following paragraphs.

TITLE:

Senior Salesmen, Residential

JOB SUMMARY:

Under supervision of Sales Manager secures listings for properties, plans advertising and prepares rough copy for all listings secured, plans and executes sales campaign for all listings secured, shows properties, completes deposit-receipt agreement. Work often entails irregular hours and week-end and evening work.

When not engaged in direct selling, must take turn in office, meeting all persons entering office. Has some responsibilities for supervising and giving informal training to new salesmen.

From time to time, will be expected to lead discussions among sales force on current selling problems.

DUTIES:

1. To meet listing and sales quotas as established by sales manager.
2. To prepare classified advertising.
3. To prepare listing agreements and deposit-receipt agreements.
4. To supervise floor activities one half-day weekly.
5. To show his own prospects and others when directed to do so by sales manager.

QUALIFICATIONS:

1. Five years of real estate sales experience.
2. Five additional years of business or selling experience.
3. Two years or more of college completed.
4. Licensed as a broker.
5. A record of selling not less than 24 homes a year during last two years.
6. Ability accurately to complete listing agreements and deposit receipts.
7. Knowledge of real estate financing sources and means of acquiring financing.
8. Male, not less than 35 nor more than 60 years of age.

OTHER JOB REQUIREMENTS:

1. Must have car not older than two years.
2. If married, wife must not be working.
3. Willingness to work not less than 45 hours per week.
4. Passing score on job tests.
5. Ability to finance own living expenses for six months.

COMPENSATION:

One-half of all commissions paid to office from sales, plus 10 per cent of commission for selling own listings when they are exclusives. All commissions returned to office in excess of $6,000 annually will give___ % commission to salesman.

Figure 5-5. Job Description, Senior Salesman

JOB TITLE:

Junior Salesman, Residential

JOB SUMMARY:

Under the supervision of a senior salesman secures listings for properties, shows properties, and completes deposit-receipt agreements. Minimum hours per week, 48, including week-end and evening selling.

When not engaged in selling, must take a turn in the greeting of clients, answering telephone inquiries, and preparing rough advertising copy.

Will be expected to complete successfully the six-week training program offered by the firm.

Figure 5-6. Job Description, Junior Salesman

DUTIES:

1. To meet listing and sales quotas established by the sales manager.
2. To prepare listing agreements and deposit-receipt agreements.
3. To spend at least one half-day each week as a floor man in the office.
4. To show prospects as directed by the sales manager or senior salesman under whom he is working.

QUALIFICATIONS:

1. Licensed as a real estate salesman.
2. 25 years of age but not more than 35 years of age.
3. One year of real estate sales experience or equivalent business experience.
4. Completion at night school or in college of courses in principles of real estate, real estate law, real estate finance, and real estate practices.

OTHER JOB REQUIREMENTS:

1. Must have a car not older than three years.
2. If married, wife must not be working.
3. Ability to finance own living expenses for at least six months.
4. Passing score on interview tests.

COMPENSATION:

One-half of all commissions paid to the office from sales made, plus 10 per cent of commissions received from sale of exclusive listings secured by him.

Figure 5-6 Continued.

Sales Training and Education

A real estate salesperson usually needs education at three levels: (1) prior to and immediately after licensing, (2) after licensing and some years of experience, and (3) upon the assumption of some type of managerial duties, either as a sales manager or as the owner of an office. Although this education must and usually does focus on the knowledge, skills, understanding, attitudes, and techniques needed for daily sales duties, it should also include some materials on general business and the economic, social, political, and geographic forces which affect land uses, land values, and real estate markets.

The methods of training vary widely, with the small and medium-size offices tending to put most of the burden of training on the experienced personnel. For example, more than 75 per cent of the small and medium-size offices but only 44 per cent of the large firms put emphasis on having experienced personnel give the new persons assistance and guidance in listing properties and closing sales. Sixty-eight per cent of the small firms, 76 per cent of the medium-size firms, and 50 per cent of the large firms supplement this assistance with additional instruction in the techniques of these processes. By contrast, an overwhelming majority of the medium-size and large firms hold regular sales meetings and also require the new persons to spend additional time in observing and working with the experienced salesmen.

The inexperienced salesperson can expect to spend anywhere from one to six months in training before he will be allowed to sell. The medium-size and large offices will prefer three to six months and the smaller offices one to three months of training. However, even after he is on the job, the new salesperson will have a period of adjustment in learning to apply what he has been taught and in working up to his maximum sales potential. In small offices, this period of adjustment may take an additional 2 to 11 months and in the medium-size and large offices as long as 36 months.

Who Should Do the Training

Although many salespersons are left largely to their own devices in securing sales training, such organizations as the National Institute of Real Estate Brokers place training responsibility upon the experienced brokers. They point out that an experienced broker can give the new man the benefit of past mistakes and mold and inspire him to avoid these pitfalls. The Institute has adopted the slogan, "Learn more, earn more, serve better," which suggests that one of the important places for a new man—and even experienced men—to look for training is in those offices which have membership in the Institute.

The Need for Training

A survey among families who had purchased homes in a suburban area provided some valuable insights into the shortcomings of real estate salespersons—shortcomings which could be corrected through training. The most frequently mentioned complaint was that salespersons would not take the time to help buyers analyze their needs and their abilities to purchase, and that they were often delayed in finding the house they felt they should have. The second major type of complaint, which covered almost all of the remaining comments, was the lack of familiarity on the part of the salesman with his product and with the factors which made it valuable. For example, salespersons usually had inadequate answers to such items as the age of the house, the dimensions of various rooms and the over-all size of the house, the lot size, costs of taxes and utilities, ages and condition of appliances, school district and church district boundaries or locations, and shopping and other facilities available in the neighborhood.

It is clear that, from the employing brokers' and the clients' viewpoints, salespersons generally lack many of the basic selling tools which they need. An analysis of these shortcomings reveals that it is not the lack of "natural" sales ability which keeps the average salesperson from being a success, but his failure to acquire the right tools and sales habits. Experiences of approximately 80 real estate brokerage offices in a suburban area show that the foundation for successful selling lies in continuous sales training.

Current trends in real estate brokerage offices also suggest that offices cannot and will not continue to hire the untrained salesperson, or else, when he is hired, will insist that he secure additional training. Rising costs of operating brokerage offices, the wider knowledge of real estate which buyers and sellers are now acquiring, the necessity for reducing sharply the unproductive periods in real estate selling, the desire of firms to be able to put sales forecasting and profit anticipation on a more organized and regular basis, all suggest that even mere survival in real estate brokerage dictates continued sales training for all sales personnel.

Characteristics of Real Estate Sales Training

The salesperson who is looking for the most effective sales training program for himself should recognize that training practices differ widely among real estate brokerage offices, so that he should study the training practices of a firm before he commits himself to employment with it. For example, all of the large firms, 90 per cent of the medium-size firms, and only 56 per cent of the small firms have sales meetings. The bulk of the large and medium-size firms and only one-half of the small firms hold these meetings weekly, and semimonthly meetings are the next most frequently held. On the other hand, almost one-third of the small firms seldom hold meetings.

Small firms tend to favor as subjects for their meetings such things as discussions of selling and listing problems facing members of the sales staff, new ideas or techniques for securing listings and sales, and visiting properties on which new listings have been secured. Medium-size firms also discuss problems and new ideas, but they tend to spend an almost equal amount of time discussing newly listed properties but less time in visiting them. The large firms tend to duplicate the training-program content of the medium-size firms, but they also add an additional relatively large block of time for the discussion of business and real estate markets and market trends.

Training for New Sales Personnel

Although not all real estate offices offer training for new salespersons, almost all of them tend to agree on what should be included in such training. Many offices do not offer this type of training because they feel that the new man can pick up most of it through other means. This, they feel, is particularly true in matters relating to license and real estate law. The form which the training program takes is not so important as the content; thus, any salesman who wishes to build a background of fundamentals can take advantage of training opportunities which present themselves, once he understands what the content of the training program should be. The areas in which a new salesperson must gain, and in which an experienced salesperson must maintain, competency are:

1. Knowledge of the firm
2. Knowledge of the community and markets served
3. Licensing law, property law, and legal procedures
4. Fundamentals of listing and selling property
5. Understanding clients
6. Evaluating the competition
7. Keeping abreast of market trends
8. Developing a sales "executive" attitude

Knowledge of the firm. When starting to work with a firm, the new man will want to meet everyone in the firm and to discuss with them their jobs, duties, and responsibilities. Later, when he needs help or wants to render better service to a client, he will know to whom he can turn for assistance. In the process of getting acquainted with the other personnel, he will also want to learn about the firm's policies and methods of operating, the functions of each of the departments which may exist, and what the general objectives of the firm are. Finally, he will want to study carefully all of the listings which the firm possesses and, by an analysis of past sales, to learn about the listings with which he should become particularly familiar. With the permission of the chief officers of the firm, he can do much of this type of training on his own.

Knowledge of the community and markets served. This is also an area of training in which the individual can do much of his own training and set his own pace. He will want to study in detail atlases, maps, census and business information which will inform him of the locations of public facilities, transportation routes and services, and shopping, recreation, and school facilities. Equally important, he will want to know about the typical family who buys homes in the markets served by his office so that he will understand what size, style, and price of house appeals to it and which it will buy. A review of those listings which sold the most quickly, the terms on which they were sold, and the kinds of families who purchased them will tell him immediately the kinds of markets served by the office for which he is working. It should also provide him with numerous clues as to where to look for properties to list and to sell.

Licensing law, property law, and legal procedures. Some firms do give some elementary training in law, but the salesman will find that he can better absorb the law training which his firm gives if he first attends one or two basic courses in law, which are usually available in all localities in adult evening schools or in special real estate schools. Once he has mastered these fundamentals, he is ready to learn how the firm wants him to handle such procedures as escrow closing, preparation of contracts, deeds and leases, title insurance purchases, special legal problems, and dealing with various types of governmental agencies such as the Federal Housing Administration, the Veterans Administration, and Building and Safety and Planning Commissions. It is very important for him to learn what he can and cannot do in the field of law so that he will not be guilty of practicing law.

Fundamentals of listing and selling. Many offices feel that earnest efforts to list a property at the proper price are more productive than attempting to sell a property which was accepted at an unrealistic listing price just so that the listing contract could be obtained. For this reason, sales personnel must learn accurately to estimate potential selling price and then to convince the seller that he should accept such a price. In many communities, owners deliberately ask a higher price for their properties than what they expect to receive so that they can have some room to "bargain." Although this practice is widespread, the most successful salesmen have found that insisting on accepting a listing at the proper price is the most effective means of maintaining a good inventory of salable properties.

Properties may be listed for sale on an open, an exclusive-right, or an exclusive-agency contract. Practices vary among offices and communities; therefore, the salespersons are usually trained to understand the advantages and disadvantages of each and the techniques of using each. Each office will also have a preference for a particular type of listing form and particular procedures for processing the form after the listing has been signed. Usually, a review of past listing agreements will provide information on these items.

The volume of sales which a given set of listings will produce is not necessarily related to the volume of listings which an office holds. Offices with high stable sales volumes tend to limit the number of listings which they will accept and to limit the number of listings which are given to each salesperson. Research has established, and experience has proven, that six to ten listings will take the full time of a salesperson and, if properly selected to match the clientele he serves regularly, will help him maintain a high personal sales volume. A large inventory of listings is useful primarily for the unusual property request or for meeting the demands of a particularly meticulous client.

Many of the most experienced salespersons feel that selling cannot be studied but must be experienced, and that those best able to learn from experience will, in time, become the best salespersons. This is a difficult and expensive method of developing sales abilities, and there are shortcuts which can be learned which will reduce, but not eliminate, the amount of sales experience needed to develop successful sales habits. For example, in training sessions, sales personnel can be given sales talks to memorize, or they may be given the opportunity to practice dealing with clients on an informal basis; telephone and personal greeting techniques can be reviewed and practiced; suggestions can be made to the salespersons on how to improve their personal appearance and the impressions which they make on clients; case studies can be presented on difficult sales which were completed and on sales which were not completed.

Exclusive Authorization and Right to Sell

CALIFORNIA REAL ESTATE ASSOCIATION STANDARD FORM

In consideration of the services of..,
herein called Broker, I hereby employ Broker, exclusively and irrevocably, for the period beginning ....
...., 19....... and ending at midnight..., 19......., to sell the property
situated in...County of ....,
California, described as follows: ....
....
....
....
....
....
....
....
and I hereby grant Broker the exclusive and irrevocable right to sell said property within said time for....................
....($...............................) Dollars
and to accept a deposit thereon...
Terms: ....
....
....
....
....
....
....

I hereby agree to pay Broker as commission..............................per cent ....
....of the selling price
if said property is sold during the term hereof or any extension thereof by Broker or by me or by another broker or through any other source. If said property is withdrawn from sale, transferred, or leased during the term hereof or any extension thereof, I agree to pay Broker said per cent of the above listed price.

If a sale, lease or other transfer of said property is made within three (3) months after this authorization or any extension thereof terminates to parties with whom Broker negotiates during the term hereof or any extension thereof and Broker notifies me in writing of such negotiations, personally or by mail, during the term hereof or any extension thereof, then I agree to pay said commission to Broker.

Evidence of title shall be a California Land Title Association standard coverage form policy of title insurance to be paid for by ....

If deposits or amounts paid on account of purchase price are forfeited, Broker shall be entitled to one-half thereof, but not to exceed the amount of the commission.

I hereby acknowledge receipt of a copy hereof.

Dated .... 19............ ....

...., California ....

....
(Address of Owner)

....
(City) (Zone) (Phone) Owner

In consideration of the execution of the foregoing, the undersigned Broker agrees to use diligence in procuring a purchaser.

....
(Address of Broker) Broker

.... By..
(City) (Zone) (Phone)

Size of parcel:...Taxes: $...per year.
Loan Information...
....

For these forms address California Real Estate Association.
117 West Ninth St., Los Angeles 15.

Some of the time in basic sales training will also be spent on learning how to secure financing for properties and how to prepare loan applications. No training is complete, in fact, unless the salespersons are shown each of the types of forms in use in the office and are given some brief instructions on how these are to be completed. Many sales have been lost becaues a sales contract form or sales closing instructions were not properly prepared; therefore, learning to use forms has to be an integral and finishing touch in basic sales training.

Understanding clients. The typical real estate firm does the majority of its selling within a two- to three-mile radius of its office, which means that the characteristics of the housing and population within this area will set the limits for the sales that can be made. Many offices have found that the most effective means of learning about the local market is to take their entire sales force on periodic trips through the surrounding neighborhood and to stop and examine each property which has been newly received for listing. As the properties are examined, the staff is invited to give comments on the type of buyer who might be interested in the property, to point out features which would make good selling points, and even to give quick demonstrations on how they believe the properties might be sold. When an office does not follow this practice, a salesperson can do the same thing for himself for the properties on which he is working.

The ability to match properties and buyers is perhaps the most important element in the sales process and one on which a great deal of time can be spent in a sales training program. Included in such training should be advice and techniques for differentiating the client who is "just looking" from the one who is seriously interested in buying. Experienced salesmen believe that it is easier to find a property for a serious potential buyer than to attempt to persuade an unqualified prospect to buy a particular property.

Evaluating the competition. The rivalry which is traditional among real estate brokerage offices is often balanced by various forms of cooperation among these same offices. For this reason, basic sales training should include an introduction to the characteristics of the typical salesperson in the other offices, the kinds of situations in which cooperation is encouraged and how cooperative selling is carried on, and the points at which one office has an advantage over the other offices. An important part of this type of training is the list of reasons which can be developed why a client should deal with one office rather than with another. For example, an office can point to the long number of years it has been in business, its large inventory of listings from which buyers can select, the amount of advertising it does, its consistent ability to obtain the price which the seller asks, the knowledge which its staff has of the community, its lists of qualified prospects who are ready to buy, the detailed procedures which it regularly follows in listing and selling properties, and its ability to secure any type of financing the buyer may need.

Keeping abreast of market trends. A detailed and expert knowledge of real estate markets is not needed by the typical salesman, yet informed opinions on market conditions and trends may help. A portion of the basic sales training time can be spent very profitably in a discussion of average sales prices, the amounts which buyers expect to receive as down payments, the level of rents, the costs of construction, and what some of the professional forecasters are saying about future real estate trends.

DEVELOPING A "SALES EXECUTIVE" ATTITUDE

Countless interviews with all types of real estate salespersons indicate that the attitude of a person toward his selling job influences to an amazing extent his actual performance. The best attitude is one in which the salesperson looks upon himself as an independent business executive. As such, he recognizes the value of constant attention to and retraining in developing good work habits, of a knowledge of his clients and properties, and of the ability to plan and execute his own business activities. He feels a personal responsibility for helping his office maintain a good sales volume so that he can profit from being with a successful brokerage office. Many offices fail to see the necessity for building this attitude and do little to build morale among their sales personnel. In such offices, training focuses almost exclusively on sales techniques and little time is spent in giving attention to the individual problems of the sales staff. Perhaps the most important criteria which a new person should look for in evaluating an office is the degree to which the office encourages the older, more experienced men to give personal attention to the selling problems of the new salesmen.

Training for Experienced Sales Personnel

Opinions of brokers are divided on the value of training for experienced sales personnel; as a result, the regularity with which meetings are held and the items discussed at these meetings differ widely. The strongest argument advanced in favor of regular meetings is that they provide a means of keeping the entire staff informed on company policy and permit the new, less experienced men to gain the advantage of sharing in the experiences of the successful men. Those offices which do not have regular meetings or do not require attendance at sales meetings feel that to do either would encroach on the independent-contractor status of their sales force.

Many experienced salesmen can see no advantage in sales meetings; but when the meetings are well planned and directed to the needs of the sales staff, even the most skeptical older man will accept some sales training. The offices which favor regular sales meetings find that the meetings must not only be well planned and well run, but they must be held continuously. Variety can be introduced and interest maintained if the meetings are a combination of lectures by the staff and outside experts, sales demonstrations, property visits, and group discussions. Group discussions are usually favored by sales personnel because they permit the group to reach its own decisions, and such decisions are more likely to be accepted and used by the majority of the group. Such meetings are particularly effective places for allowing the staff to "blow off steam" on items which have been bothering them. These advantages must, of course, be weighed against the time that group discussions consume and the necessity of limiting groups to 10 or 15 persons.

Experienced salespersons who are reluctant to participate in sales meetings can turn them to their benefit by suggesting topics for discussion at the meetings. Topics which salesmen have found to be particularly interesting and useful in many offices include:

1. Personal improvement: personal efficiency, memory training, personal qualities of successful salesmen, and methods which inspire in clients confidence in the salesperson's abilities
2. Improving sales methods: creative selling, the art of negotiation, selling aids, the sales kit, essentials of salesmanship, case histories of sales, polishing the demonstration, new listing methods, new sources of prospects, answering objecttions intelligently, and reviews of basic sales training
3. Specialist selling: building a clientele through property management, using better appraisals as selling tools, augmenting income and sales through insurance selling, brokerage of industrial, commercial, and investment properties, developing residential properties, developing residential income properties for investors, and creating new real estate investments
4. General business topics: income taxes and real estate investing; what is happening in real estate financing markets, in sales markets, and in leasing; meeting competition; trends in business conditions; and government home-financing programs

SALES TRAINING SUPPLEMENTS

The individual salesperson can do a great deal to make the formal training which he receives more effective if he supplements it with activities on his own. If he is not participating in regular sales training sessions, he can use these supplements to create his personal program. The first and most obvious thing he can do is to attend evening adult courses in real estate. Often he will find that an office which does not have organized sales training sessions will pay part or all of the costs of his attending such courses. Second, he can attend the conventions and sales meetings which are sponsored by organized real estate groups. For example, a state Real Estate Association will hold periodic sales seminars, and many local Realty Boards will sponsor sales training programs conducted by Board members. Third, he can build a library of materials on real estate and real estate selling. This personal library can be added to if he subscribes to selected professional publications in real estate, and it need not be large if he also uses the books and other publications owned by the local realty board library, his office, and the public library. Finally, he must educate himself on what it takes to be successful in real estate selling and plan and follow a program of personal development which will help him become one of the successful real estate sales executives.

SELLING AND HUMAN RELATIONS

One of the most obvious reasons for the failure of many real estate salespersons and sales managers was found to be related to the emphasis which they placed on securing more and more technical information about real estate selling while neglecting the human-relations element almost entirely. Perhaps the most important ability which a salesperson can develop is that of becoming sufficiently sensitive to be able to understand how other people react to him. The ability to do this can sometimes be developed over a long life of selling experience, but it can be developed more effectively and quickly through conscious study and attention to it. Almost all salespersons recognize this, but, in their rush to earn high incomes as quickly as possible, they tend to forget it. It is for this reason that too much real estate education deals with the "tricks" and techniques of selling rather than with some of the more fundamental materials.

IS THERE A PLACE FOR AN EFFECTIVE SALESPERSON?

A series of studies completed recently indicate quite conclusively that a higher standard of sales performance is definitely needed in real estate brokerage. Not only is there a large incidence of over-all poor sales performance, but there are also many indications that too many sales personnel are being used inefficiently and ineffectively by the majority of the real estate brokerage offices. Even in those instances in which sales personnel are being managed properly, this seems to have been accomplished more by chance than by a consciously planned program.

Because the owners of real estate brokerage offices do not appear to recognize the tremendous waste which is occurring through poor personnel practices, the sales personnel must take the initiative in asking that good practices be followed. It should be pointed out to the offices that the higher percentage of successful salespersons which would be produced from an effective program would more than offset the costs of developing such a program. It is quite clear that real estate brokerage offices which desire continuity of profits and operations over reasonably long periods of time cannot afford to have less than the best in their salesmen.

Principles of Selecting and Training Real Estate Sales Personnel

1. *Successful salespersons.* There are no universally accepted criteria for judging a successful salesperson. Success is related to the size of the firm, the types of markets served, and a variety of other factors.
2. *Unity.* Success in selecting and training real estate personnel is not possible unless a total, unified personnel program is used that involves recruting, interviewing, testing, training, and compensating.
3. *Universality of training.* All successful sales personnel engage in a continuing program of training and education.
4. *Maximum production.* Maximum sales production can be achieved only if the sales personnel are matched to the sales jobs required of them, rewarded for superior performances, and given measurable and attainable sales goals.
5. *Selection.* Selection of the proper salesperson begins with a full job description.
6. *Personal characteristics.* There is no evidence that a particular combination of personal characteristics can be used to predict success or failure in selling real estate.
7. *Testing.* Testing is most successful when it is used to support judgments already made or when additional evidence is needed to guide these judgments.
8. *Job descriptions.* Success in selecting a top-quality salesperson is most likely to be achieved if each applicant is compared with a carefully prepared job description.
9. *Training programs.* Training programs should always be designed to fit the needs and resources of the firm that is conducting the training and the kinds of persons to be trained.
10. *Sales training supplements.* Training by the firm should be supplemented with attendance by the trainees, and by all persons on the sales force, at conventions, sales conferences, and similar types of events.

CASE STUDY

Introduction

The President of this firm finds that, although his sales are being maintained at a proper level in the Brokerage Department, they have not been increasing as they should. Several of his weaker salesmen are just meeting their minimum quotas and nothing else. He has tried sales contests and special prizes, but they provide very short and temporary sales stimulation. He has checked with the Sales Manager, and finds that one or two newer offices with younger salesmen are providing some stiff competition. He is wondering what he can do to meet this competition and to stimulate his staff to higher productivity.

Identification

Income: Averages $600,000 gross annually, with $50,000 absolute net to the owner.

Size: Corporation with one president, two sales managers, 40 sales personnel, 20 in nonbrokerage activities such as appraising and property management, and 10 clerical and secretarial personnel.

Age: The firm started operations in 1952.

Location: There is one central office located in a central business district of a small community adjacent to a large city. Three branches are located in various parts of the community. The small community was settled at an early date by families in the upper-income brackets and since that date has managed to maintain a special reputation for having middle- and high-income families exclusively.

Organization

The company is organized as a corporation with closely held stock, so that the president is in control of the company. The company has been departmentalized, with the following departments: (1) Brokerage—divided into residential, industrial and commercial, (2) Leasing and Property Management, (3) Financing—loan correspondence and servicing, (4) Appraising, (5) Accounting and Record-Keeping, and (6) Subdividing (improving vacant land with utilities and streets and then selling). Each department is headed by a Vice-President, who sits on the Board of Directors (without a vote) and is responsible to the President.

Staffing

Department Vice-Presidents act independently in hiring staff personnel. They set criteria, interview, and make final decisions, except in rare instances, when they may consult the owner. A survey of the staff indicated that they worked well together and enjoyed the prestige of working for this company.

In the Brokerage Department, emphasis is placed on hiring persons of attractive personal appearance and with a "refined" manner about them. This term was used by the owner and his vice-presidents but never clearly defined by them; neither do they have a job description which defined what they mean. They feel that personal observation plus interviews with the applicant and his family will give all the necessary information for deciding about hiring.

Every applicant for a sales position must be able to carry himself financially for at least six to nine months and must be living in the area where he will be doing his selling. None are allowed to sell before serving three months with the company. The firm has adhered strictly to this policy, so that they are constantly searching for persons to add to the staff. The securing and retention of good personnel is a major problem.

A survey of present sales personnel indicates that all had had previous real estate sales experience before coming to work for this firm. When this was checked with the President, he stated that experience was not required, but that evidently the selection process had worked out that way. The initial training for these persons consisted of going out with experienced salesmen of the firm and observing their actions. The new salesmen are then required to read the policy manual thoroughly and to attend a series of informal meetings with the Sales Manager for the purpose of discussing the implications of the various policies. After this, the Sales Manager reviews listings and prospect reports of completed and pending sales and lets the new man observe closing transactions in the office. This entire training period takes from two to four weeks, depending upon when the salesman feels that he has learned enough to start on his own.

Once accepted as a part of the sales force, the salesman is given a sales quota and a listing quota to meet. The sales quota provides that he must return to the office not less than $3,000 in commissions each year or earn a total of $6,000 in gross commissions for retention. As a matter of practice, the firm usually expects at least twice this amount in commissions after the man has been with the firm at least two years; of these do not materialize, they will suggest indirectly that he should leave.

To assist the sales force, advertising is increased as business declines, but there is no organized budgeting. Salesmen write their own ads and submit them to the sales manager, who rewrites them for publication.

The firm feels that it is its prestige and strong advertising program which make possible the high volume of sales. They point to surveys made in the office indicating that from 45 to 55 per cent of all sales completed came from referrals by satisfied clients. The commissions are split uniformly 50–50 between the office and the salesman; the office does not pay for a car but pays for all advertising (no budget limits) and furnishes a telephone and a desk.

Sales meetings are held on an occasional basis with topics selected by the President or the Sales Manager on items which they believe are important and of interest to their sales staff. Attendance at these is not compulsory, but they are held at a local restaurant in the early morning with breakfast furnished. Salesmen who are not meeting their quotas are expected to attend or to give a satisfactory reason why they have not attended.

Once the man begins to produce at a satisfactory level, he is allowed to pursue whatever course of selling he feels will be most successful. Each man is required to take certain floor time, but none object to this because they feel it is an important source of business. The Sales Manager makes himself readily available to any salesman for consultation. He says that he "will not force himself on any man, because they are all mature and experienced and intelligent enough to know when they need help."

Chapter 6

MANAGING SALES ACTIVITIES

The consistent failures of many real estate salespersons can be traced in large measure to the poor programs of sales management that are characteristic of many real estate brokerage offices. To some degree, this condition arises from the reluctance of brokers to attempt much control over sales personnel for fear of interfering with their independent-contractor status. On the other hand, there is much that a real estate brokerage office can do to aid salespersons in developing good selling habits. In this chapter, reports are offered of methods that have been used successfully to induce good sales habits. In addition, the experiences of some of the most successful salespersons are summarized so that owners and sales managers can gain some insight into the attitudes and practices of successful salespersons.

SALES PLANNING

Successful selling begins with good planning; therefore, all salespersons should be encouraged to plan their selling time. Good planning is done on a daily, weekly, and annual basis.

The Annual Sales Plan

The simplest method of determining how to aid a salesperson in planning a typical sales day is to determine what the annual sales goals of the firm are going to be. Sales activities can then be prorated among salespersons, who can then prorate their projected sales over the year on a daily basis. For example, assume that a real estate office has determined that it needs $1.5 million annual sales to pay all expenses and a satisfactory profit. If there are four salespersons in the office, each will have to sell annually $375,000 of properties. (Figure 6–1.) Based on past performance, the sales manager then determines that each man must sell in a year 25 properties with an average sales price of $15,000.

Annual income to be earned	$ 13,500
Total annual commissions which have to be returned to office	$ 22,500
Total annual sales volume needed to produce desired office commissions	$375,000
Total annual number of homes needed to be sold @average of $15,000	25
Total buying prospects to be contacted, @15 per sale	375
Total listings needed, @10 per sale, to be made	250
Total listings contacts needed to produce 10 good listings per sale	2,500

SUMMARY: Weekly average activity goals, based on 50 working weeks per year:

Sales	1 (every other week)
Prospect contacts	8
Listing agreements signed	5
Listing contacts	50
Dollar sales volume	$7,500

Figure 6-1. Planning for Effective Real Estate Selling

Office records will provide the sales manager with an estimate of the number of properties that each salesperson will have to show in order to make 25 sales. In the same manner, the total number of contacts that must be made to produce a reasonable number of listed properties can be estimated. Figures 6–2 and 6–3 indicate the manner in which this information can be used to prepare sales plans for individual salespersons. In the illustrations, it has been assumed that each listing requires 8 personal contacts and that each sale demands 16 personal contacts.

In Figure 6–2, the sales manager can see that the salesperson failed to make as many personal contacts as he should have made, and that he has finished January with three fewer listing agreements than his plan called for. His sales plan shows (Figure 6–3) that he has sold the number of properties he had planned to sell, but that their total value was lower than he had planned. His sales plan chart also shows that he made one-fourth fewer personal contacts than he should have made. From these analyses, the sales manager knows that the salesperson did not meet his listing and sales quotas primarily because he did not make as many personal contacts among prospective buyers and sellers as he should have made. This shortcoming is usually the major cause of listing and selling failures.

The Weekly Sales Plan

Once weekly goals have been established, the sales force should be left to work out their own detailed weekly programs and to keep track of their

Total listings to be secured for the year 250; per week 5
Listing contacts to be made for the year 2,500; per week 50

Week Ending	Personal Contacts				Listing Agreements Signed			
	Planned		Actual		Planned		Actual	
	For week	*To date*	*For week*	*To date*	*For week*	*To date*	*For week*	*To date*
January 7	50		40		5		3	
14	50	100	56	96	5	10	4	7
21	50	150	62	158	5	15	7	14
28	50	200	30	188	5	20	3	17

Figure 6-2. Property Listing Plan

Total number of properties to be sold for the year 25; per week 1/2 (1 every 2 weeks)
Total dollar volume of properties to be sold $375,000; per week $ 7,500
Prospect contacts to be made for the year 375; per week 8

Week Ending	Prospect Contacts				Properties Sold							
	Planned		Actual		Planned				Actual			
	For week	*To date*	*For week*	*To date*	*For week*		*To date*		*For Week*		*To date*	
					No.	*Value*	*No.*	*Value*	*No.*	*Value*	*No.*	*Value*
January 7	8		8									
14	8	16	7	15	1	15,000						
21	8	32	6	21					1	10,000	1	10,000
28	8	40	9	30	1	15,000	2	30,000	1	18,000	2	28,000

Figure 6-3. Property Selling Plan

results. Figures 6–4 and 6–5 show a weekly planning and analysis scheme that is a composite of some of those used by successful offices and sales personnel. The use of these types of exhibits will probably require one or two hours of work filling them out each week. Although sales managers will sometimes find resistance among salespersons to the use of these forms, the advantage of a planned day is so evident that salespersons should be given strong encouragement to develop one.

Week Ending__________

WEEKLY LISTING-ACTIVITY PLANNING AND ANALYSIS

Total contacts to be made 50 . Listings to be secured 5

Name of contact	Address	Phone	Comments
1. New, in-person contacts, canvassing			
2. New, phone contacts			
3. New, in-person contacts, meetings			
4. Follow-up on previous-listing contacts			
5. Follow-up on current-listing contacts			
6. Follow-up on expired-listing contacts			
7. Listings secured			

Summary	Type of contact*						
	1	2	3	4	5	6	total
Total contacts made							
Total listings secured							

*These numbers relate to numbers above

Figure 6-4. Weekly Listing—Activity Planning and Analysis

The exact content of an activity form depends upon the characteristics of the business done by a particular office. Figure 6–4 indicates that this office obtains its listing contacts by personal canvassing by sales personnel, telephone contacts from advertising, at meetings which various members of the staff attend, follow-ups on persons who have been contacted previously and who indicated that they might be selling at a later date, and telephone calls to persons who had already signed listings but who might know of

Week Ending ________

WEEKLY PROSPECTING-ACTIVITY PLANNING AND ANALYSIS

Total prospect contacts to be made __8__. Total properties to be sold __1__

Name of contact	Address	Phone	Comments
1. New, in-person contacts, office drop-ins			
2. New, in-person contacts, phone calls			
3. Follow-up on previous prospects			
4. Follow-up on current sellers, listing contacts			
5. Contacts, phone and personal, in neighborhood			
6. Properties sold			

Summary	Type of Contact					
	1	2	3	4	5	Total
Contacts made						
Properties sold						

Figure 6-5. Weekly Prospecting-Activity Planning and Analysis

other persons planning to sell. Following up expired listing contracts made by other offices may create some complications in future contacts with these offices; also, the seller may be disgruntled because his property was not sold. Many experienced salespersons would not use this method. When the activity sheet has been used, the summary at the bottom of the sheet can then be transferred to the annual planning sheet.

The weekly prospecting-activity sheet resembles the listing-activity sheet in many ways, because the two activities are somewhat similar. In this case, the office has found that good prospects are obtained from office visits made by persons replying to advertisements or simply attracted to the office by its appearance, telephone calls to the office—usually in response to advertising—calling on previous buyers, who often recommend the office to others (this will happen in a good office, with as many as 40 per cent of the total prospects obtained in this way), and personal calls upon and telephone calls to neighbors asking if they have suggestions about friends or relatives who might wish to move into the neighborhood. It is clear that this office has to spend more time securing listings because this activity is greater, but the listings obtained must be good ones because of the much smaller degree of prospecting activity required.

Monthly Summaries

Each month, the weekly activity sheets can be summarized so that working plans for the next month can be developed. Figure 6–6 presents a summary based upon the plan shown in Figure 6–1. The monthly summary indicates that the salesman has worked diligently in contacting clients and obtaining listings and sales prospects, but his activity has resulted in the achievement of only 93 per cent of what he had planned. His comments reflect his analysis of the trouble. Apparently, he has not worked diligently enough with the listing and sales prospects which he obtained, or he has not been sufficiently discriminating in picking the ones with whom to work more closely. As a first step in seeking a better balance between his listing and prospecting activities and his commissions earned, he plans to make a careful review of his present prospect lists and to eliminate all but the most promising. In doing this, he can refer to his past files of completed sales and determine which prospects he has been most successful in selling. He could also check with the other sales personnel, and could also study any information he can obtain about the local real estate markets, to determine whether he may have to revise his planning and do much more personal contacting than he had thought would be necessary.

Although the paper work involved in maintaining these summaries may seem excessive, successful salesmen have found that this type of paper work is the most effective means they can use for taking advantage of their past

January _____, 19_____

	Listing				*Prospecting*		
	Number of active listings at beginning of month		25		Number of active prospects at beginning of month		25
Less:	Number of canceled listings		−6	Less:	Number of prospects dropped		−5
		Total	19			Total	20
Less:	Number of listings sold		−2	Less:	Number of prospects sold		−3
		Total	17			Total	17
Add:	New listings obtained		17	Add:	New prospects being processed		30
	Listing inventory for next month		34		New prospects to be processed next month		47

Achievement of Sales and Listing Quotas:

	To Date		
	Quota	*Actual*	*Per cent of quota achieved*
Listings	20	34	170%
Prospects	32	47	146%
Number of property sales	2	2	100%
Dollar volume of property sales	$ 30,000	$ 28,000	93%
Commissions earned	$ 1,800	$ 1,680	93%

Comments on plan for next month:

Concentrate more on current listings and prospects before seeking new ones.
Review current files and eliminate the least likely prospects.

Figure 6-6. Personal Monthly Summary of Selling Activity

experiences. These records of successful and unsuccessful sales, the history of what was planned and what was achieved, the comments on events which lead to successful sales, and how recurrent problems were solved are all very useful aids during periods of slow listing and selling.

LISTING

Because good listings provide the inventory from which successful sales can be made, nothing is more important, nor typically more difficult, for both the new and the experienced salesperson than the securing of a constant flow of good listings. Experience shows that the salesperson who maintains a file of good listings has the best potential for earning a high income, not only because he has more personal sales opportunities, but also because his associates will turn to him when they have good prospects and need good listings to show them. Moreover, the salesperson will be economizing his time and efforts when he is able to show good prospects listings which fit their needs. A good inventory of listings can be obtained if attention is paid to sources of listings, the use of the proper type of listing agreement, avoiding poor listings, and knowing how to secure the best listings.

Types of Listing Contracts

The most frequently used basic listing contracts are the open, the exclusive right, and the exclusive agency. The open listing permits the brokerage office which sells the property to collect the commission regardless of which office obtained the listing. The exclusive right provides that the office which secures the listing will receive a commission if the property is sold, regardless of who sells it; and the exclusive agency requires payment of a commission to the listing office if any but the owner sells the property. The multiple-listing contract is often mentioned as a fourth type, but it is simply the exclusive-right listing with the added provision that any office which is a member of the multiple-listing system may show the property and will receive a share of the commission if it sells the property. The bulk of practice favors either the open or the exclusive-right listing, with the latter gaining increasing favor. The reasons for this are discussed in later paragraphs.

Sources of Listings

The most successful firms and salesmen find that they secure listings from the following sources, which are listed according to their effectiveness, with the most successful method first: (1) Former clients, (2) responses to newspaper advertising, (3) public relations activities in the community, (4) telephone calls to the office from persons seeking assistance and directed to the office by the activities previously mentioned, (5) office visitors, and (6) door-to-door soliciting.

(1) *Former clients.* More than 40 per cent of the sales and listings of successful offices are obtained from referrals made by satisfied clients. Although many of these clients may use the office only once, they are quick to mention good service to their friends, because it is so rare in many real estate offices. In some sections of the country with a high mobility of population, a client will often deal with a real estate office at least two or three times rather than just once.

(2) *Responses to newspaper advertising.* A variety of advertising media are used by real estate offices, and they will be discussed in detail in another chapter; however, it is important to emphasize that consistent, well-planned, and well-written advertising is the principal mainstay for the majority of real estate offices seeking to build good listing inventories.

(3) *Public relations activities.* Every member of the real estate firm must remember that he can build good will for his firm by working in a variety of civic projects and service clubs. He need not be aggressive in mentioning his business association, but he will find that, if he does a good job in his service work, he will automatically call attention to the high quality of service which his office can render.

(4) *Telephone calls.* Telephone calls are usually in response to some form of advertising—usually, newspaper ads or "yellow pages" listings. For this reason, a salesman must learn to cultivate a pleasing telephone personality so that he can encourage the caller to permit a face-to-face visit. Telephone solicitation can often be used effectively to obtain listings if the salesman selects an area he knows well and if he uses a reverse phone book (one which lists properties by addresses rather than by names) and concentrates on careful coverage of his market.

(5) *Office drop-ins.* Many offices are so located as to encourage passers-by to call at the office. The manner in which such callers are greeted and their questions answered will determine whether they can become good prospects. Such callers may be very good prospects, because they have made a conscious effort to seek out the office. When drop-ins can be expected regularly, the importance of regular floor time and of attention to the appearance of the office must not be overlooked in creating the image which will cause the "looker" to become a good prospect.

(6) *Door-to-door soliciting.* Sales managers are divided sharply in their opinions about the effectiveness of this method. Those who favor it are usually located in large middle-priced development or tract areas where there is a reasonably high turnover of families. Some offices insist that a salesperson assume responsibility for becoming thoroughly acquainted with the homeowners in a particular area; such offices must plan various devices for calling attention to the services the salesman offers. For example, each month

he may distribute some small gift or simply leave his business card. The danger in such a process is that he may make his calls too frequently and become rated as a nuisance.

(7) *"For sale by owner" signs.* In some markets, owners are constantly tempted to be their own salesmen, because they see the apparent ease with which homes are being sold. When an "owner" sign has been up for some time, an effective salesperson can often convince the owner that, even if he pays a commission, he will obtain a better net price in a shorter time and will be freed from the annoyances of constantly showing his property and negotiating with a variety of strangers. More important, the owner will probably have only a vague notion of how to prepare a sales contract, secure financing, and complete title transfer; therefore, if these are discussed with him, he can usually be convinced of the wisdom of letting an experienced salesperson handle his property.

(8) *Direct mail.* Direct mail is typically used to call attention to the services which an office can render rather than to seek to sell a particular property. The most effective direct mail is the personalized letter which provides some useful information while bringing in some indirect sales ideas. Direct mail for selling particular properties is most effective when a new listing has been obtained: neighbors are informed of the fact and invited to offer suggestions concerning persons whom they would like to have as neighbors. Friends and relatives of the lister can also be solicited in this manner. Letters can be used effectively to introduce a new buyer to his neighbors, thus calling the attention of the neighbors to the ability of the office to sell property.

(9) *Other sources.* A variety of unusual sources have been used very successfully from time to time by individual offices on a regular and a one-time basis. Such methods have included using rental departments for leads to prospective buyers, spot announcements primarily of an institutional type on TV and radio, placing signs on properties, and through the promotion of exchanges.

Setting Selling Prices

The "good" listing which successful salespersons say is the key to effective selling is one which is priced at an amount and on terms which are consistent with market trends. For example, in a rising market, the listing price can be set slightly above the price at which properties have been sold in the past, because price increase will absorb the extra margin. In falling markets, however, prices must be keyed directly to past sales; otherwise, the listing should be refused until the seller is convinced of the wisdom of accepting a reasonable price. Some offices feel that a slightly overpriced listing can be accepted if the owner has a good reason for selling, because he will be amenable to lowering his price when, as time passes, he sees that he is not obtaining an offer to purchase. In one metropolitan county, for example, multiple-listing records show that over one-half of all properties listed with the Multiple Listing System have their listing prices cut by approximately 5 to 10 per cent before a sale is made.

Research has shown that real estate firms do tend to accept listings at prices which they believe are too high. More than one-third of the firms surveyed felt that at least 25 per cent of their listings were priced too high and would need some adjustment before they could be sold. An additional one-fourth of the firms felt that at least 50 per cent of their listings were too high, and another one-fourth felt that almost all of their listings were priced too high. Larger firms showed more of a tendency to accept overpriced listings than did small firms.

Some of the more frequent reasons given for accepting overpriced listings are: (1) owner has a good reason for wanting to sell, or he has to sell whether or not he wants to; (2) the seller is known to the office and can be persuaded to accept a lower price later; (3) the office has a basic policy of letting the owner influence the selling price so that the listing can be obtained, with the full knowledge that an additional sales effort might have to be made later to get him to accept a lower price; (4) the listing price is not too far from what the office believes it should be; (5) the owner will sign a long-term listing contract and cooperate actively in trying to obtain the higher price; (6) as a means of meeting overpriced listing practices of competitors; (7) the owner shows a disposition to listen to a lowering of price after efforts have been made to sell the property at the higher asking price.

The offices which do not accept an overpriced listing feel that too much time and money can be wasted in a futile effort to sell such a property. Moreover, they feel that they injure their reputation by accepting a listing at one price and then returning to the owner and admitting that the price is too high. Certainly, a salesman hurts his image as a real estate "expert" if he has to ask the owner to lower the listing price.

The advantages in obtaining a properly priced listing are overwhelming and are well known to the successful salesman. The properly priced listing sells readily, thus establishing the salesman as a truly professional man who knows his business. This type of professional approach establishes a good client relationship upon which additional business can be built. Moreover, the client will not have time to become unhappy over the poor service which he would feel he received from having to wait while an overpriced listing was being sold.

Setting an accurate listing price begins with a careful inventory of the physical characteristics and the legal rights associated with the property. These include such things as the condition of the property; needed repairs;

RESIDENTIAL-APPRAISAL SUMMARY SHEET

DATE____________

SUMMARY OF VALUATION:

ADDRESS________________CITY________________

PHONE NO.____________________________________

NEAREST MAJOR CROSS STS.______________________

____

PRESENT MKT. VAL.__________DATE____________

COST TO REPROD.____________DATE____________

PURCHASE PRICE_____________DATE____________

DOWN PYMT.___________________________________

SQ. FOOTAGE__________________________________

AREA: White Mixed

Listing From__________________

2nd Orig. Amt.__________Bal. Due__________Payable______@_________Due____________

1st Orig. Amt.__________Bal. Due__________Payable______@_________Due____________

1st Held by: Institution ____________________Private Party____________________

SUMMARY OF APPRAISAL:

LOCATION: 10 9 8 7 6 5 4 3 2 1 Poor				PROPERTY: 10 9 8 7 6 5 4 3 2 1 Poor			
ITEM	GOOD	SATIS	POOR	ITEM	GOOD	SATIS	POOR
Neighbors, properties				Structural soundness			
Zoning, deed restrict.				Resistance to elements			
Nat., artifi. barriers				Resistance to use			
Utilities				Functional			
City growth				Mechanical equipment			
Transportation				Natural light, ventilation			
Shopping facilities				Architectural analysis			
Schools, churches, rec.				Location on lot			
Assessments				Operating costs			
Taxes				Maintenance costs			
COMMENT:				COMMENT:			

Figure 6-7. Residential-Appraisal Summary Sheet

floor plan; sizes of rooms; electrical, plumbing, and mechanical equipment; easements; covenants of use; and taxes and special assessments. The better offices usually have a simple check list-type appraisal form which they expect the salesperson to complete. An example is shown in Figure 6–7. The use of such a check list provides an easy method of noting both the

LOT: FRONTAGE__________FT. on__________ST.__________DEPTH

HOUSE: YR. BLT.__________X__________DIMENSIONS__________SQ. FT.

GARAGE:__________X__________DIMENSIONS__________SQ. FT.

INTERIOR ROOMS

ITEM	NO.	FLOORS	WALLS	TRIM	DIMENSIONS
Liv. Rm.					
Din. Rm.					
Kitchen					
Built-ins.					
Extra Facilities					
Svc. Pch.					
Study					
Bed Rm.					
Den					
Carpets					
Drapes					
Bath					

EXTERIOR DESCRIPTION

FOUNDATION	EXTERIOR WALLS	ROOF	FENCE
Concrete	Stucco	Wood shake	Landscaping
Stone	Wood	Wood shingle	Paved streets
Brick	Brick	Composition	Paved sidewalks
Concrete blck	Masonry	Gravel	Patios
Cement pier	Concrete blck	Tile	Extras
		Rock	

COMMENT:

PLUMBING:	HEATING	MACH. EQUIPT.	Adeq.	Inadeq.
Public sewer	Forcd air	Water htr		
Public water	Gravity	Capac ( ) Auto. ( )		
Septic tank	Furnace	Laundry sinks		
Baths; Stall shwr	Wall htrs	Dishwasher		
Tubs	Thermostats	Garb. disposal		
Lavatory	Air-condition.	Elect. fuse box		
Toilet	Heat pump	Elect. circ. breaker		
Shwr over tub				

COMMENT:

THE AREA: BOUNDARIES__________NORTH__________SOUTH__________EAST__________WEST__________

AVERAGE SGL-FAM. HOME VALUES $__________TO $__________AGES__________TO__________

TYPICAL ARCH. STYLE__________SIZES__________SQ. FT. TO__________SQ. FT.

Figure 6-7. Residential-Appraisal Summary Sheet (continued)

good and the bad points of the property and calls attention to the items which are most likely to produce a good selling price. The summaries of the location and the property on the first sheet, in which the best properties are rated 10 and the poorest 1, provide an easy means of comparing properties and adjusting prices. On the second sheet, the last item also permits notation

MORTGAGE PATTERN: 10 9 8 7 6 5 4 3 2 1	BORROWER: 10 9 8 7 6 5 4 3 2 1 Poor
ITEM GOOD SATIS. POOR	ITEM GOOD SATIS. POOR
Loan-to-value ratio ( )	Motivation
Term, princ. int. rate	Credit reputation
( ) ( ) ( )	Stable income
Loan pymts to rent ( )	Additional assets
Loan pymts to income ( )	Other liabilities
Price to ann. inc. ( )	Cash for purchase
Size 1st TD ( )	Effective income
Loan term — prop. life ( )	Assocns.
Amortized payments	Attitude, credit behavior
Market patterns	Net worth
Economic background	Employed by: Name
COMMENT:	Address
	Phone No.
	Nearest relative: Name
	Address
	Phone No.

Figure 6-7. Residential-Appraisal Summary Sheet (continued)

of how the property compares with others like it in the neighborhood and also establishes a realistic range within which the listing price should be set.

One of the most overlooked qualities in a home, but one which is most important to buyers, is the functional plan of the house. In its simplest terms, "functional" quality refers to the ease and comfort which will be enjoyed in using the home. Figure 6–8 lists some of the most important items which affect functional quality and can be used in conjunction with Figure 6–7, because comments or check marks can be placed next to those items relating to the home being appraised.

Architecture and Design:

Type: Modern or obsolete
Attached or detached
Position with respect to street, lot lines, other structures in area
General appearance

Living Room:

Favored location
Proportions—ratio of three-to-two preferred; long, narrow rooms hard to furnish
Placement of doors, windows, registers, radiators, electrical outlets as related to circulation, ventilation, heating, lighting, and furniture placement
Fireplace—position with respect to traffic and possible furniture grouping; provision of ash dump
Circulation—direct, requiring as little floor space as possible, convenient with respect to furniture groupings
Position of windows and doors with respect to assuring privacy
Location of closets and stairs with respect to living room
Adequacy of floor and wall space

Figure 6-8. Check List for Functional Plan of a House

Dining Room or Area:

Necessity of dining room for size house involved
Proportions—dining rooms best if square or nearly so, consider proportions in relation to furniture
Position of doors and windows, electric outlets, electric fixtures, radiators, registers as related to circulation, ventilation, heating, lighting, and furniture placement
Ease of access to kitchen
Privacy—position of doors and windows

Bedrooms:

Adequacy of floor area and wall space for essential furniture
Provision for cross ventilation
Position of doors and windows with respect to privacy, furniture placement, ventilation
Position of radiators, registers, and electrical outlets in relation to heating, lighting, and furniture placement
Position of room in relation to bathroom; protection against noise from bathroom

Kitchen:

Efficiency of arrangement with respect to "work centers"; placement of equipment—L-shaped or U-shaped; sequence of work centers (For example, in order: refrigerator, sink, range)
Position of windows, doors with respect to work arrangement
Provision of ventilation—exhaust fan
Provision of light for work centers
Condition of walls, floors, ceilings; attractiveness, ease of cleaning
Work surfaces, height, convenience, quality, ease of cleaning
Adequacy of floor and wall area for essential equipment

Bathroom:

Location with respect to other rooms; provision for privacy
Fixtures—quality, placement
Adequacy of floor area
Position of windows and doors with respect to arrangement of fixtures, privacy, ventilation
Lighting arrangements
Floors and walls—adequacy of floor and wall covering, ease of cleaning
Safety—protection against falling, such as grab-bars and rails
Storage space—medicine closet, towel closet, clothes hamper, waste basket, and other space
Provision of shut-off valves—convenience of location, ease of repair
Provision of towel rack and other accessories

Halls and Stairs:

Safety provisions—lights, handrails, steepness or narrowness of stairs, balanced use of hall space, position of stairs and halls with respect to other rooms
Condition of outside stairs and provisions for safety

Basement Area:

Size and condition—adequacy of floor area and height, dryness of basement
Provision for light and ventilation, window space and location
Arrangement of equipment, adequacy of space for furniture, storage, etc.
Convenience of stairs
Possibilities of special uses—playrooms, laundry, etc.

Figure 6-8. Check List for Functional Plan of a House (continued)

Closets:

Number and location with respect to need: at least one per bedroom
Coat closet—location and size
Linen closets
Broom and special-equipment closet
Storage closets—size, location, and ease of use
Dimensions of closets—not less than 22 inches deep, preferably; not over 2½ feet for clothes closet; others in accordance with use.

Other Storage Provisions:

Basement storage—dryness, convenience, lighting, safety
Attic storage—adequacy, safety, lighting, ease of access
Kitchen and accessory storage—food storage, seasonal equipment, tools and equipment, such as cleaning utensils, paint, etc.
Fuel storage
Laundry storage
Waste—garbage, trash, etc.

Accessory Buildings—Garage, etc.:

Condition
Adequacy for purposes
Special provisions for workshops, tool storage, etc.

Figure 6-8. Check List for Functional Plan of a House (continued)

Estimating the Sales Price

Sales price can be set by using one or all of the three most acceptable approaches—comparison of sales, cost to replace, and investment value.

Market comparisons. The easiest and most frequently used method of deciding at what price a property should be sold is to find a group of properties which are comparable to it and, by matching various features, to establish an estimated selling price. An example of the types of factors which usually influence the price of a property is shown in Figure 6–9. The average characteristics for properties in the area can be placed under the column designated for "comparable properties" and the characteristics of the property being offered for sale can then be listed and compared with these. In setting a listing price, particular attention must be paid to the terms on which the property is sold. Usually, when a second trust deed is involved, the price will be higher, because the seller has to wait longer to receive all of his cash from the sale. The list given is not exhaustive, but it provides an initial basis on which to do a listing appraisal, and it can be adapted for use in a particular market area after only a short period of use.

Often the market-comparison method is the only method that needs to be used, particularly when the property is located in an area where no further building can take place and the area is one which constantly attracts buyers. A very effective method of using this system is to ask other members of the sales staff to make their estimates of what the listing price should be and

Comparison Factors	Characteristics of Comparable Properties	Characteristics of Property Being Listed
1. Lot size (dimensions)		
2. House size (sq. ft.) ; Rooms (total, bedrooms, baths, etc.)		
3. Age of property in years		
4. Architectural style		
5. Costs of repairs to make property salable		
Sales information:		
6. Date of sale		
7. Terms of sale:		
Down payment		
	1st loan 2nd loan	1st loan 2nd loan
Sizes of loans		
Length of loans		
Interest rates on loans		
8. Conditions of sale:		
Value of personal property		
Reasons for sales		
Days from listing to sale		
Sales price as per cent of asking price		
Information analysis:		
Highest average prices in area		
Typical prices in area		
Lowest average prices in area		
9. Estimated price at which property should be listed		
Length of listing agreement and financing terms		
Other conditions:		

Figure 6-9. Market-Comparison Check List for Setting Listing Price

then to average their estimates as a basis for setting the price. When a hesitant seller is shown what other properties have sold for and what an experienced sales staff would recommend, he is usually ready to accept whatever listing price is suggested.

Cost to replace. The cost to replace is one of the most popular methods of setting a sales price in areas where there is construction under way and the buyer has the choice of buying an older existing home or a newly finished home or of building a home. In such an area, the square-foot or cubic-foot cost of building a home can be established, land and lot-improvement costs added, and a reasonable estimate developed of the costs of building a new home which would be an acceptable replacement for the home being listed for sale. In such estimates, the inclusion of the costs of landscaping the property and adding some interior improvements should not be overlooked, because they are often the chief difference between the listing prices of older and newly finished homes. Usually, the older home will have a somewhat lower value than a newly finished or about-to-be-built home because there will be some repairs, painting, and other improvements which may have to be made in order to put the home in the best possible sale condition, and such costs have to be subtracted from the estimates of replacing the home with a new home in which such improvements would not have to be made. The final listing price which is established should recognize that a typical buyer will not willingly pay more for a used or older home than he would pay for a new home unless he sees some advantage in owning a particular home; he does not want to incur the costs of finishing a new completed home (that is, pay for drapes, rugs, and decorating), and he does not wish to wait while a new home is being built for him.

Investment value. Single-family homes are rarely purchased for their investment value, but sometimes such an approach provides an additional clue to the sales price of the home and an additional selling point to present to buyers. Such an approach is particularly applicable in an older area in which some homes are being offered for rent. One approach in this method is to find the average annual gross rental charges for homes and compare this with the average selling prices of homes. For example, homes in a particular area may be renting for $1,200 gross annual rent and the average sales price may be $12,000, which gives an annual gross rental multiplier of 100. The home listed for sale might be somewhat better than the average home in the area and rentable at $1,300 per year. Multiplying $1,300 × 100 produces an estimated investment value of $13,000. In developing the multiplier, it is important to compare homes which are closely similar in size, condition, and costs of operation.

Another method of establishing investment value is to estimate what amount of net income might be left if the home were rented and certain minimum expenses, such as taxes, painting, and repairing, were paid. The net amount could then be capitalized at a comparable market investment rate and a value derived. For example, if the home rented for $1,300 a year, as in the previous assumption, and taxes, insurance, and maintenance payments equaled $600 a year, then the net income would be $700. If first mortgages carried an interest rate of six per cent, which would be an indication of the investment returns expected by mortgage lenders, then $700 divided by .06 (6 per cent) indicates an estimated investment value of $11,666, or $11,700 rounded to the nearest hundred dollars.

When each of the methods is used to establish a listing price, and when these estimates are reinforced by the opinions of the other salesmen in the office, the owner is usually ready to allow the weight of this expert advice to guide him in setting his selling price. Usually, an owner knows what the price should be but feels that the "rules of the game" require that he set a higher price and then, through a process of bargaining, eventually accept a somewhat lower listing price. Some salesmen recognize this and, even after they have used a variety of means to establish a reasonable listing price, may set the price approximately 5 per cent higher. In this way, some bargaining with potential buyers will be possible and the owner will finally lose all reservations he may have had about signing the listing contract.

Securing Good Listings

The securing of good listings is a constant problem in almost all real estate offices, but the offices with the fewest problems are those which have studied and utilized the most effective methods of securing not only good listings but exclusive listings. There of the most important blocks to securing good listings are: the unrealistic prices which owners set on properties and which they refuse to change for any reason; the keen competition to secure listings, which often causes a salesman to accept a listing at an unrealistic price just to prevent a competitor from getting it; and the inability of inexperienced or average salesman to convince owners that properties should be listed at the prevailing market levels. The more successful offices meet these problems—which indicates that they approach them in an organized and realistic manner.

Securing listings for a particular office. Successful offices have found that the most effective means of securing listings is to maintain a file of sold listings and to have salesmen show this file to each prospective new lister. This file is usually supplemented with examples of the types of advertising which the firm does and some indication of how many of these homes were sold, reports of the activities of the firm in the community, and other items which show that the office has had an outstanding reputation for community service over a number of years. These items are all matters of fact which can be proven and which can be checked with others, if the lister wishes to have references.

There are less tangible evidences which are used by many successful offices to supplement these statements. For example, some offices have prepared a list of services which they provide for each owner who lists. In this list, they mention that they will (1) photograph the property and prepare a detailed listing statement complete with the photo, which will be distributed immediately to each salesman; (2) list the property at once with the local multiple-listing agency or, when there is no multiple, will announce the availability of the property to all of the cooperating real estate offices in the area; (3) arrange financing at once (or they will state that they have sources which can secure financing on terms which the buyer wishes); (4) provide a weekly summary of all persons who visit the property, together with their comments, so that the seller can make changes, if this seems desirable, in prices or terms; (5) use classified advertising to call the property to the attention of prospective buyers and maintain a consistent program of advertising until the property is sold (this may not mean that that particular property will be advertised every week, but it does guarantee that similar properties will be); (6) place signs on the property announcing its availability, but prospective buyers will be advised to call the real estate office and not bother the occupants; (7) advise neighbors of the property's availability and ask them to suggest potential buyers; (8) contact the most likely prospective buyers among names on file in the office; (9) canvass the entire area carefully to make sure that all prospective buyers are contacted; (10) hold an open house or send special invitations to selected prospects to visit the house.

Securing exclusive listings. From the viewpoint of the real estate office, the finest listing is an exclusive listing, because it provides some assurance that a commission will be paid if the office devotes time and money to selling a property. In many areas, the open listing is still used, so that a firm can only urge that its office be used and then work more diligently than competing offices. The most important argument given by a successful office against the use of the open listing, and for the exclusive-right listing, is that it can neither afford to waste time nor give the quality of service necessary to sell a property if it is given an open listing. Some firms may accept open listings but they will not advertise them; they give them a low priority when showing properties to buyers; and the salesmen give them only limited attention. Some of the fears of an owner that his property may not be given proper attention if he signs an exclusive-listing contract are allayed by giving him the opportunity of withdrawing his listing if the office fails to give the service it promises, and by showing him that other offices will be given an opportunity to sell the property on a cooperative basis.

The inability of many offices to obtain an exclusive-right listing is often due to their failure to explain to an owner the special characteristics of such a listing. For example, an owner who lists his property on an open-listing contract with several offices might, under a given circumstance, owe a commission to each office which presents a legally "ready, willing, and able buyer." Moreover, the owner tends to forget the old adage that "what is everybody's business is nobody's business," and that neither an office nor any salesperson will have much interest in trying to sell a property when they know that someone else may be working on the same property and complete the sale earlier. The weight of evidence is that the most successful offices will not allow their sales personnel to accept any but exclusive-right listings.

Many offices also advise the owner that, if he wishes to obtain the maximum sales price, he should accept suggestions that the office has about the showing of the property. For example, many offices furnish the owner with showing instructions, which advise him to take care of any obviously needed painting, to keep the outside of the home in a neat-appearing condition, to keep the house clean and in order so that it can be shown at any time, and so on. Experience suggests that all offices should submit such a list to every owner even though many may not follow the advice.

The sale of a property, no matter how carefully the price has been determined, will take time; therefore, many offices feel that an exclusive listing cannot be handled properly unless the office is given a minimum of 90, and preferably 120, days in which to seek to sell the property. Properties with unusual characteristics may often take longer. The length of the listing contract will be determined in a large measure by what is being done locally; therefore, there is no general rule as to listing-contract length. Contracts do tend to extend over longer periods of time when markets are slower and qualified buyers are more difficult to find.

FINDING QUALIFIED BUYERS

In the kinds of active markets that have been prevalent since 1960, the finding of qualified buyers has been more difficult than finding properties to sell, because the early postwar imbalance between the supply of and the demand for homes has been rather well corrected. The rapid rate at which housing prices have risen in many areas has further complicated the problem by reducing the number of families which are qualified to buy the more expensive homes. For these reasons, the search for qualified buyers by successful salesmen begins with a careful study of the listed property in order to determine exactly what type of buyer might wish to buy it. Once this has been done, an effective sales campaign can be developed and executed, because this analysis will indicate what size family will find the property most attractive, the type of tastes they should have in order to appreciate and enjoy the property, the degree to which the property's neighborhood will meet their needs for shopping, schools, employment, recreation, and similar itms, and what financial capacity the family will need to pay for the home.

Sources of Qualified Buyers

The sources of qualified buyers are closely similar to the sources for good listings, so that what has already been said about these sources applies to finding qualified buyers. The successful offices report that their best sources of qualified buyers, in order, are: (1) former clients' referrals, (2) classified advertising, (3) signs on the property, (4) holding open houses, which produces prospective buyers for that house as well as for other houses which the firm has for sale, (5) in-person visits to the office, (6) telephone calls to the office, usually in response to advertising, (7) contacts by members of the firm in activities not related to business, and (8) such miscellaneous sources as rental services, direct-mail letters, institutional advertising, and nonbrokerage services of the firm.

Qualifying Buyers

Once the prospective buyer has contacted a salesman, it is the salesman's responsibility to qualify the prospect's interest and ability to buy the property suited to his needs and buying capacity. This qualification process usually includes obtaining information about the buyer's reasons for wanting to buy a home, his financial ability, and his family's social aspirations and interests.

Countless lists have been prepared on why families buy homes. The most evident reason is that they want shelter; but beyond this, good salesmen have found that the home must also meet such diverse needs as those of meeting the neighbors' standards of living, a desire for security, and a place for centering family life. There is no single list of such items which is universally useful; rather, the successful salesman slowly builds his own list, which he learns to use to meet each selling situation.

Early qualification of the family's financial capacities is perhaps the most important ingredient in qualifying prospective buyers, according to the views of successful salesmen. Information on financial capacity can be obtained by direct or indirect questioning, but it should establish that the family has the resources to make the required down payment, that it has no large outstanding debts which would hinder its credit-obtaining ability, and that the principal breadwinner has a steady income which is in proper proportion to the price of the property (this usually means that a family should not pay more than two to three times its gross annual income for a home, or that not more than 20 to 25 per cent of the breadwinner's take-home monthly income can be allocated for all housing outlays).

The family's social aspirations are much more difficult to determine, but good salesmen find clues in the way the members of the family are dressed, the kind of automobile they drive, and the kind of home or apartment in which they currently live. Careful questioning will also bring out the type of social life the family likes, what clubs the adults and children have joined, what they do with their leisure moments, what schools they attend, and so forth.

SELLING TECHNIQUES

More volumes have probably been written on successful real estate selling techniques than on any other subject, so that research can add little to this subject. The high volume of writing is due not so much to the discovery of new techniques, but to the changing emphasis on a few known techniques as buyers and markets change and require differing sales methods. For this reason, successful offices tend to emphasize the necessity for constant review of techniques and changes in them as markets change; therefore, the single most important technique is that of flexibility and sound knowledge of the basic principles of selling real estate. Techniques can be grouped into three major classes: (1) showing properties, (2) closing the sale, and (3) preparing the closing papers.

Showing Properties

Successful salesmen indicate that showing a property consists primarily in directing the buyer's attention to those items which the qualification process has already shown him to be interested in and, in the process, in guiding him to a final decision to buy. For this reason, all of the various types of advice on how to show properties can be summarized as: (1) arranging ahead of time for appointments to see only a select list of properties in which he will be most interested and alerting the sellers that the showing will take place, (2) determining the most appealing features of the neighborhood and the property and making sure that the buyer sees these, (3) keeping the confidence of the buyer by also pointing out the weaknesses of the property while showing how they can be modified or minimized, and (4) gaining the confidence of the buyer so that he trusts the salesman and looks upon him as a competent home-buyer counselor.

One experienced salesman has suggested that showing a property involves pointing out important individual features in each room of the house being shown; pointing out deficiencies—because the buyer will see them himself—but have remedies ready for the buyer to consider; giving a true estimate of repairs or, at least, making sure that any estimates about which there may be some question are quoted on the high side; showing the prospective buyer through the home in an informal, relaxed manner, allowing him to review items by himself if he wishes; listening attentively to any comments so that any lingering doubts on his part can be turned into positive feelings toward the property.[1]

Sometimes new salesmen are given prepared sales speeches to memorize or are shown "trick" techniques which may surprise or trap the buyer into signing a contract, but the majority of good salesmen reject such practices. Not only is the buyer likely to be upset by such tactics and seek to renege

---

[1] These comments are taken from one of a series on brokerage published by the National Institute of Real Estate Brokers, 22 West Monroe Street, Chicago 3, Illinois. Several such volumes are published each year and cover such topics as: *Today's Home—Know It, Show It, Sell It; Greater Profits From Listings; Real Estate Advertising;* and *Business-Building Letters and Forms.*

Deposit Receipt

CALIFORNIA REAL ESTATE ASSOCIATION STANDARD FORM

...., California..,19........

Received from..

herein called Buyer, the sum of...

Dollars ($..............................) evidenced by cash ☐, personal check ☐, cashier's check ☐, or..........................

....

as deposit on account of purchase price of..

....Dollars ($..............................)

for the purchase of property, situated in...

...., County of..., California, described as follows:

....

....

....

....

....

....

....

Buyer will deposit in escrow with...

the balance of the purchase price within......................days from date of acceptance hereof by Seller, as follows:

....

....

....

....

....

....

....

(1) If Buyer fails to pay the balance of said purchase price, or to complete said purchase as herein provided, the amounts paid hereon may be retained by Seller at his option as consideration for the execution of this agreement by Seller.

(2) Title is to be free of liens and encumbrances other than those set forth herein. Title subject to..........................

....

Evidence of title shall be a California Land Title Association standard coverage form policy of title insurance issued through ...., to be paid for by.............................. If Seller is unable to convey a marketable title, except as herein provided, within three months after acceptance hereof by Seller, or if the improvements on said property be destroyed or materially damaged prior to transfer of title or delivery of agreement of sale, then upon the demand of Buyer, said deposit and all other sums paid by Buyer shall be returned to Buyer, and this agreement as between Buyer and Seller shall be of no further effect, and Seller thereupon shall become obligated to pay all expenses incurred in connection with examination of title.

(3) Taxes, premiums on insurance acceptable to Buyer, rents, interest and other expenses of said property shall be pro-rated as of the date of transfer of title or delivery of agreement of sale. The amount of any bond or assessment which is a lien shall be paid by.., except that the amount of any delinquency now existing shall be paid by Seller. Seller shall pay cost of revenue stamps on deed and any expense connected with the removal of title defects.

(4) Possession of said property to be delivered to Buyer on closing escrow ☐, or not later than.................................. ....days after closing escrow ☐. ....

....

(5) This offer shall be deemed revoked unless accepted in writing within..................................days after date hereof, and such acceptance is communicated to Buyer within said period.

(6) Time is of the essence of this contract, but Broker may, without notice, extend for a period of not to exceed one month the time for the performance of any act hereunder, except the time for the acceptance hereof by Seller and date of possession.

.... By...

Real Estate Broker

Address..Telephone.....................................

The undersigned Buyer offers and agrees to buy the above described property on the terms and conditions above stated and acknowledges receipt of a copy hereof.

Address.. ....

Telephone.. ....

Buyer

Buyer to take title in name of..

....

Please Print

For these forms address the California Real Estate Association,
117 W. 9th St., Los Angeles 15. Revision Approved 4-24-54

Figure 6-10. Deposit Receipt Form (Front)

ACCEPTANCE

The undersigned accepts the offer on the reverse side hereof and agrees to sell the property described thereon on the terms and conditions therein set forth.

The undersigned agrees to pay Broker therein named and employed by the undersigned to sell said property as commission the sum of..Dollars ($..................................)
or one-half of the amounts paid by Buyer in the event the same is forfeited, provided such one-half shall not exceed the full amount of said commission.

The undersigned acknowledges receipt of a copy hereof.

Dated.., 19.......... ....

....

....
Seller

Address..

....

Telephone..

Figure 6-10. Deposit Receipt Form (Back)

on his agreement, but many buyers will soon see through such practices and go to another broker. The best selling has been defined as "telling the truth attractively," which means that the salesman prepares himself well enough in advance to be able to answer all questions truthfully about the property, to give all pertinent information about the property, and to make the buyer see the advantage to him of buying the particular property. Such procedures cannot be memorized but must grow with practice and experience; however, its start begins with knowing the property thoroughly—room size, age of building, ages and capacities of mechanical equipment, taxes, zoning and deed restriction, the neighborhood, and other facts which make the property unique and attractive.

Closing the Sale

Experienced salesmen are generally agreed that new or unsuccessful salesmen usually make the mistake of never asking the buyer to buy the property. At some point the buyer will show clearly that he is interested and willing to buy the property which has been shown, but he will rarely admit this until he is asked. This means that at this point the salesman must ask directly if the buyer is ready to sign the deposit receipt (Figure 6–10.) Usually, the receipt must be explained and the buyer informed that it is a contract which binds him to buy, if the seller accepts, but that he can modify the seller's offering terms. The terms of the deposit receipt will usually be drawn directly from the terms of the listing agreement. All terms on which the seller and buyer agree must be spelled out so that they can be included in the sales contract. Usually, the primary reason for sales failing to be consummated by a closing is the failure of the salesman to spell out exactly what the buyer and seller are to do, thus leaving this task to the escrow clerk. The result under such conditions is always failure of the sale.

Preparing the Closing Papers

The items which usually cause trouble at a closing because they are not spelled out are: (1) disposition and price of personal property, (2) proration of taxes and insurance, (3) methods of financing the purchase and what mortgage terms are acceptable, and (4) additional conditions which the seller is to meet in repairing or modernizing the property. Usually, good salespersons avoid bringing the seller and buyer together until the deposit is accepted and the mortgage arrangement is closed, and often not even then; however, salesmen often assist buyers and sellers in finding good legal assistance or title insurance assistance, but they never make the mistake of performing these services themselves.

THE KEY ROLE OF FINANCING

Eighty per cent of the homes sold today are sold with some type of financing in which the buyer's equity is a relatively small amount. For this reason, the most successful brokers quickly develop a thorough knowledge of the fundamentals of real estate financing. Such fundamentals can be acquired only through experience and study. They cover such topics as the types of instruments which can be used to finance the purchase of a home, analysis of borrowers in preparation for securing loans, trends in mortgage terms and interest rates, sources of funds, and the use of FHA-insured and VA-guaranteed loans.

SALES COMMISSIONS

Sales commissions are probably the most often discussed topic among salesmen and their employing brokers, probably because there is no uniform method of determining what the commission rate should be or how it should be paid. Many real estate brokerage firms favor paying the salesmen 50 per cent of the commission received by the office whenever the commission has been received from the escrow office. Offices located in areas where securing listings is a problem favor paying a special percentage, varying between 10 and 15 per cent of the total commission to the listing salesman with an additional 40 to 50 per cent of the commission to the selling salesman, with the firm receiving the remaining 35 to 40 per cent of the commission.

The successful salesmen are not too concerned about the percentage which they receive on each sale so long as it is competitive with that paid by other real estate brokerage offices in the area. Furthermore, they organize their personal financial lives so that they do not have to wait anxiously for their share of the commissions to be paid. All too often, the unsuccessful salesman has arranged his personal finances so poorly that he spends more time worrying about how soon he will be paid than he does worrying about how to make the next sale. However, much of the anxiety among all salesmen concerning commissions arises from their failure to reach a mutually satisfactory understanding with their employing brokers concerning the rate which they will receive and the time and manner in which they will be paid.

Commission Splits

The portion of the sales commission that the salesman receives is primarily a function of the type of listing he sells, the size of his firm, its competitive position in the market, and whether he secured the listing. For example, a limited number of small firms located in highly competitive markets will pay a commission even if the salesman sells an open, unsigned listing. All firms will pay the highest commissions for the signed exclusive listings, although many firms in smaller towns pay almost as much for signed open listings. Salesmen who sell their own listings will usually receive 10 to 15 per cent more commission than if they sell the listing of another salesman.

If the firm is a member of a multiple-listing system, the system will collect a small percentage of the commission for its services and then split the commission between the listing office and the selling office according to some predetermined percentage, usually 50–50. The amount received by the selling office will then be split according to its policies. When firms cooperate in selling a property and there is no multiple listing, the commission is usually divided equally between the selling and listing offices. Some brokerage offices will take off a small percentage of the commission received and allocate this to their advertising budget and then split the remaining amount with the selling and listing salesmen; however, the majority of the offices take nothing from the commission received and split the entire amount with their salesmen.

Commission Rates

A great deal of confusion always arises when salesmen discuss what commission rate they are paid, because few mention the manner in which a commission is split. The most common methods of splitting commissions which the office receives are: (1) 50 per cent to the selling salesman, 10 per cent to the listing salesman, and 40 per cent to the office; or (2) 50 per cent to the selling salesman, 15 per cent to the listing salesman, and 35 per cent to the office. Commissions from cooperative sales, either with other offices or between salesmen, are usually split 50–50, except that the commission received by cooperating offices is split 50–50 but cooperating salesmen receive only that portion of the total sales commission normally paid to a single-selling salesman and must then split this portion 50–50.

The biggest mistake salesmen make, however, is becoming too concerned about the commission rate which they are paid. Experienced, successful salesmen will accept a smaller commission rate if they can work for an aggressive office, located in a good market, which advertises aggressively. Furthermore, even the best of salesmen have great difficulty in receiving a more favorable commission rate than that paid other salesmen in the same office. Offices which pay higher than usual rates typically are faced with difficult sales problems or they do not maintain a sufficiently high advertising outlay to attract good listing and sales prospects. Rather than becoming concerned about the commission rate, a good salesman will be more interested in the average annual dollar earnings which can be produced in a particular office.

Bonus and Incentive Plans

Many offices have found it to their advantage to offer additional bonuses or other incentives to salesmen who consistently produce a high volume of sales. Typically, for example, between 30 and 40 per cent of all real estate brokerage firms in one state have some form of bonus plan. In the typical plan, bonuses are paid whenever the total volume of sales in a particular time period exceeds a stated amount. The purpose of bonuses is to encourage salesmen to maintain a consistent volume of sales; therefore, bonuses are usually paid when the salesmen exceed a given monthly quota. For example, one office increases the commission from 50 to 60 per cent if the salesman sells more than $15,000 in property per month, and another pays 60 instead of 50 per cent whenever within the year the salesman has earned more than $5,000 in commission. Sometimes the salesman is paid a flat amount in addition to his regular commission for each sale he makes in excess of a stated quota.

Many offices have regular sales contests in which the winners get cash or prizes. Some offices bring the wives into the picture by offering prizes which the wives might want, thus hoping that wives will encourage the salesmen to greatest sales efforts. Contests and special incentive plans are used quite often when an office wants to increase its salable listings.

The continually successful salesman will find that employing brokers will often go to great lengths to keep them with the firm, and they may be offered a share of the annual profits or stock in the company or even an opportunity to participate in the management of the company and in its profit distribution as well. In any case, incentives and bonuses are not a reliable source of income; therefore, wise salesmen treat them as unexpected windfalls and do not include them in their family financial planning.

Buying and Selling for Own Account

Some offices permit salesmen to buy properties from the office for their own investment, after they have paid the usual commissions charged all buyers. The results of such practices are mixed, because many salesmen become so engrossed in managing their property investments that they fail to maintain their sales volume. Successful salesmen do a very limited amount of investing for their own account, and then they usually turn over the management of the property to an experienced property manager. If a salesman finds investing more interesting and lucrative than selling, then he should devote his full time to this, because he will find that dividing his attention between investing and selling does not produce satisfactory results.

Principles of Managing Sales Activities

1. *Planning.* Successful selling begins with good planning; therefore, all salespersons should be encouraged to plan their selling time.
2. *Annual planning.* The daily sales activities of selling personnel should be derived from the annual sales planning goals of the firm.
3. *Records.* Minimal written records are necessary for the control of sales activities.
4. *Local influences.* The kinds of records used to maintain control over sales activities must be derived from the types of properties sold and the markets served.
5. *Record functions.* Records should be maintained only as long as they aid in developing successful selling programs.
6. *Listing inventories.* Listing inventories are developed in the same manner as are good prospect lists.
7. *Listing prices.* A "good" listing price is one that consists of an amount and terms that are consistent with current market trends.
8. *Setting listing prices.* The final listing price should be based on careful analyses of the property, the seller, and the market.
9. *Exclusive listing.* The most effective listing for both sellers and real estate offices is an exclusive listing.
10. *Buyers and sellers.* Equal attention should be given to securing good listings and good sales prospects, but different methods will be used to secure these from time to time, depending upon competitive conditions in the market places.
11. *Commissions.* The amount of commissions is less important than the total sales program planned by an office in determining what salespersons will actually earn.

CASE STUDY

The A & A Realty Company is a partnership consisting of two partners and two salesmen. They operate in a community of about 40,000 adjacent to a major metropolitan area and specialize in the sale of properties in the $12,000 to $22,000 class. They have been in operation since 1928 and have a membership in the local real estate board. They believe that the success of their firm is built on their selling program, the chief characteristics of which are:

1. Select a location.

   Each of the men in the firm is assigned to a particular section of the town, and it is his responsibility to know about all properties which are being offered for sale in this area and to know about all persons who might wish to purchase property in this area. Each man is expected to spend a good portion of his time going from door to door in his area asking about properties which might be for sale or seeking persons who might wish to purchase properties. Their slogan is: "Ring doorbells, ring doorbells, ring doorbells," and they believe that this is the cornerstone for any brokerage operation.

Do you believe that the emphasis on a policy of this kind will be successful in a majority of real estate sales? How would you supplement such a program in order to develop sales projects? What kind of training would you give the men who are going to do the doorbell ringing?

2. Get to know the neighbors.

   The firm urges each salesman to get acquainted with the people in the neighborhood in which he operates. They believe that this is important, not only because a friendly neighbor will encourage sales, but because it will also make it easier to find prospective clients. Neighbors often know friends or relatives who would be interested in moving next door.

3. Having something to offer.

   Each salesman is encouraged to return to the persons in his area who have had business with the firm and to offer the services of the firm to them. This includes such things as helping them to find contractors when they want to repair their houses, keeping them informed as to new city activities which might affect their neighborhood, and similar services. They believe that if the former clients come to rely on the salesman both as a friend and as a source of valuable information, they will be willing to keep him informed about possible future business.

What other services do you believe this firm could render? How would you make such services "services" and not "nuisances"?

4. Get listings in writing.

   This firm believes that all the listings which they obtain should be exclusive listings, and the reasons why they believe this are:

   4.1 While listing is given to a number of agents, no one works on it.
   4.2 An exclusive listing means that one office is concentrating its interest and talents on the property.
   4.3 One person will be responsible for obtaining the best offer and there will be only one offer and, therefore, no confusion.

The listing contract which they use is the one advocated by their real estate board and it provides for exclusive listing.

Do you believe it is necessary to get listings in writing? Do you think this firm is correct in insisting on an exclusive listing? What other device can be used with exclusive listings to disseminate information about the property? Do you think that the information listed on the listing contract is sufficient, or would you want additional information about the property?

5. Use a check sheet in selling property.

When a listing has been obtained through the firm, this listing is then assigned to one of the salesmen. The information is furnished the salesman on a sheet of paper which fits into a small notebook, and he is expected to follow up on the listing until he has obtained a client. On the reverse side of the notebook sheet are listed the steps which the salesman is expected to follow in selling the property. These steps include:

5.1 Calling on any prospects which the salesman has developed through his own contacts.

5.2 Talking with the persons who are currently occupying the property which is to be sold.

5.3 Calling on the neighbors in person, notifying them that the property is to be offered for sale and asking them if they have anyone who they would like to have move in. The call is then followed up with a letter within the next few days.

5.4 Salesman should arrange to place a sign on the property announcing that it is for sale.

5.5 Classified advertising is prepared and an insertion schedule is arranged. This firm specializes in the use of the morning paper.

5.6 Property listings with the local Realtors' group.

5.7 Letter is sent to other agents telling them about the property, particularly when the property has unusual characteristics which might meet someone's particular needs.

5.8 Letters are sent to the various personnel men throughout the city, particularly those with big companies, informing them that the property will be available in the near future.

5.9 The salesman is required to determine how much of a mortgage can be obtained on that property and to be fully informed about any financial plans in connection with the property.

5.10 Salesman handling the property is expected to call the owner at least once every two weeks and to tell him what has been done and what is being done in order to sell the property.

5.11 After the property has been sold, a card is sent to the neighbors introducing them to the new owner of the property.

6. Show property to prospective clients.

Before a prospective client is taken to a home, the salesman should inform the people occupying the property and arrange for an appointment. As the prospects are being taken to the property, the route should be arranged so that they will be shown the most favorable parts of the neighborhood in which they will be living. When they arrive at the house, the salesman should first talk about the outside of the house, pointing out both the strength and the weakness of the house. This firm has found it successful to point out the defects and let the prospects sell the salesman on how easy it would be to remedy them. This firm emphasizes that women buy houses, and that the sales talk should be built so as to appeal to the women. They also believe that emotions sell houses and that the sales program should be designed to emphasize those factors which would appeal to the emotions, such as beautiful fireplace, unusual views, and unusual architectural treatments inside and outside the house.

When the firm has arranged for an appointment to show a house, they send the people occupying the house a small pamphlet (Exhibit C) which shows how the people living in the house can help the sale; however, this will be successful only when the people occupying the house are selling the house. Many times, the persons in the house will be renting it and will not be anxious to have it sold. In this case, the salesman must plan his program so as to have minimum interference with the occupants of the house.

Evaluate the strength and weakness of this program, and indicate how you would improve it. What steps would you take to show a house which is occupied by persons who do not want the property to be sold? Do you think a sales training program of any kind is necessary for a salesman in this program? If so, what would you include in such a program?

7. Close the sale.

After the prospect has indicated that he will be interested in buying the property, the salesman is encouraged to put the prospect's offer in writing and to urge the giving of earnest money. They believe that the earnest money should be an amount equal to the commission that the firm will receive for the sale of the property. Once the offer has been written out, the firm presents the offer to the owner and lets the offer speak for itself. They urge the seller to review the offer and to try to decide whether he would be willing to sell the property under the terms and conditions as outlined in the offer. Once the seller has agreed to sell, the firm calls in their attorneys and, with the attorneys, completes the papers necessary to close the transaction.

What items do you think should be included in the written offer? How would you convince a prospect that he should be willing to put his offer in writing? How would you encourage the prospect to give earnest money? Suppose the prospect was willing to give earnest money but did not have cash or did not have enough in his checking account to pay for the earnest money in the near future. What could you do to insure the receipt of the earnest money?

8. Supply a salesman's handbook.

The firm believes that each salesman should be encouraged to keep with him a handbook in which he has the following information:

8.1 Prospects
8.2 Listings
8.3 Payment books from savings and loan associations
8.4 Tax rates

Can you think of any other items which should be included in the salesman's handbook? How would you expect the salesman to use this handbook?

Chapter 7

MARKETING PRACTICES AND POLICIES

Personality, training, and experience are all that a superior salesman needs to maintain consistently good sales results, but unfortunately there are not many superior salesmen. There is the struggling neophyte who is eager to become an effective salesman in the shortest possible time but finds that each day he meets new problems while he is still struggling to overcome yesterday's mistakes. There is the old-timer who suddenly hits a slump and cannot seem to regain his old selling abilities. There is the average salesman who enjoys just enough success in selling to maintain but not improve his earnings. There is the harrassed sales manager who always hopes that the next salesperson he hires will know how to sell effectively. All of these persons need assistance in order to improve, and they need the kind of assistance that fits their special needs.

Sales training can meet some of the needs of these persons, and, when they can get it, advice from the sales manager or the owner of the real estate brokerage office also helps. In most cases, however, the salesperson is left to his own devices in deciding how to improve his selling results. Fortunately, this need not always be true. A few of the most successful offices, and an increasing number of others, are finding that the single most effective aid they can provide their sales personnel is a complete, up-to-date sales policy manual. The major elements of such a manual are discussed in this chapter.

THE POLICY MANUAL

A policy manual may consist of anything from a collection of typed or mimeographed instructions to the sales force on procedures or policies to an elaborate, printed looseleaf notebook. Only about one-third of the small offices have a manual of the latter type, but one-half of the medium-size offices and 60 per cent of the large offices have them. The small and medium-size offices have less need for an elaborate printed manual than do the large offices, because answers to many of the questions taken up in the manual can be obtained immediately by asking the owner of the firm or the sales manager.

All offices need at least a minimum policy manual, but the need is more urgent in some than in others. The owner of an office can determine whether he needs a manual and how elaborate it must be if he will keep a list of questions asked him by his sales personnel over a period of one week. If he finds that he is answering some questions constantly, he should prepare written answers to which he can refer his staff so that he can be free to answer the more unusual and difficult questions. If the owner, or the sales manager, finds that the same questions arise over a period of time and he cannot remember what answers he gave previously, he should prepare written statements on these matters. If the owner or sales manager finds that his staff is accusing him of being inconsistent or of "playing favorites" because he gives different answers to different persons, a policy manual is needed.

Sales personnel have an even greater need for a policy manual than do the owner of the firm or the sales manager. If a salesman finds that he does not know how to proceed in some aspects of the sales process, he needs the guidance of a policy manual. If he makes promises to clients and then finds that the firm will not carry through on these promises, he needs written statements on these matters to avoid this error in the future. If a salesman finds that he needs new ideas on how to find clients, how to advertise a difficult property, how to cooperate with another office, he needs the manual. If a salesman wants to know when commissions will be paid to him, whether he can have a drawing account, or how much of his car expenses will be paid for by the office so that he can do some personal financial planning and budgeting, he needs a policy manual to guide him.

A policy manual can be developed initially in a number of ways. For example, as has already been mentioned, a list of questions asked by the sales force can be compiled by the owner of the firm and written answers prepared. The list can be added to and changed from time to time. Sales personnel might also be asked to keep a list of questions to which they have found they need answers that can be supplied only by the owner of the firm, and these lists can be submitted, compiled, edited, and answered.

Copies of manuals used by other firms can be used to develop a manual. Sometimes a manual can be started with a printed copy of the code of ethics of the National Association of Real Estate Boards and with supplementary discussion explaining the need for each of the items in the code and the manner in which the owner of the firm wishes the items applied in his office. The practices listed in other chapters in this book can be summarized and adopted by an office as a first start on a policy manual.

The advantages of a written policy manual may be summarized as:

1. Policies, procedures, and practices are stabilized so that they are understood and applied with fairness to all members of the firm.
2. The owner of the firm and the sales manager are freed from the time-consuming task of answering routine questions on practices and procedures.
3. The sales personnel have a readily available source to which they can turn for information, ideas, and inspiration that will help them become more efficient and effective.
4. The manual saves for future use those past experiences that have proven to be most applicable to successful selling. The sharing of these successes develops the neophytes into experienced salespersons more quickly and helps the experienced salespersons when they are having difficulty.
5. A policy manual provides for continuity and stability in operations that lead to continuous high-level profits for the firm and the same type of commission earnings for the sales staff.
6. A currently revised manual is the single most important supplement to the training, education, and experience of the sales staff.

A survey of policy manuals used by a group of the most successful real estate brokerage firms reveals that the following items are usually included in a manual:

1. Introductions and explanation of the purpose of the manual and how it is to be used
2. Broker-associate relationships
3. Office procedures
4. Deposits, receipts, and closing procedures
5. Commissions, bonuses, drawing accounts
6. Nonselling departments
7. Sales personnel
   a. Listing
   b. Records
   c. Floor conduct
   d. Advertising
   e. Open houses
   f. Buying and selling for own account
   g. Sales meetings
   h. Selling procedures and policies
   i. Real Estate Board activities

Item 1 through 6 are basically administrative in nature. The others are related to daily sales activities. In the remainder of the chapter, a series of questions are given to which an office should develop its own answers;

however, beside each series of questions is a list of suggestions on how the questions might be answered. An effective manual would not have to contain all of the materials listed. Each office should develop a manual only large enough to fit its needs. Salespersons should be encouraged to review the entire manual periodically, and sections of the manual should be discussed at the sales meetings. A small manual, much used, is more desirable than a large, impressively printed manual that is rarely used. Furthermore, the policies should not be so restrictive that a salesperson cannot adapt them to his own methods of operation.

ADMINISTRATIVE POLICIES

Administrative policies should be planned to provide minimum interference with the work of the sales staff. The administrative staff is provided only to support the sales efforts. Salespersons consistently refuse to do any but the most minimal administrative work; therefore, the policies in this section should be prepared with this limitation in mind.

Basic Rules for the Preparation of a Manual

1. The language should be simple and clear. Avoid wordy expressions and phrases.
2. All policies necessary to guide your associates in their daily operations should be included.
3. The manual should not be too long or too detailed.
4. The manual can be developed initially from corrective actions you have had to take in order to avoid losses of commissions or good will.
5. The manual is an outline of suggested business procedures, not a book of rules. Any impressions of making rigid and unchangeable rules will defeat the purpose of the manual.
6. Members of the firm should be encouraged to participate in the writing and interpreting of policies, in making additions to the manual, and in making changes in the manual.
7. Avoid creating the impression that every conceivable business situation has been covered. Let your associates feel that they have considerable freedom of action within rather broad policy limitations.
8. Do not include any policies which you do not intend to follow or to enforce impartially among all members of the firm. Be firm but fair when a violation of policy is discovered.
9. A copy of this manual should be given to each member of the firm.

Introduction to the Manual

Each firm will want to develop an introduction that explains why the manual is used and that summarizes what the manual contains. The following questions should aid in developing such a statement; the questions are followed by comments and by one statement used by some offices.

I. FOREWORD OR INTRODUCTION

1. Are your sales based on proven business principles?
2. Do you require your associates to adhere to a particular code of ethics?
3. Is it necessary that your principles and policies be followed closely by your associates?
4. Are your policies based on experience, and have they proven themselves over the years? Do they encourage teamwork and cooperation?
5. What procedure is followed in changing a policy?
6. Do you describe the contents of your policy book and the use that is made of it?
7. Do you provide for maximum distribution of the manual in your office?

Comments:

1. Adherence to a code of ethics does not stifle competition but provides a framework within which competition best survives.
2. If you have added to or subtracted from the printed codes of NAREB and your local board, be sure to inform your associates of this fact. (See the complete treatment of this problem in Section IV.)
3. Never publish a policy unless you expect it to be followed. Be sure that each policy has been tested and is workable. Many offices have large and detailed policy books to which they never refer.
4. The majority of policies can only be developed from experience. The policies outlined in this manual have been developed from the experiences of many Realtors and are intended to correct errors in operations which have cost thousands of dollars.
5. The most successful policies are typically those in which the associates have had some share in their preparation. However, the owner or manager should always reserve the right to make the final decision. Once a change has been made, it should be communicated to all associates in written form and put in all copies of the manual.
6. Policy manuals are most successful and useful when the reasons why they have been developed are carefully explained. In addition, issues raised in the manual should be discussed from time to time, and associates should be reminded of the constant need for letting the manual guide them in their daily operations.
7. The policy book should always be available to all associates. In some firms, the manual is so large that only the owner has a copy, and he rarely lets any member of the firm know what is in the manual until *after* trouble concerning policies has arisen.

One introduction to a policy manual reads: "Successful real estate operations in which accomplishment and remuneration are paramount are dependent upon personal factors that are associated with good leadership and freedom of enterprise. With this basic concept as a guide, the (*Broker or company name*) has devised a system of business operations in which associates are treated as entrepreneurs, masters of their own destinies, in their chosen field of real estate selling. Associates can expect friendly assistance and cooperation but not supervision. Alertness, enterprise, resourcefulness, and sales accomplishments will determine the rewards an associate can earn under this system.

Purpose of the Manual

"The purpose of this manual is to provide each associate with information on the policies and guides for the conduct of real estate business in this office. The manual is to be referred to when problems or questions arise about the procedures and the principles which govern conduct in this office. Since these policies represent the joint thinking of the members of this firm, each associate is invited to offer any suggestions that he believes will improve the operations of this office.

"In seeking to meet the objectives that have prompted the creation of this manual, this office asks each associate to sign a written statement in which he and the broker set forth mutual promises, as presented in this manual, that define the services this firm will provide the associate and that he will provide the firm. Agreement on these policies will provide the basis for future productive, mutual cooperation.

"This office is an active member of the __________ Board of Realtors and each associate is expected to become a member of this Board and the __________ State Association. In addition, each associate is expected to familiarize himself with the Code of Ethics of the National Association of Real Estate Boards and to conduct himself at all times in accordance with its principles.

Use of the Manual

"Associates are expected to make constant use of this manual in daily operations. When the manual does not provide adequate guidance, or when clarification is needed, the associate should first discuss this with the sales manager and, if the associate desires, with the owner of the firm. These policies are intended to promote close cooperation among all members of the firm. They have proven themselves through constant use and application. Associates will find high rewards in using this manual for constant guidance in their daily tasks. This manual will improve as each associate contributes his knowledge and experience to applying the policies intelligently and in recommending new policies or changes in current policies.

"The most important goal of this policy manual is to aid associates in creating a favorable impression of the firm among the general public. Each associate *is the firm* when he deals with the public, and his actions and judgements will be accepted by the public as the actions and judgements of this firm. He will find that this policy manual will assist him in meeting this goal efficiently and effectively.

"We hope that this manual will provide the basis for a lasting, pleasant, and profitable association. Welcome to our office; we are pleased to have you as an associate."

Broker-Associate Relationships

Although a salesperson is usually an independent contractor, he is still expected to adhere to certain basic policies of the firm. These policies are not intended to restrict his actions but to define for him the standards of performance that he must meet.

II. BROKER-ASSOCIATE RELATIONSHIP

1. Do you have a written agreement or contract with your associates?
2. Do you invite consultation with your associates? (That is, owner gives help to associates in what situations?)
3. Are there situations in which associates are required to consult you or someone else in the firm?
4. What do you agree to furnish your associates? (That is, desk, telephone, stenographer service?) Describe.
5. What does your associate generally agree to do for you? (That is, follow policies, work hard? Furnish a bond, car, public liability and property damage insurance, and so forth?)
6. Do you require the associate to sign the policy book and agree to its contents?

Comments:

1. The majority of the successful firms have a policy manual or a written agreement to be signed by all new associates or both senior and new associates. If there is no policy manual, then the contract of employment should contain a detailed explanation of how commissions are split and when they are paid. For instance, to say that the commission split is 50 per cent is not enough. Is it 50 per cent of the gross commission collected? Fifty per cent after deductions for advertising? Fifty per cent of what?

   A written agreement between the firm and the associate guarantees a businesslike arrangement which outlines the responsibilities of each party. It is not a sign of distrust.
2. The amount of consultation occurring depends upon the type of persons in the office. A firm with many experienced personnel will expect the sales personnel to solve most of the problems themselves. Effective consultation is possible only when a real problem exists—usually, the problems center around financing. Consultations can also be an effective means of letting

associates air their complaints directly to the head of the firm rather than disturbing the other associates.

3. Situations in which consultations are required most often are: (1) when completing closing details (this is done with the escrow officer), (2) when unusual financing must be arranged, (3) when there is a dispute between members in the office, (4) when an associate wishes to go counter to policy.
4. The majority of offices furnish desk space, telephone service, listing books and files, and an advertising allowance or budget. A few also furnish limited secretarial services.
5. Associates are usually expected to have a late-model car which is always kept in a presentable appearance; to belong to the local board; to give priority to their business interests; and to work diligently. Some firms may also expect associates to carry a limited amount of insurance for public liability and property damage and to furnish a bond.
6. Associates may be required to sign a statement that they have read the policy book, and this statement is filed; they may simply sign such a statement which is permanently affixed to the front of a master policy book; or they may be asked to sign each page of their own copy of the policy book when they finish reading the page. The majority of firms take some type of action to insure that the policy book will be read.

Office Procedures

Clear policies are needed on the conduct expected of associates while they are in the office in order that clients may be received properly and the administrative personnel permitted to work without constant interruption or harrassment. The questions listed do not include all that may be asked, but they should generate additional ideas of what the individual office needs.

1. What are your office hours?
2. What hours are associates expected to keep?
3. Do associates have certain days off?
4. Should associates call into the office at certain times during the day for messages, and so forth?
5. Do you encourage associates not to speak of other offices and their employees unless they have something worth while to say?
6. Have you indicated to your associates what you expect in dress, office conduct, neatness at desks, and so forth?
7. Is your office considered a place of business only? Do associates have assigned desks and work areas?
8. Are associates expected to keep in touch with buyers and sellers after the sale is made?
9. Do you stress courtesy, sincerity, and honesty as basic operating policies in your firm?

10. Have you assigned responsibilities for answering inquiries about listings and sales?
11. Are your associates required to hold open house or do other specified work at certain times?
12. Who opens and closes the office?
13. Do you require that certain reports be kept?
14. Do you expect your associates to answer correspondence and calls as soon as possible? And do you see that they do it?
15. What expenses may associates charge to the firm?

Comments:

1. Office hours should be prominently posted and adhered to for the benefit not only of associates but also of clients.
2. Policies on associates keeping hours are widely divergent. In almost all
3. cases, associates who are not coming to the office are expected to phone
4. in the first thing in the morning, in the afternoon, and in the evening to receive messages and instructions. When associates are expected to be in the office during certain hours, these should be posted well in advance. The same policy should be followed in arranging for days off. Days on which associates must be on duty should always be announced.
5. Associates who have complaints against other offices should refer them to the manager or owner at once. These complaints should never be discussed with other salesmen or with clients.
6. The majority of offices do have minimum standards of dress for their associates, but many of them fail to tell the associates. They also expect the office area to be kept in a neat condition and desks cleared except for current working papers. Each associate should be assigned desk space and instructed not to use any other desk nor to use closing rooms or other space reserved for use with clients.
7. Personal problems or the problems of clients should not be discussed in an office, and such practices are usually discouraged.
8. Many offices provide cards or form letters that associates can send to both clients and prospects. Some offices, the larger ones particularly, send follow-up "thank you" letters on behalf of the associates.
9. Are courtesy, sincerity, and honesty hallmarks of your operation, or only superficial conveniences to be used when expedient in making a sale?
10. Usually one person is assigned to answer all phone or drop-in inquiries. He then refers the caller to the associate who can help him. A uniform telephone greeting is usually used and written messages taken for anyone not in the office. If a particular salesperson is asked for and he is not in, a note is left for him. A standard form to be filled out for leaving phone messages is usually provided. It indicates the name of the person called, person taking the message, the date, the time, and the message.

11. Usually, salespersons are not expected to do any work not directly connected with selling. Holding open house is generally required of the salesperson who secures the listing, or he must arrange for open-house showings. If holding open-house showings is a regular procedure, not many offices do this, but rather, the sales manager assigns hours and dates. Some firms find open-house showings a good source of sales leads, but there is growing opposition to them.
12. The majority of brokerage offices have regular opening and closing times, but they expect the administrative staff to open and close the office at these times. The sales force opens and closes the office only at other times or on special occasions.
13. Many offices keep a record file on each property that is listed and on all sold properties. All information on the property is placed in this folder and salespersons refer to it whenever information on the property is needed. Copies of listing agreements, closing or escrow papers, sales agreements, and deposit receipts are kept in this folder.

    All correspondence relating to any aspect of the firm's business is usually handled through the office secretary, who maintains the file and gives information from it to the sales staff. The sales staff are not expected or allowed to place materials in this file or to take material from it, although they are allowed information from it. All contracts and agreements in original copies are kept in this file, and copies of these items are placed in the property files.

    Some offices supply each salesperson with a printed time organizer that contains suggestions on how he should plan each day of work. This organizer is particularly useful in training new sales personnel.
14. Each salesperson should be assigned a secretary to take care of his ordinary secretarial work. Normally she should not be asked to prepare large volumes of sales literature unless she has free time. If a salesperson needs additional help, or if the secretary normally assigned to him is busy, he should be asked to contact the sales manager, the owner of the firm, or the office manager. Secretaries should not be used to make appointments or to take personal calls: these things should be taken care of by the salesperson. Copies of all correspondence should be sent to the owner of the firm or to the sales manager for their information and review.
15. Salespersons are usually not permitted to obligate the firm for any expenses without prior permission from someone in authority. All office expenses are paid by the firm. Expenses of associates who are asked to assist in listing or selling property should be paid by the person asking for this assistance.

    Practices vary on other expenses. Some offices expect a salesperson to pay all of his car expenses, including insurance. Others allow a fixed sum or mileage for these items. Legal expenses arising from a transaction may be shared between the salesperson and the office or be borne entirely by the office, but normally a salesperson is not obligated to pay more than the amount he would receive as commission on the sale. The firm usually reserves the right to decide when to institute suit. Costs of collecting unpaid commissions are usually shared on the basis of the commission split.

Many offices pay for public liability insurance covering injury to any client who is in the office, in an automobile being used for company business, or while at property being shown.

Deposits, Receipts, and Escrow Procedures

Before policies are developed on these matters, competent legal counsel should be secured in developing answers to the questions raised. Some suggestions are offered, but they cannot be substituted for valuable legal advice.

III. DEPOSITS AND RECEIPTS

1. Do you stress the importance of filling out deposit-receipt forms completely and correctly?
2. How much deposit or down payment do you require?
3. Do you have a minimum deposit limit?
4. To whom are checks made payable?
5. What do you do with buyer deposits after they are accepted by associates?
6. Who handles the refund to the buyer if an offer is not accepted?
7. What is your policy regarding refunds when a buyer backs out of deal? Is it flexible enough to fit each individual case?
8. What is your policy regarding associates who desire to instigate legal suits?
9. Do you clearly set forth the legal responsibilities where more than one offer is received on the same property prior to any acceptance by the seller?
10. Who is charged with the responsibility of setting up your escrow?
11. How do you handle deposit checks?
12. If you have an escrow department, does it handle the transaction until completion, answering all questions, and so forth?
13. Do you emphasize the importance of opening the escrow as soon as possible after acceptance of an offer?
14. Who is charged with the responsibility of following through until close of escrow?

Comments:

1. Sales personnel are expected to use only standard printed forms in preparing deposit receipts and to refer any special contracts to the manager of the office. Offices usually require that all completed deposit-receipt forms must be checked by the sales manager before they are submitted to the seller.

2. Offices usually encourage their sales personnel to secure the maximum down payment but always specify the minimum amount to be accepted. Typically, the deposit should equal the difference between the sales price and the amount of money to be secured through a loan. Some offices provide each salesperson with forms for promissory notes, counter checks, and savings-withdrawal slips so that these can be completed as soon as the buyer agrees to buy.

   It should be stressed that all deposits are the property of the seller of the property and must be deposited in a trust account until the transaction is completed or the deposit is returned. All deposits should be returned immediately if the offer to buy is not accepted.

3–9. The answers to these questions should be developed only after consultation with a lawyer skilled in these matters. If suit must ever be instituted, the manner in which these items were handled will probably determine the outcome of the suit.

Closing practices differ widely from community to community, but the problems relating to escrow are the same. The following principles should be observed in setting up escrow procedure:

1. In nearly all small firms, the responsibility of the associate ends when the deposit receipt has been completed. The owner of the firm or his secretary takes over and completes the paper work involved in closing.
2. In many firms a well-trained secretary, escrow clerk, or other person will assist in supplying the details necessary to close a sale. This frees the owner or manager for more important work.
3. All details of a transaction should be completed and in writing before escrow is begun. Many offices were observed doing such a poor job prior to going into escrow that they had to resell the entire transaction in escrow. Too many brokers do not really begin to sell until they reach escrow.
4. A complete file of all completed escrows provides valuable sales and listing information.

Commissions, Bonuses, and Drawing Accounts

The amount of commission that a salesperson should receive is usually determined by the rates paid in the local community, with modifications that reflect the preferences of the office for which he works. A basis for determining what the rate should be is discussed in Chapter 4. The materials on commission that are included in a policy manual discuss the administrative details of paying commissions and the standard rates paid for the majority of sales work. The payments of bonuses and drawing accounts must also be included, because they are an integral part of the over-all compensation scheme for sales personnel.

IV. COMMISSIONS, BONUSES, AND DRAWING ACCOUNTS

A. *Charges to Clients*

1. Do you follow an established schedule of commissions charged to clients?
2. What is your policy regarding changes in commissions?
3. Do you allow commissions in excess of the quoted rate?
4. Do you notify all parties in a trade of the fact that each is to pay the established commission?

B. *Schedules of Commissions Paid to Associates*

1. Do you have a complete and definite commission schedule covering listings, sales, exchanges, bonuses, and splits?
2. How and when are commissions paid?
3. What fees or expenses are deducted from the commission before it is paid?
4. Is the commission schedule listed in the associates' contract, or is it a separate written agreement?
5. What split, if any, is made with any other member of the organization for referrals or other help (or service)?

C. *General*

1. What is your policy regarding the acceptance of notes in lieu of cash commissions from the seller?
2. Do you require or suggest a quota to your associates?

D. *Disputes*

1. How are controversies between associates handled?
2. Who makes the decision to decide a dispute?

E. *Compensation—Bonuses—Drawing Accounts*

1. Do you have incentives that increase with length of service?
2. What benefits do you offer your associates that are not common with your competitors?
3. Do you offer a profit-participation program?
4. Do you encourage or offer any accruing security programs for the associate and his family?

Comments:

What is a proper commission rate?

Many offices fail to realize that a commission is an incentive, and that the more opportunities for commission, the more selling that will result. High commission rates cannot be used to overcome poor business practices, and it is for this reason that large, established, and efficiently run offices can pay smaller commissions and still keep their sales associates.

Payments for listings should not be done automatically but only if the firm needs listings. The amounts paid for various kinds of listings should reflect the listing needs of the firm. If the firm wants its sales associates to secure exclusive listings, then the highest listing commissions should be paid for these. If the firm wants sales associates to sell their own listings, then the highest commissions should be paid for this.

The proper commission rate:

1. It is not a fixed amount.
2. It must be related to the services the firm provides for the sales associates.
3. It must be competitive with those paid by competing offices.
4. It must reflect the objectives of the firm.

Bonuses

An increasingly greater number of firms are using various types of incentive and profit-sharing plans to keep their sales at consistently high levels and also as a means of retaining the services of their experienced, high-production sales associates. These general conclusions can be made about incentive plans:

1. The more complicated and comprehensive plans are used by the larger offices; the simpler plans are used by the smaller offices.
2. The majority of plans are based on a minimum quota plus varying percentage rates on commissions as the minimum is exceeded.
3. The most successful plans appear to be those which provide bonuses when a goal is reached, with the goal based on a monthly or periodic achievement basis.
4. Reasonable or achievable minimums or goals are much more successful than high goals with high percentages for exceeding the minimum.
5. Incentive payments to associates for group achievement are less successful than those for individual achievement. For instance, a plan of this type which rarely succeeds is one in which a bonus is paid for extra sales within a given period, with the sales associates sharing in the bonus according to sales made.
6. Profit-sharing plans are rarely understood or appreciated by associates. A true profit-sharing plan is one in which a given percentage of profits is paid after all firm expenditures have been made.
7. Opinion is divided on the merits of sales contests. Some offices never use them; others use them regularly. In most cases, a well-planned and executed sales plan does provide a temporary stimulus to sales.
8. The simpler the plan, the easier it is to administer and the more readily it will be accepted by sales associates.

Drawing Accounts

Opinions among owners of real estate brokerage offices on the use of drawing accounts is sharply divided. Some feel that they weaken the entire commissions incentive system; that they permit salespersons to develop poor financial habits. Those who favor the use of drawing accounts recommend that they be used for the following:

1. A new staff person with little experience but lots of promise whom you hope will develop into a good salesperson within not more than six months.
2. High-producing salespersons who are in a temporary slump.
3. Salespersons with completed sales in escrow who have an immediate need for cash for family financing needs, or who wish to maintain relatively level monthly income.
4. An experienced salesperson earning large commissions in another type of business who wishes to train with your office, earn a license, and then join your sales staff.

A. *Charges to clients*

1. Offices normally follow the commission schedules recommended by the local real estate board.
2. Any deviations from the published schedules must usually be approved by the sales manager or the owner of the firm. Cutting commissions for any reason is usually discouraged. Salespersons may not cut commissions by taking less than their proportionate share and passing the savings on to the seller of the property.
3. Commissions in excess of the quoted rate are permitted when extra services must be provided or when the property represents an unusual sales problem.
4. Many offices have the commission schedules posted prominently, provide printed brochures that give the rates, and include a statement on the amount of commission to be paid in all sales contracts. A firm statement that the commission will be based on a printed schedule will usually discourage buyers and sellers from asking for cuts in the rate.

B. *Schedules of commissions paid to associates*

1. Associates should be furnished with a complete and definite commission schedule covering all types of compensation situations. Any changes should always be put in writing and the notices distributed to all sales personnel.
2. Most of the controversies over commissions arise because the sales staff does not know for sure when the commissions they have earned will be paid. Some offices prepare weekly or bimonthly statements for each salesperson showing how much he has earned in commission, the amounts to be paid as the result of successful closing of escrows, and the amounts he owes the firm either because of a drawing account or for other expenses. Other firms issue commission checks as soon as escrow is closed and the office has received its commission check. Many troubles can be avoided if the rules on paying commissions are known to all and followed to the letter.
3. Practices vary on what amounts should be deducted from the total

commission before the associate's share of the commission is calculated. Here again, the amounts or items to be deducted are not important as long as the sales staff knows that they are to be deducted and agrees to the deductions. In every case, the salesperson should be given an itemized statement of commissions earned and expenses incurred that were deducted from the commission.

4. Commission schedules are usually printed up by themselves and not included in any part of an agreement. Sometimes the associate may be asked to sign the schedule to indicate that he has read it and agrees to it.
5. The usual practice is to pay 50 to 60 per cent of the commission received by the office to the person selling the property and an additional 10 to 20 per cent to the person who listed the property. Firms usually expect to keep not less than 30 to 40 per cent of the total commission collected for selling a home.

C. *General*

1. Many offices will accept a promissory note or a signed bank withdrawal slip in lieu of a check or cash for the commission. Promissory notes are used most frequently when second trust deeds must be used to finance part of the purchase price. A few offices refuse to accept anything but cash for their selling commission.

E. *Bonuses, drawing accounts*

1. Bonuses that increase with the length of service are sometimes used by offices that wish to keep an experienced and effective salesperson.
2. Other benefits besides bonuses are: payment of premiums on health, accident, and sickness insurance; payments on some form of retirement system; paid vacation plans related to total sales made in the previous year. The payment of one-half to three-fourths of the premium for a good health insurance plan is being done by more and more offices because of the peace of mind such a plan brings to the salesperson who is worried about his family.
3. The use of profit-sharing programs is very limited and not often successful because it diverts the salesperson's attention away from his function of selling to concern over how the business is being run. Firms find that incentive plans tied to better selling results are much more effective than profit-sharing plans. Some incorporated firms offer shares of stock to those salespersons whom they would like to keep as participating managers.
4. Many firms provide Social Security benefits to their sales personnel instead of treating them as independent contractors. Others pay premiums on some form of group retirement program. There is little

evidence as yet to indicate that salespersons have a strong desire for such plans.

5. If drawing accounts are used, the rule relating to them should be printed and made available to all in the office. Special drawing-account privileges for some and not for others creates mounting ill will.

Nonselling Departments

As a real estate office grows, the owner of the office is often tempted to expand his operations to include such nonbrokerage activities as insurance, mortgage financing, and property management. If departments are created for such activities, large amounts of capital must be invested in the departments in their early years if they are to become profitable. Otherwise, such departments should not be created, and if insurance, mortgage-financing, and property-management services are to be offered, they should be used primarily as extra service benefits to the clients of the office and as aids to selling rather than as independent profit-making activities.

1. Do you have a rental, insurance, or loan department?
2. What is the purpose of these departments?
3. Do your associates tell everyone they meet of these extra services?
4. What is your policy regarding the obtaining of sales prospects from these departments?
5. Do you have cooperation between all of your departments?
6. What is your commission schedule for rentals?
7. Do you advertise rental listings?
8. Do you make a charge for loans?

A large majority of real estate offices feel that a rental office or service is a necessary part of any brokerage operation and should be offered for the benefit of clients even if it is not a profitable operation. A smaller number of offices offer property-management and insurance services. Only a few of the older offices earn substantial profits from these services; however, all offices which have these services find them to be good sources of prospects.

A small commission to the brokerage personnel for securing rentals or property-management business—plus the opportunity for them to have priority on any sales prospects developed from these services—usually results in the best arrangement for these service departments.

If any of these services are to be offered by a firm, regardless of the size of the firm, the sales staff should be given some incentive for bringing in this type of business. In such cases, the relationships between the service departments and the sales departments should be set forth in detail.

Normally, these services would not be offered until the firm has been established and has begun to grow. Offices with limited associates do not have the facilities for proper handling of these departments and are usually the ones which are the most dissatisfied with the results from having such services.

Some of the larger offices are loan agents for banks, savings and loan associations, and insurance companies, but the majority of offices use the local lenders to secure loans. Maintaining good sources of mortgage-loan money is an important part of building a large sales volume.

SELLING POLICIES AND AIDS

The previous chapters discuss the management of the selling process and the sales staff; the purpose of this section is to provide a series of questions and minimal content as guides to creating a policy book. Much of the material that is included in the policy book will have been covered in sales meetings; therefore, the policy-book statements can be brief. The questions listed are those that the majority of successful firms find must be answered by policy statements in order for them to maintain harmonious working arrangements with their sales staff. Additional suggestions on possible answers to these questions may be obtained from materials published by the state real estate associations and the National Association of Real Estate Boards. It must be emphasized that policies recommended in this book or in materials published by others should not be adopted blindly but should be studied and tested and rewritten to meet the needs of the local office. In connection with developing selling policies and aids, a manager will find that, if each policy is discussed with his sales manager and staff first and then written up, the policy book will become a vital aid to all selling efforts.

Listing

A. *General policy*

1. How do you normally obtain listings?
2. Do you have standard listing forms?
3. Do you require your listing forms to be completed in detail?
4. Do you have quotas?
5. Does the lister have special rights to listings he obtains?
6. What policy do you follow when listing a property regarding: (a) price; (b) length of time; (c) types?
7. Do you know why the seller wants to sell?
8. Do you find out what kinds of neighbors live near the property? Do you ask them for suggestions about possible buyers?
9. Are your associates well acquainted with certain neighborhoods—do they specialize?
10. When is the listing commission paid?

11. Do you try to obtain listings of other offices after their listing contracts have expired?
12. Do you define the area you normally serve?
13. Must listings be turned in to the office immediately?
14. Do you report to the seller at various intervals what has been done to sell his property?
15. Do you approach the owner for a relisting before the expiration of an unsold listing held by the office?
16. Do you thank owners for a listing by writing them a courtesy letter?
17. Do you accept listings only when you are able to offer skilled and conscientious service?

B. *Types of listings*
1. What types do you handle?
2. Do you turn down a certain type?

C. *Residential*
1. Do your associates specialize in a certain area?
2. Are they familiar with all listings in a certain area?

D. *Nonresidential*
1. How do you define nonresidential or income properties?
2. Do your associates specialize in them?

E. *Setting Listing Price*
1. How do you determine the price at which the property will be listed?
2. How do you approach the seller regarding the listing price?
3. Do you maintain a comparable "sales" file?
4. Do you sell owner on your ability to set price?
5. Do you sell owner on services of your firm?

F. *Forms*
1. Are you alert to the opportunities for improving your forms?
2. Do you keep a file on all listings, past and present?
3. Are the completed forms approved before they are distributed to the associates?

Comments:

A. *General policy*
1. The majority of firms find that they must pursue an aggressive policy in order to keep a supply of good listings. Usually this involves advertising plus personal contact by telephone or calling on homeowners each week.
2. Only one listing form should be used in any single office. Standard forms, such as those developed by state associations, are used by many offices. Very few offices have prepared their own listing forms.

   The information on a listing form should provide the following:

(1) Sufficient information to permit the preparation of advertising copy,
(2) Complete information on the terms that the seller will accept,

(3) Extensive enough description of the property so that all sales associates can describe the property to clients by a quick review of the form, after the sales associate has visited the property, and
(4) An indication of the progress being made in selling or showing the property.

3. No listing quotas are needed when sales associates are well trained and properly compensated. In the majority of firms, listing quotas are quite often used but rarely achieve significant results.

   Too many firms assume that they have a good reputation in their community, and that that is sufficient to guarantee a continuing flow of listings. Referrals are a good source of listings but a minor source not available to a great number of offices.
4. In only very few firms are listers given special rights to the listings they obtain. Usually they are given a share of the commission when the property is sold, but even this practice varies widely among firms and with the kinds of listings firms may wish to obtain.

   Exclusive rights to listings are successful only when special types of properties are involved and only when the lister has sufficient technical background to show the property as it should be shown. Such practices are usually followed in commercial and industrial listings.
5. The majority of firms will admit that they can be in error in setting a listing price by five per cent, either higher or lower. Many offices feel that they do not wish to argue with a client and therefore accept the listing at his price, with the intention of asking for a lower price when the property does not sell. Those firms who insist on listing at their price usually have accurate and complete market information on which to base their listing appraisal.

   Some offices deplore the competition for clients through exaggerated listing prices, but they still follow the practice. In several instances where this was going on, the listing usually changed hands when the price was lowered.

   The office which gets the listing at the "right" price may have fewer listings, but the listings are sold more quickly and total sales are higher. The majority of offices follow this practice. The typical listing is for 90 to 120 days. In a few instances, the time is extended to 180 days where high-priced or unusual properties are involved. When moderate-priced properties are listed for long periods, too many offices do nothing to sell the properties during the majority of this period.

   Types of listings taken vary from community to community. The basic rule is to take the type of listing that can be sold for the best commission. Too many offices will take a listing they are not prepared to service simply because they can get it on an exclusive basis.
6. Almost all offices agree that the reason for the sale should always be

known before a listing is taken. If the reason is a good one, then the property can be taken at a slightly higher price.

7. Opinion and practices are divided on the merits of assigning special listing areas. Usually, however, areas near the office should be assigned in some manner so that all possible listing sources are covered systematically.
8. The time at which a listing commission is paid is not so important to sales associates as is consistency in payment policy so that the salespersons can anticipate payment.
9. In almost all offices, at least 50 per cent of the listings being worked on have expired or are about to expire. A system of checking listings for expiration dates is needed. The majority of offices contact owners one to two weeks before the listing expires to discuss renewal.
10. Contacting neighbors often produces possible buyers among the friends or relatives of the seller.
11. The offices that have overcome the problem of listings not being turned in will require each sales associate to report in each night on listings obtained. No excuses are accepted for "pocket" listings.
12. Many offices have plans for contacting sellers and keeping them informed, but few of them do this.
13. If an honest effort has been made to sell the property, the owner should be contacted.
14. Successful offices use form letters for this purpose but always have the letters typed.

Records

1. Does each one of your associates carry a sales kit?
2. Does he keep complete records on each prospect?
3. Is a record kept in the office of all prospects?
4. Do you have a daybook or daily log?
5. What information is kept in the log or daybook?
6. Who records information in the log?

Comments:

The problem of what records a sales associate should have is one of deciding what he needs versus what he can carry. Whether or not the associate wishes to carry a large kit, he should have a complete sales kit in his car, at his desk, or some place where it is available when he needs it.

Included in a good sales kit are such items as:

1. Prospect file
2. All blank forms necessary for closing a sale

3. Advertising matter—pamphlets, recent ads, types of ads used, souvenirs, and so forth
4. A file of current listings
5. Reference materials on financing
6. Maps of the neighborhood
7. Information on neighborhood facilities
8. Information on recent sales
9. Promissory-note forms

Logs or Daybooks

Logs or daybooks appear to be a necessity in any firm with more than two sales associates. The log should be used to indicate new listings, sold listings, inquiries, wants, financing information, and similar items that are needed to keep sales associates informed on new developments.

A manager will find a log useful in determining how long it takes from listing to sale; where prospects are coming from; to whom properties are being sold; average terms of sales; and similar items. The log can be maintained easily by a secretary, who could post all information from the previous day's business in the log at the start of the next day.

Floor Conduct

A. *General*

1. Who takes floor and telephone calls, and how are they defined in various situations?
2. How do you greet new clients who telephone? New clients who walk in?
3. Do you take *complete messages* for others in the office?
4. Are you always courteous?
5. Do you keep a "log" and note every drop-in and telephone call?

B. *Schedules*

1. How are schedules determined (that is, by floor days or fixed days)?
2. How and when are floor schedules announced?
3. Do you notify someone in the office when you are unable to keep your schedule?
4. Does the scheduled floor man forfeit his floor time if he is late?
5. Who takes care of telephone calls and drop-ins when the scheduled floor man is busy or out?

C. *Duties and Responsibilities of Floor Men*

1. What is expected of the floor man?
2. What procedure do you follow for directing a drop-in or caller to the proper person to assist him?
3. Are there other responsibilities of the floor man?

D. *Relations to Other Associates*

1. When the floor man is out, what is your policy regarding the greeting of customers and clients by other members of the organization?

2. What is your policy when customers or clients ask for a particular associate?
3. Do you ask clients or customers if they have been working with another one of your associates?
4. When a client or customer asks for a particular associate and he cannot be located, what is your policy toward the assistance that the floor man may give him?

Comments:

The major functions of the floor man are to answer telephone calls about properties listed or sold and to greet all persons who call in person at the office to discuss buying or selling a property. When he is not busy greeting clients, the floor man may be asked to bring listing files up to date, check advertising, or do other tasks that the sales manager may ask him to do. He may also use the time preparing his own correspondence or telephoning his own prospects if he does not neglect his primary floor responsibilities.

If the floor man has to leave the office for any reason, he should be responsible for finding a substitute or for notifying the sales manager to determine whether a substitute is needed. Because the floor man is in an advantageous position to obtain the first contact with prospective buyers and sellers, the sales staff should be consulted in the creation of the floor schedule and in setting policies on how prospective buyers are to be assigned to other members of the sales staff. A firm policy should be established that, when a salesperson is asked for by name, he is to be notified of this fact; and, if the client asks for a service that the floor man cannot render, the client should be referred to the proper person so that the firm will not lose a client or create bad feeling by rendering poor service.

A. *General*

Successful offices treat the greeting of clients as an integral part of their advertising and public relations, and insist that all clients be greeted in a sincere and uniform manner. Usually a salesperson gives his name, his position in the firm, and offers to assist the client.

Almost all offices require that a "log" or note be made of every call and of every person calling in person at the office. When messages are involved, they are delivered by the person taking the message.

B. *Schedules*

A surprisingly large number of firms do not have floor days but prefer that their associates spend all of their time out of the office. Offices who do schedule floor time usually do it by half-days on a rotating basis, so that all associates will have an opportunity to be on the floor during both the best and the poorest hours and days. Only the owner or manager can excuse an associate from floor time. In some cases the floor schedule may not result in an equitable distribution of prospects, and in these cases the manager may have to allocate some prospects on a different basis. Firms who do not schedule floor time do require that someone be in the office at all times. Typically, a firm does not have a floor schedule when the firm is small. In the larger offices, the new associates and trainees are usually not assigned floor time until they have served a period of apprenticeship.

Advertising

(See the Chapter on Advertising for suggestions on how to create policies that answer these questions.)

1. What purpose do you have in advertising?
2. What types and media of advertising do you use?
3. Do you have planned campaigns?
4. Who writes the advertising?
5. Is it important that you explain your advertising program to your clients?
6. Do you or your associates promise clients that you will advertise their property? If so, in what situations do you do this?
7. Do you analyze your transactions to find their source as to clients or customers, and do you maintain checks on advertising results?
8. Do you allot a certain amount of advertising money to each associate for a period?
9. When do you advertise, and what determines the volume?

Open House

1. When are your hours for open house?
2. Who holds open house?
3. Do you arrive early and locate your flags and signs?
4. Are you friendly and courteous?
5. Do you obtain necessary information from the owner?
6. Do you try to secure new listings and clients from drop-ins?
7. Who is responsible for lost flags and signs?
8. When can you leave an open house to show other properties?
9. Where should the associate locate himself at the open house (that is, in his car or in the house)?
10. If a client is referred to the open house by another associate and buys the house, does the referring associate participate in the commission?

Comments:

Opinion is sharply divided on the merits of holding open house. Some areas discourage it or even prohibit it; some are very much in favor of it; some tolerate the practice.

Open houses are usually considered to be a necessary part of mass selling.

The principal attraction of open houses is that they do provide a list of prospects.

Buying and Selling for Own Account

1. Are associates allowed to buy or sell property for their own account?
2. What is your policy if they are allowed to do so? (Clearly and completely defined.)
3. Do you recognize that the normal buying public has priority over a salesperson in purchasing property?
4. When and how do you let the listing owner know that a member of your sales staff is buying the property?

Comments:

Firms do not take an intermediate position on this problem. Associates are allowed to buy and sell as many properties as they choose or they are not allowed to engage in any type of buying and selling.

Firms do not permit this practice for the following reasons:

1. They do not wish to give the impression that they are competing with their clients.
2. Sales associates have, in the past, taken advantage of their special role as intermediary in a sale, and have worked to the disadvantage of either the buyer or seller or both.

Firms which permit this practice usually have the following limitations:

1. Any property bought or sold must be listed with the firm, and full listing commissions, cooperative sales commissions, and other expenses must be paid.
2. Failure on the part of any associate to meet the above conditions results in severe and immediate disciplinary action.
3. Such transactions should not be undertaken unless they benefit the buyer or seller (that is, the seller may desire a quick sale, knowing that he is selling at a lower-than-market price).

An increasing number of instances are arising in which a buyer or seller would be assisted if the firm or the sales associate purchased a property. Any policies adopted with respect to this problem should be reasonable and should reflect the practices of the local community, and policies established on this matter should be followed to the letter by all persons associated with the firm.

Sales Meetings

1. When are sales meetings held?
2. What are the objectives of the meetings?
3. What are typical agenda?

4. How long are your sales meetings?
5. Is attendance mandatory?
6. When are properties visited by salespersons? Do they go as a group or individually?

Comments:

There are few offices, regardless of size, that do not have sales meetings. The meetings may be planned on a regularly scheduled basis or may be held whenever the owner feels the need for one. The most important item in the agenda is the discussion of selling problems and the exchange of sales information. Typical agenda in firms which use sales meetings effectively would include the following:

1. Activities or policies of the firm—particular emphasis on advertising, selling, and listing policies. Old policies are reviewed and discussed, new policies announced, and policy changes reviewed. The bulletins from the Real Estate Commissioner's office are discussed.
2. Market information—changes in money markets, sources of funds, new market developments, average prices, and price changes in local markets.
3. Current business discussion of the firm's listings and prospects, sales completed, good properties available, properties wanted by prospects, and similar items.
4. Educational activities—guest speakers, changes in governmental lending policies, escrow procedures, or other items intended to broaden the background of the sales associates.

Selling

A. *General*

1. Are you always courteous and friendly?
2. Do you have planned quotas or objectives?
3. Do your associates try to sell or qualify another man's prospect?
4. What is your policy for working on other company's exclusives?
5. Do you send "thank you" letters to the seller and buyer?
6. Do you always try to avoid conflicts and disputes with your clients?

Comments:

Good sales associates typically plan their selling program from one week to six months in advance. Many firms do not set quotas, but invariably a good associate has his own quota, in terms of either the number of properties or the total dollar volume of sales.

A principal source of strained relations in many offices are the attempts made by sales associates to sell each other's prospects. A clear statement of policy is needed on how prospects are assigned.

When an office cooperates with other offices on the sales of exclusive listings, some form of written agreement should be developed. An understanding is particularly important—cooperation extends beyond the terminal date of the listing agreement.

B. *Closing*

1. Who handles the closing?
2. Where should closing take place?
3. Do you insist upon extreme care in the preparation of documents?
4. Do you try to settle all conditions before entering into escrow?

Comments:

The majority of offices prefer that all closings take place in the office. However, this is sometimes not possible; therefore, every sales associate should be equipped with a complete kit of all materials needed to close a sale.

C. *Cooperative Sales in the Office*

1. Do you encourage cooperation among your associates (that is, share information)?
2. Are prospects registered for a certain length of time with one associate?
3. If so, for how long?

Comments:

Firms expect associates to cooperate with each other in selling so that clients will receive the best possible service. However, each associate should keep the other persons on the sales staff notified of all persons with whom he is working so that members of the staff will not be competing with each other. If an associate cannot sell a property and the listing expires, he should be required to allow some other member of the staff to attempt to relist the property and then attempt to sell it.

D. *Cooperation with Other Offices*

1. What is your policy regarding sharing of information with other offices?
2. Who gives information to other offices?
3. What is your policy on accepting or seeking assistance from another broker on open listings?

Comments:

Successful firms normally cooperate with other offices if these offices offer an equivalent quality of service and if they subscribe to the same code of ethics. The need for cooperation arises when a client sees a property listed by another office and wishes to see it, when a client has a special need that can be met only by properties listed by other offices, or when a client has asked the office to accept his property as a listing and the office does not ordinarily sell this type of property.

E. *Giving Addresses*

1. Do you give addresses of properties listed by you to prospective buyers?
2. Do you convince a prospective buyer that you, as an expert, are the one to show the property inside and outside?

Comments:

Firms almost universally will not give out the addresses of properties to prospective buyers nor will they allow the buyers to visit the properties without some member of the firm accompanying them.

F. *Keys*

1. Where are house keys kept?
2. How long are keys to be kept by a salesperson?
3. How do you account for keys to furnished and unfurnished properties?
4. Are keys marked so that they will be returned if lost?
5. Do you ever let anyone other than a member of your organization use a key?
6. When you enter a home, do you knock or call out? If the owner is not at home, do you leave your business card so that the owner will know when you were there?
7. Do you always make sure that all windows and doors are locked when you leave?

Comments:

Keys should be kept in one place and checked in and out by one person, usually the secretary. If this is not possible, then each key should be clearly labeled and anyone taking a key be required to place his card on the board in place of the key. Keys should be returned after each showing. Because a real estate office can be held liable for damages to a property occasioned by showing a property or by careless attention to who has the keys, each office should establish and enforce policies on keys.

G. *Telephone Answering*

1. Do you remind associates to be courteous and to take complete messages?
2. Do you have recommended stock answers to be used by all associates?
3. Do you restrict the amount of information that may be given over the telephone?

Comments:

The telephone company will assist in training all persons in good telephone-answering techniques. Because this is usually an initial contact by a client, the telephone call must be exploited to the fullest if advertising that prompted the call is not to be wasted.

Standard methods of answering telephone inquiries should be developed and their use required of all personnel.

Sales associates should be trained to arrange for a person-to-person meeting with the caller. Little information about properties should be given over the telephone; instead, appointments should be arranged.

H. *Representation*

1. Are representations in writing cleared by the office?

2. Do your associates know the limits of their contractual ability?
3. Who clears expenditures?

Comments:

The policy should be that all offers or representations as to what the firm will do must be in writing and approved by the sales manager or the owner of the firm. The same should apply to all expenditures over a given amount, such as $10 or $15.

I. *Showing Property*

1. Do you require that associates arrange all property showings by prior appointment with the seller?
2. Do you require associates to call the seller when an appointment cannot be kept?

Comments:

All property showing should be by appointment only. This gives the seller an opportunity to put the property in the best possible shape for showing and permits efficient use of showing time. The seller should always be notified if the appointment cannot be kept.

J. *Other Brokers' Listings*

1. Do you obtain permission to show them?
2. Do you treat other brokers' owners as if they were your clients?
3. Do you tell the customer that you cooperate with other offices?

The listings of other brokers should always be respected and the listing broker contacted when his property is to be shown.

K. *Loans*

1. Do you charge fees for obtaining loans on property refinanced by private money?
2. What financing services do you provide?

L. *Protection*

1. In what instances will an associate be protected on sales prospects?
2. For how long is an associate protected on property that he has shown to a certain prospect?
3. How do members of the office identify their prospects so that there will be no misunderstandings?

M. *Prospects*

1. How are prospects normally obtained?
2. Do you make a daily report on all prospects furnished by the office?
3. Can a prospect be taken away from an associate for a certain reason?
4. How are prospects qualified, classified, and distributed?
5. Do you have a prospect commission for an associate who refers a client to another associate?
6. Do you allow two or more associates to try to sell the same prospect?

Real Estate Board Activities

1. Do you give an explanation to your associates of the services of the local board?
2. What is your policy regarding board membership by your associates (that is, mandatory membership)?
3. What is your policy regarding support of Realtor programs and activities?
4. Do you post a list of board activities for your associates?
5. Do you require attendance at educational programs?

Comments:

Real estate board activities are an integral part of public relations and educational work. The degree to which a firm participates in any of these activities usually depends upon the interests of the owner of the business. Some offices require their sales associates to participate actively in all community service activities. Opinion is divided on the degree to which sales associates should be required to join or participate in board activities. Some boards will not permit associates to become members.

Termination

1. What is your policy regarding termination?
2. What is your policy concerning any unfinished business that your associate may have created?
3. Does the associate have any rights in listings he has procured? If they are sold before expiration?
4. Is associate required to give notice if he intends to leave?
5. What materials are the associates required to surrender when leaving?
6. If an associates is terminated for cause, do you report this to:
   a. State licensing agency?
   b. Local board?

Comments:

This is one of the most badly neglected areas in the operation of real estate offices. Many offices never know that a sales associate has left until after he has failed to report to the office for a week. Few firms give notice or expect to be given notice.

Firms are generally agreed that listings remain the property of the firm when a sales associate is terminated; beyond this, there is little agreement. Some firms will pay commissions on all transactions in escrow at the time of termination; others will pay partial commissions if deposit receipts have been signed.

Termination of licensed associates is covered under the Real Estate License Law of most states, but too many firms fail to follow the requirement of the law.

CASE STUDY

(Author: Dr. L. Burns)

History of the Firm:

The Neuhouse Realty Company is a relatively young firm. In the course of a two-hour interview, you discover the following information about Neuhouse, his three-year-old firm, the community which he serves, and his business policies.

W. I. Neuhouse has lived his 40 years in this metropolitan community of about 200,000. Neuhouse seems somewhat embarrassed when he tells you that his education consists of two years of high school and a real estate course completed at a local junior college. He spent three years traveling as a salesman for a nationally known clothing wholesaler before entering the real estate business. His first exposure to real estate was as a speculator, buying and selling houses from funds he had set aside for a "golden investment opportunity." Finally, at the urging of friends, he took a job as a salesman with a large local office, Avalan Acres Realty Co. Together with another salesman, T. Old, he completed an average of eight out of every ten of the office's sales.

Believing that they were a good team, Old and Neuhouse left Avalan Acres to form a partnership, known appropriately as Old and Neuhouse. However, even this partnership was eventually dissolved—according to Neuhouse, because of "incompatibility of business philosophy and the lack of freedom to make my own decisions." Although Neuhouse believed that the business was worth $75,000, he sold his interest for $3,500.

Neuhouse is currently studying the mechanics of trades and exchanges and plans eventually to supplement his education with some work in financing and tax problems of income property.

The population of Mixopolis has increased at an annual rate of four per cent. This is somewhat less than average for similar communities in this section of the country. The number of licenses granted to real estate salesmen in this city has increased at almost double this rate. The city's economic base is about evenly divided between agricultural production and income generated seasonally by light manufacturing, government officials, tourists, and retail trade.

Present Organizational Structure of the Firm

The staff consists of six full-time salesmen and a secretary. In his first full year of operations as a sole proprietor, 90 per cent of Neuhouse's activity was devoted to real estate brokerage and 10 per cent to building and property speculation for his own account. With regard to the latter, Neuhouse owns some properties for investment or speculation. In the course of the past year, he has bought and sold three houses for speculation. In addition, he holds several small second mortgages which he took in lieu of commission cuts. There is no insurance or business opportunity department, but Neuhouse was considering the possibility of establishing one.

The 90 per cent of activity devoted to real estate brokerage consists of an average of 85 hours a month (according to owner's estimate) split between sales activity and "office affairs."

Financing is easy to secure, says Neuhouse, because of his stature in the community. In his words, "we promote the good name of our firm by being active in civic organizations and real estate groups. I regularly attend local meetings and do my share of donating. These activities help my business a lot. Because of this outside activity, I have established a reputation and can get a loan for anywhere up to $6,000 from the bank without their ever having seen the property." Referrals account for about 70 per cent of the firm's business.

The firm seeks to maintain cooperative working relations with all other realty offices serving the same area. "I always make it a point," says Neuhouse, "never to discredit the reputation of my competitors by casting disparaging remarks, criticizing, or agreeing with customers who do so." He reports that the only recurring ethics problem is that of a competing salesman who tells sellers who have listed with Neuhouse that he has a buyer who will purchase the property if the listing is turned over to his office. Neuhouse's standard reply is, "I will give up the listing if the competitor produces the buyer."

Neuhouse recalls no deals that have fallen through prior to or during closing nor any serious problems with buyers. Disputes among salesmen are rare; but, when they do arise, the owner says that he relies on "policy" for a solution.

Neuhouse's income as a salesman working for Avalan Acres varied between $12,000 and $18,000 annually. As a partner with Old, he typically took home profits of about $8,000, which included the commissions from his own sales. Net profits, including commissions, since 1954 have averaged about $10,000, reaching a high of $13,500 in 1957 and declining thereafter, even though total gross income increased slightly in 1958 over 1957.

Staffing and Directing

Although Neuhouse requires no previous sales experience of applicants for sales positions, he emphasizes neatness, willingness to work, honesty, willingness to study and learn, character, and ability, although he does not always use these criteria. He checks references, and he interviews the spouse as well as the applicant. He says that he is not particular about criteria, but later emphasizes that he will not take "just anybody." Nevertheless, he would like to add another salesman so that he could eliminate his own selling activity. He does not believe that good salespeople are good managers.

Neuhouse relates one unfortunate hiring experience: "Not too long ago a retired air force officer—quite a fellow—asked for a selling job with my firm. Said he'd heard good things about the Neuhouse Company and wanted to be part of it. As it turned out, he just could not—or perhaps would not—talk to people who were less educated than he was, as, for instance, factory employees. Another thing he never could quite understand was why the average customer wouldn't buy one house for every two he was shown. To top it all off, he left the firm, and sold seven properties to prospects he'd been given while he worked for me!"

Most of the present sales force are experienced and have held positions with one of two large local competitive offices, one of which Neuhouse says he "doesn't like." One-half of the sales force has turned over each year in the three-year experience of the firm. One cause, according to the interviewee, was that Neuhouse had periodically released the part-time help.

Older people, he believes, are more difficult to direct, because they have already formulated their own methods of operations. Neuhouse believes that, "Because I pay all the bills, I feel that it's my right to be able to tell the salespeople what to do when they're not producing. Still, one of my major operating problems is salesmen who just sit in the coffee shop all day. You know, it's pretty hard to get salespeople to do anything. I'm glad I don't have to stick around this office very much. You know, they spend more time around this place than I do. I've got to admit that I've lost business, not from lack of salesmen, but from lack of good, trained salesmen."

Neuhouse hopes sometime in the future to train his salesmen just as he did in his previous office (the partnership). His method was to get together men who wanted to learn real estate selling and meet with them twice weekly for training which stressed two things: first, how to pass the licensing exam; and second, how to sell. "I've also encouraged them to take real estate courses," he says, "but they ignore me."

Neuhouse sells, too, and he feels that because of this he is different from other brokers. He is proud of a system which he has learned from books and lectures that taught him how to sell real estate. He practices this system faithfully and believes that if his salespeople follow it, they will make money. It's that simple.

The staff gets together for weekly sales meetings. The first item in the agenda is usually a discussion of each new listing. Then they may discuss articles from real estate magazines, rules and regulations relating to financing, and materials which the owner secures from the local FHA office. In addition to weekly meetings, the staff meets monthly or twice-monthly with an invited guest, such as an FHA appraiser, who discusses a specialized phase of real estate.

Presently the office has 65 listings. This is too few, says Neuhouse, who believes that a qualified salesman can easily handle 25 exclusives. Neuhouse secures the bulk of the listings, all of which are exclusives. The principal source of listings is personal referrals, with a relatively few from advertising. About one exclusive in four is eventually sold. He believes that this is about average for the area. His personal average, however, is about nine exclusives in ten listings. To persuade prospective sellers to list their property with his office, Neuhouse cites a list of properties sold through the firm and in some cases even conducts the prospect through the office, "so they can see the set-up." Every exclusive is advertised and photographed, and the owner receives copies. Photographs are distributed to the salesmen for inclusion in their personal files and another is placed in the office window; when a potential customer stops to look at the photo, Neuhouse runs out and qualifies him on the spot.

"We take about 70 per cent of our exclusives at prices we know are about the market price. But we thing this is O.K. because, once we have the listing, we can show the seller comparable properties available for less. I know when they're priced right because I used to watch FHA appraisers, and I learned their techniques. Often I go to the property and make an appraisal that's just as complete as FHA. Another way we try to arrive at a fair market price is to ask the owner how he figures his asking price, and then, if he answers by saying that he made a comparison of the asking price of a house just sold down the street, I tell him that, while the house may have been listed at that price, the owner was really ashamed to reveal the final selling price. A third gimmick is to get an FHA commitment and use this as a means for setting true market value. Anyhow, we don't worry much even if we do have to keep an overpriced listing at an unrealistic price, because, if it is a long-term listing, any property will sell."

Neuhouse maintains constant personal contact with each seller, attempting to keep fully informed on details of the listing and preserving a personal feeling with the property owner. An individual file is set up for each listing at its inception.

Neuhouse qualifies customers by attempting to find out from the "suspect" in the course of a half-hour discussion where they work, how much they plan to pay down, and so forth. Open houses are one of the best sources of clients, although Neuhouse does not know how many sales or clients resulted from open houses.

Neuhouse keeps a sales kit but does not believe that the salespeople use them. Instead, he believes that they use "fly-by-night systems." Furthermore, most of them have no methods for scheduling their time or planning their activity, nor do they use devices such as prospect files or appointment books. (When interviewed personally, the salesmen generally agreed that they found themselves devoting too much time to real estate, working unusually long hours.)

Neuhouse proudly points to the fact that his firm gives the customer the utmost in service. They attempt, for example, to complete as much as possible of the detail work involved in closing a deal without bothering the customer, even delivering papers to his home in the evening if his work schedule conflicts with a visit to the office. In addition, each customer receives one potted plant, which Neuhouse believes his customers appreciate.

Planning

Most advertising campaigns are formulated without advance thought. For example, Neuhouse mentions that he will sometimes decide "just on the spur of the moment" to advertise the name of the firm to see what happens. The bulk of advertising placed is in classified ads. They use little direct mail, but occasionally they canvass an area, leaving "Choose your neighbor" and "Sold" cards. Neuhouse explains that he would like to try new things that he's read about, but his people have been just too busy.

The plans for the future include expansion of the sales force and consideration of the possibility of adding insurance, building, and financing departments.

Table 7–1

The W. I. Neuhouse Income Statements
19—19—

	19	19	19	19	19 (6 m.)
Total gross income	$ 30,000	$ 40,000	$ 45,000	$ 48,000	$ 21,000
Expenses:					
Salaries	2,400	3,000	3,400	3,600	1,900
Commissions to salesmen	12,000	11,200	12,400	13,300	5,500
Advertising	3,600	4,800	5,200	5,100	2,400
All other expenses	6,000	10,000	12,000	12,500	6,200
Total expenses	24,000	29,000	33,000	34,500	16,000
Net profit before taxes	6,000	11,000	12,000	13,500	6,000
Average sales price	15,000	12,500	13,000	12,500	12,500
Sales volume	$ 900,000	$ 1,200,000	$ 1,350,000	$ 1,450,000	$ 700,000
Number of sales	40	95	105	115	55

*Firm still a partnership. All first-year figures are halved to represent Neuhouse's interest.

Controlling

Neuhouse keeps no detailed records of the effectiveness of his advertising expenditures. However, how does allocate the expenditures made to different advertising media, and then goes "right down the list to see what has been spent on each item."

No checks are kept on the effectiveness of open houses or other sales efforts. However, complete and up-to-date listing records are maintained.

Questions

1. What is the most important factor to which the success of this firm may be attributed?
2. What sort of standards does Neuhouse have?
3. Why is the rate of employee turnover so high?
4. Criticize Neuhouse's image of a manager.
5. What do you think of Neuhouse's statement that a qualified salesman can easily handle 25 exclusives? And what do you think he meant by "qualified"?
6. What evidence is there that Neuhouse budgets his expenditures?

Chapter 8

MAXIMIZING PROFITS THROUGH CONTROLS

Controls are used to determine the degree to which goals and objectives are being met and to indicate where action should be taken, if performance is below standard. As plans are finalized, a system of controls must be introduced as a means of coordinating activities and personnel. The most effective controls are those that correct deviations before they occur.

In real estate brokerage offices, controls enable the chief executive to discover whether advertising expenditures are providing the expected sales; whether unnecessary expenses are being incurred; whether expenses are being kept within allowable limits; how much is being spent for classified advertising, telephones, and similar items. Controls permit him to discover which sales personnel are producing the most profitable sales, as well as which ones are wasteful and inefficient.

MAJOR AREAS OF OPERATIONS NEEDING CONTROL

Successful real estate brokerage operations require control over three major areas of the firm—personnel, time, and money. Personnel control is exercised primarily through sales management, which is discussed in the previous chapters. Time control is exercised primarily through good planning, which was discussed. The focus of this chapter will be on the control of money, with only incidental references to the control of time and personnel.

Table 8-1

INCOME AND EXPENSE RATIOS FOR A TYPICAL REAL ESTATE BROKERAGE OFFICE

Gross Income:		
From brokerage activities:		
Single-family home sales	74%	
Other property sales	20	94%
From nonbrokerage activities		6
Total Gross Income		100%

	Expenses as per cent of gross income		*Expenses paid as per cent of total expenses*		*Office expenses as per cent of gross income retained by management*
Expenses:					
Paid to salesmen:					
Commissions		38%		53%	
Gross income retained by office for:					
Salaries (secretaries, receptionists, and bookkeepers: none for management)	7%		10%		11%
Advertising (newspapers, brochures, mailing pieces, cards, signs, etc.)	11		15		18
Office occupancy (rent, janitor, furniture, etc.)	6		9		10
Utilities:					
Telephone and telegraph	3				
Other (light and heat; not occupancy)	2		6		9
Other business expenses (travel, office supplies, auto, entertainment)	6		7		11
	35			47	
Gross income retained by management	27	62			
Total expenses		100%		100%	
Sales manager's override					7
Retained by the office for capital investment, management salaries and profits, sales training programs, taxes, etc.					34
TOTAL					100%

The necessity for better financial controls is becoming increasingly evident as the higher commission rates paid to sales personnel, rising clerical and secretarial costs, and the slow upward push of other operating expenses are sharply reducing the income left to the firm. At one time, for example, a real estate brokerage office could expect to keep at least 50 or 60 per cent of each dollar of commissions produced by its sales force. Today the firm is fortunate to be able to keep 25 to 40 per cent of this dollar. The firms which are included in this study, for example, reported that over a period of five years expenses absorbed between 61 and 82 per cent of their gross earnings; and that 88 to 98 per cent of their gross earnings came from brokerage activity.

A breakdown of income and earnings for a typical, average-size real estate brokerage office is given in Table 8–1, and a breakdown for various sizes of firms is given in Table 8–2. The expense patterns of the small and medium-size firms are somewhat similar, because they depend primarily upon brokerage to produce their income. The somewhat lower net income which the large firms show is offset by the profits which they produce through investing and building, the income from which is not included in their gross income statements. The 13 per cent of gross income which these firms report from their nonbrokerage activities comes largely from property management.

In many instances, real estate brokerage offices do not keep sufficiently complete financial records to be able to prepare the kinds of income and expense ratios which are shown in the two tables. In such firms, all records become valuable primarily for their historical uses, as in the payment of income taxes, rather than as means of measuring actual performance against planned performance and for taking remedial action. Although minimal

Table 8–2

INCOME AND EXPENSE RATIOS FOR VARIOUS TYPES OF BROKERAGE OFFICES

Income and Expense Description	*Type of Office*				
	Small	*Medium*	*Large*	*Small and Medium Firms*	
				Low-Income	*High-Income*
Gross Income:	100%	100%	100%	100%	100%
From brokerage activity	98%	96%	88%	98%	93%
Nonbrokerage activity	2	4	12	2	7
Expenses (as per cent of total gross income):					
Sales commissions	28%	45%	45%	41%	35%
Advertising expenses	9	10	8	10	10
Office-occupancy expenses	7	6	6	8	6
Salaries	7	7	15	6	7
Travel, auto, utilities, and related expenses	9	8	10	7	9
Miscellaneous expenses	2	1	0	3	1
Total expenses as per cent of total gross income	62%	77%	84%	75%	68%
Per cent of gross income remaining for owner's salary, sales training, capital investment, etc.	38%	23%	16%	25%	32%

ASSETS

Current:	*Fixed:*
101 Operating cash	110 Land
102 Deposit cash	111 Buildings
103 Petty cash	112 Reserve for deprec.—bldgs.
104 Accounts receivable	113 Furniture and fixtures
105 Notes receivable	114 Res. for dep.—furn. & fix.
106 Real estate held for resale	115 Automobiles
	116 Res. for dep.—automobiles

LIABILITIES:

Current:	*Long-term:*
201 Deposits received from clients	211 Mortgage payable
202 OASI taxes payable	212 Loans payable
203 Withholding tax payable	
204 Notes payable	

NET WORTH:

301 Capital investment	*or* Capital stock
302 Drawing account	*or* Earnings retained in the business

INCOME AND EXPENSES:

Income:
401 Commissions earned
402 Rental income
403 Miscellaneous

Expenses:

501 Rent expense	510 OASI expense
502 Salaries	511 Other tax expense
503 Commission paid	512 Interest expense
504 Utilities	513 Contributions
505 Advertising	514 Dues
506 Automobile expense	515 Insurance
507 Travel expense	516 Miscellaneous
508 Supplies	601 Income and expense summary
509 Legal and accounting expense	

JOURNALS

1. Cash receipts and disbursements journal
2. General journal
3. Ledgers
4. Statements

SOURCE: Arthur M. Weimer and Homer Hoyt, *Principles of Real Estate,* 3rd ed. (New York: The Ronald Press Company, 1954), pp. 520–21.

Figure 8-1. A Standard Accounting System for Brokerage Offices

controls are desirable in real estate brokerage operations, a complete lack of them causes confusion among the office and sales personnel and raises the costs of operations to a prohibitive level. A real estate salesman can estimate whether control is needed in the office for which he works if he will observe the frequency with which office appointments are broken; the number of times too many appointments are made with clients, so that some of the appointments have to be rushed and others missed or canceled; the amount of correspondence which is never answered; the number of times selling or operating policies have to be ignored in order to "get something done"; the delays which occur in the payment of commissions which have been earned; and the wide fluctuations in expenditures for advertising because no one knows in advance how much can be spent. The salesman will feel the impact of lack of control directly when he finds that he can never spend enough time with the head of the firm to secure answers on crucial selling problems and when he finds the head of the firm spending long hours trying to solve many petty financial, administrative, and selling details.

Good financial control records can vary from nothing more than a carefully kept checkbook which reflects income received and paid by the firm to an elaborate set of records such as is shown in Figure 8–1. Good records, properly audited by a knowledgeable accountant, not only provide effective means of controlling operations but also provide the basis for future planning and may be used as a basis for securing credit when financing is needed for growth or to take advantage of particularly attractive investment opportunities.

ELEMENTS OF AN ADEQUATE CONTROL SYSTEM

Control is not exercised in a vacuum, but only with relationship to some goal. As we have seen in previous chapters, a salesman who is asked to attain a given income level must translate his goal into a given number of contracts and sales per week and then check carefully each week to make certain that he follows his plan. The first step in instituting financial controls is to establish financial goals, either in the form of income to be earned or expenses to be met or both. Because goals are only estimates, the control system devised to meet them must anticipate and provide for deviations from the goals. For example, sudden downturns in business may make selling more difficult and require more expenditures on advertising.

Flexibility in controls, particularly in small offices, is particularly important where plans must change constantly and where there are often many failures before a workable and achievable plan is developed. Because deviations and flexibility must be built into controls, fewer controls will make these easier to accomplish. In the typical real estate office, working relationships are so intimate that a great number of controls is not needed. Sometimes a simple chart showing percentage of income earned compared with income planned for, and percentage of income paid as compared with percentage of income planned as expenditures is sufficient. A weekly informal conference between the owner of the office and his sales staff can usually pinpoint reasons for differences between planned and actual performance. If each person knows what is expected of him in terms of the financial plan, he has a ready means of measuring and controlling his own performance and of reducing the need for action on the part of the owner of the business.

Perhaps the most persuasive argument against elaborate financial control reports and charts is that all except a very few of the very largest brokerage offices find such charts costly to prepare and relatively ineffective in maintaining control. Further, the more elaborate charts are often difficult to interpret or too general to be useful. For example, a chart on which all personnel are to report personal telephone calls, their length, and so forth, may be completely ineffective because no one has defined what is meant by a "personal" telephone call. A simple chart is as effective as an elaborate one in pointing up failures or deviations in performance, and this is what a control chart is supposed to do.

SETTING UP FINANCIAL CONTROL SYSTEMS

The most efficient financial control system is one which is created and maintained by an experienced accountant; however, before he can create such a system, he must have certain policy decisions from the owner of the firm. In turn, the owner cannot decide policy until he has worked it out with his sales staff. Therefore, the first measure of an effectively controlled real estate brokerage office is that members of the sales staff are given an opportunity to participate in creating, changing, and enforcing policy. The sales staff can contribute effectively in setting policies on (1) the number and dollar value of properties to be sold, (2) the amount of advertising to be bought per property sold, and (3) the amount to be invested in sales training programs, education, and related items which are intended to improve the selling effectiveness of each salesman.

One recommendation for an effective accounting system for a brokerage office is shown in Figure 8–1. Such a system can do three things for a brokerage office: (1) provide a daily basis for analyzing and recording financial transactions; (2) provide the statements which the office needs for measuring sales productivity and costs, for calculating tax liabilities, and for establishing credit status for submission to banks or other lenders; and (3) establish the means for measuring actual versus desired performance, so that corrective actions can be instituted on a timely basis.[1]

The recommended accounting system consists of three major portions: (1) The journals, in which all transactions are entered for later transfer to specialized accounts. For example, all transactions involving cash (money and checks) are recorded in the Cash Receipts and Disbursements Journal. Other transactions which will affect ledger accounts are entered in the General Journal. At the end of the month, entries are made to the proper

[1] Arthur M. Weimer and Homer Hoyt, *Principles of Real Estate*, 3rd ed. (New York: The Ronald Press Company, 1954), pp. 519–33.

accounts, all accounts are balanced, and income and expense statements (Profit and Loss Statement) statements of what the company owns and what it owes (Balance Sheet), and income and expense analyses are prepared. (2) The ledgers are the books in which all entries are summarized and placed in the proper accounts. The kinds of accounts to which entries are made from the journals and ledgers are listed under appropriate titles. *Assets,* for example, indicate the types of things which a brokerage office may own, with *current assets* representing items which are more easily and quickly converted to cash or credit than would be possible to do with fixed assets. *Liabilities* show the items which an office owes, with the *current liabilities* those which will become due rather soon. *Net worth* represents the amount which has been invested in various parts of the business. The *expenses* shown are those most likely to be encountered in a real estate brokerage office which should be closely watched and controlled if the business is to be a financial success.

The use of such a system may seem too complicated, but, once installed by an experienced accountant and after being used for a while, it will become an indispensable means of controlling operations. Perhaps the existence of such a system or one closely similar is something a salesman should expect any office for which he is working to have. Furthermore, the really effective offices do not hesitate to provide their sales personnel with monthly, quarterly, semimonthly, or annual profit and loss and balance sheet statements.

The types of financial records actually maintained by 80 real estate brokerage offices in one part of the country are shown in Table 8–3. This list provides interesting contrast to the recommendations on the types of records which should be kept. The table does not show, although research did, that the higher-income brokerage firms of all sizes tended to keep a greater number of financial records and to adjust operations according to what these records showed. It seems clear that brokerage offices find an *income and expense statement* and a *balance sheet* almost indispensable. Financial budgets also show up strongly, but still in much smaller percentages—probably because the preparation and use of budgets to complement the other two types of statements are not clearly understood. To some extent, the *sales ledger* performs the same function as the *financial budget,* because it indicates both expected and actual dollar volumes of sales in total and by individual salesperson, and the financial budget also shows expected and actual income as well as expenses.

BUDGETS AND STANDARD COSTS

A *budget* is a financial expression of what is planned for future operations and, as such, provides a means of setting individual sales goals and cost controls. Three budgets which a real estate brokerage office can use most

Table 8–3

TYPES OF RECORDS USED BY 80 REAL ESTATE BROKERAGE OFFICES

Type of Record	Per Cent of All Firms			
	All	*Small*	*Medium*	*Large*
Financial:				
Income and Expense Statement	91	84	95	100
Balance Sheet	85	80	95	100
Financial Budget	40	36	43	47
General Ledger	39	46	39	27
General Journal	17	15	21	14
Cash Book *or* Journal	36	31	52	27
Sales Ledger	21	15	22	32
Office Ledger	10	8	8	14
Disbursements Ledger	7	3	13	9
Nonfinancial:				
Policy Book	39	22	47	61
Correspondence File	85	81	90	89
Prospect File	63	67	61	56
Prospect Protection File	31	28	38	28
Personnel File	45	33	57	56
Telephone Calls	47	42	52	50
Sales Records by Property	69	69	71	67
File of Current Listings	96	97	95	94
File of Inactive Listings	84	83	90	78
Advertising Files	81	75	90	83
Salesmen's Reports	21	17	28	22

effectively are a *revenue and expense budget,* a *capital expenditures budget,* and *a cash budget.* The *cash budget* is extremely important because it anticipates how much cash will be needed to keep the business operating—a need which many small real estate brokerage offices fail to meet adequately and consistently. Salesmen expect to be paid their commissions in cash when the sale closes, and any office which fails to do this can expect to have a large turnover of sales personnel.

The other types of budgets are of more interest to the owner or manager of a brokerage office than to the sales personnel. The *expense and revenue budget* is simply an estimate of how much needs to be allocated to expenses on the basis of the revenues which are expected. Usually, expenses are stated on a sliding scale which relates directly to the amounts and kinds of sales made. The *capital expenditure budget* outlines those long-term and high-cost expenditures that are expected to improve the earnings of the sales personnel and the firm. For example, a firm can plan to underwrite the costs of developing an effective property management, escrow, appraising, or insurance department for the first three to five years of its existence, because it will probably take this long to develop a clientele of sufficient size to pay the costs of the department. Capital expenditures may also be planned for the opening of a new office, for expanding the present office, for installing electronic machines for processing market, listing, and sales information, or for developing an extensive library of sales training aids.

The role of budgets must always be kept in perspective, because too much budgeting tends to focus attention on details, to slow initiative, and to divert attention from the more important current problems and goals of the firm. Personnel may come to accept budget estimates as firm standards of performance and not seek to improve performance or to change it to meet situations not anticipated in the budgets. Budgets have a potential for developing tremendous rigidities in brokerage operations instead of being one of many tools for increasing the efficiency of the firm's operations.

NONBUDGETARY CONTROL DEVICES

Once an effective financial control system has been introduced a series of nonbudgetary devices can be developed which will facilitate the process of control. For example, historical data can be used to make forecasts on the assumption that the future will not differ materially from the past. Special analyses can be prepared to determine whether changes should be made in sales quotas, advertising budgets, training expenditures and similar items. Periodic audits of historical records and comparison with audits of current performance can be used to spot developing deviations from established standards.

Breakeven Chart

The most important single chart which a brokerage office can develop is a breakeven chart. This chart provides information on how much revenue and sales must be produced to meet the ongoing costs of the business (Figure 8–2). All offices have certain expenses, such as rent, utilities, taxes, and license fees, whose amounts do not change with the volume of sales. The impact of these expenses can be lessened if they are spread over a larger number of sales or more revenue. The impact of variable expenses can be controlled, because they tend to rise in steps, so that, for example, if one telephone can service two salesmen and telephone costs are a large part of expenses, then salesmen should be added to the sales force in pairs in order to minimize this cost. Or, a firm may find that if it wishes to increase the number of homes sold in a year to 10 or 15, it can add one salesperson to the staff; if it wishes to raise the number of sales to 20, it will have to add two more salespersons; therefore, it should increase the quota by another 10 to 15 instead of only 5.

Of all the devices which might be used, the most effective for the small office is simply the continued personal observations and penetrating inquiries

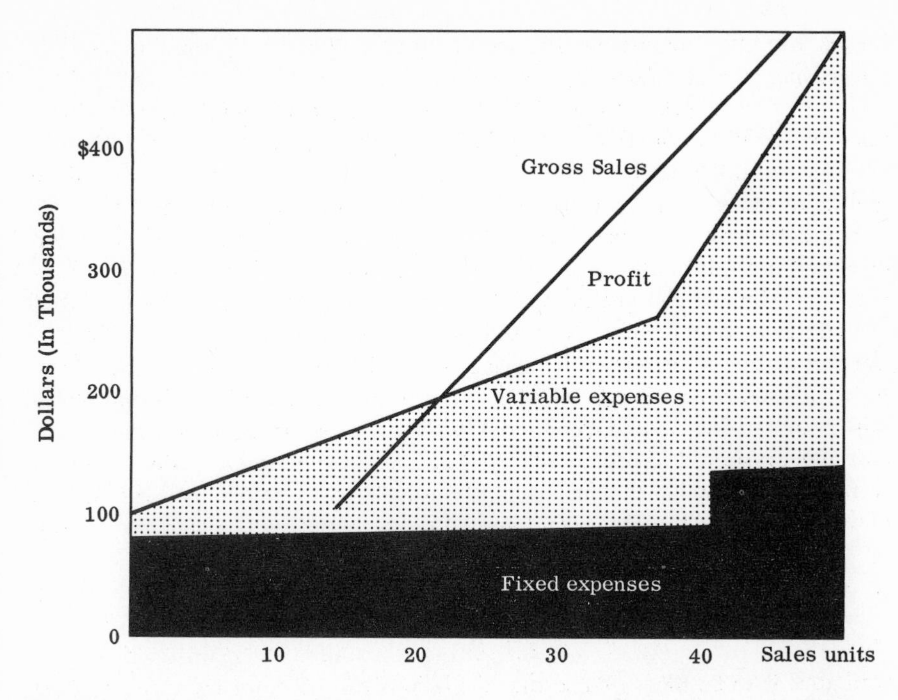

Figure 8-2. Breakeven Control Chart for a Real Estate Brokerage Office. Explanation of the exhibit: This firm has found from past experience that it must sell at least 25 homes each year in order to meet all of its fixed and variable expenses. However, its profit margin is very small when it sells only 25 to 30 homes each year. Its best profits are earned when sales exceed 35 and approach 40— the highest number the firm has ever sold. The relationships between fixed and variable expenses, and the gross sales income per unit sold have been established from historical records, which are reviewed at the end of every year. From this chart the firm can see that it must plan for minimum sales annually of at least 25 units with a total sales value of $230,000. Because each salesperson averages 12 sales per year, at least two persons should be hired and they should produce sales of 24 units, or at least $ 240,000. If profit opportunities are to be maximized, however, at least three salespersons should be hired and expected to produce $ 360,00 minimal sales per year.

by the owner or manager of the firm. As the size of the operation increases, the other types of controls which have been mentioned become more useful and necessary.

Standard Costs

Standard costs are also as effective as breakeven charts in setting cost and performance standards and may be used instead of or to supplement break-even charts. In their simplest form, standard costs need consist of nothing more than a chart that shows how much can be spent for various types of expenses for each unit to be sold. When a salesman has such a chart, he knows that, if he spends certain amounts for telephone calls, mail, newspaper advertising, travel, and similar items, he must produce a certain equivalent amount of gross sales. In this way, the salesman can decide what his own sales goals will be. Such a control device is particularly effective if the salesman is also shown that his commission earnings will go up much faster if he maintains or exceeds a certain minimum dollar and unit volume of sales.

Standard costs are very necessary for the firm which wishes to keep expenses at a minimum, because they indicate quickly what minimum standards of performance must be maintained. For example, if a firm knows that each $100 in telephone calls should produce $50,000 in gross sales, then at the end of the month when it receives a telephone bill of $300, it can check to see if gross sales were $150,000. If it also knows that each $100 in newspaper advertising should produce $75,000 in sales, then if newspaper ads cost $300, it should have had $225,000 in sales. If the sales actually produced were only $150,000, the firm should investigate to determine whether its newspaper advertising has been handled properly during the previous period.

INAUGURATING CONTROLS

Controls are merely devices for setting the standards against which performance is to be measured so that deviations can be detected and corrected before they place a brokerage office in a dangerous financial situation. Financial controls do not, however, measure many of the intangibles which can also affect sales, and they must be used as only one of several managerial devices for achieving the firm's objectives. Effective sales management, good planning, and continuous sales training programs are also useful control devices. In financial terms, the most strategic points at which controls should be used are the number and dollar volume of homes sold, the costs of selling—particularly, commissions, advertising, and telephones—and the amount of capital to be reinvested for growth.

Principles of Financial Controls

1. *Relate to activity.* Financial controls must derive from the objectives of the firm and reflect the nature of the activities to be controlled.
2. *Deviations.* Controls must anticipate and provide for deviations from objectives and policies when changes in the market place require this.
3. *Flexible.* Controls should give the personnel some leeway in making decisions when dealing with clients. In smaller organizations, plans change constantly, and controls should be designed to change as plans change.
4. *Few in number.* Controls should be few in number, understood by all, and enforced. Smaller organizations require fewer controls, because personnel are under the constant observation of the head of the firm.

5. *Economical.* The cost of maintaining charts and items related to controls should not exceed the value of the results achieved. An elaborate system of controlling advertising expenditures may inhibit the use of the advertising budget and produce fewer sales than simpler forms of control.
6. *Understandable.* The personnel who are subject to the controls should understand the need for them, know what they mean, and be able to follow them. For example, if a limit is placed on personal phone calls, have personal phones calls been defined ?
7. *Assure corrections.* Controls should provide easy and instant identification of failures and deviations, and should show where corrections can be made.

CASE STUDIES

CASE 29-G: RECORDS AND RECORD ANALYSIS IN A SMALL BROKERAGE FIRM

Assignment

1. The owner of this firm reports a declining share of gross income, as evidenced by the decline in the proprietorship account, even though business has been increasing. He asks for your recommendations on how to improve his operations. What analyses will you recommend?
2. What recommendations would you make with respect to personnel? With respect to finances? To other operations of the office?

Income

	1st Year (19—)	*2nd Year* (19—)	*3rd Year* (19—)
Gross Commissions Earned:			
Sales of own listed properties	$71,824	$80,547	$92,579
Paid to office by cooperating offices	18,811	20,395	22,011
Insurance Commissions	8,223	9,282	10,120
Property-Management Fees	2,122	3,672	7,218
Total Gross Income	$100,980	$113,896	$131,928

Expenses

Item No.	*Description*			
	Administrative:			
1	Secretary	$3,000	$3,000	$3,000
2	Stationery, supplies, misc.	150	160	185
3	Rent and utilities	6,122	6,136	6,180
4	Phone	1,200	1,420	1,800
5	Taxes and licenses	200	200	200
6	Insurance	100	100	100
7	Fees, dues, subscriptions, etc.	85	80	82
	Total administrative	$10,857	$11,096	$11,547

Sales:	*1st Year* (19—)	*2nd Year* (19—)	*3rd Year* (19—)
Commissions paid to other offices	$ 10,000	$ 9,000	$ 12,000
Commissions to salesmen	$ 45,317	$ 55,518	$ 63,025
Car expenses	6,100	7,580	9,760
Newspaper advertising	3,354	5,823	9,215
Brochures, signs, other adv.	500	1,286	3,469
Sales manager, guarantee	4,800	4,800	4,800
Total sales expenses	$ 80,071	$ 84,007	$ 102,269
Administrative expenses	10,857	11,096	11,547
Total Expenses	$ 80,928	95,103	$ 113,816
Proprietor account	20,052	18,793	18,112
	$ 100,980	$ 113,896	$ 131,928

Sales Classified By Sales Personnel and Amounts:

Sales Personnel Identification	1954 *Properties Sold*					
	Under $ 15,000	$ 15,000—49,999	$ 50,000—99,999	$ 10,000—*& over*	*Total Sold*	
1	10	2			12	
2	16				16	
3	8	4			12	
4	18	1			19	
5	4	2			6	
Sales manager	(56)	(9)	3	2	5	(70)
Total value of sales	$ 672,329	$ 358,275	$ 179,876	$ 260,000	$ 1,426,480	
Cooperative sales made by other offices					$ 1,128,692	(35)

	1955					
1	10	5			15	
2	18	1			19	
3	9	3			12	
6	10	3	1		14	
7	14				14	
Sales manager			3	4	7	
Total number of sales	61	12	4	4	81	
Total value of sales	$ 671,822	$ 359,129	$ 280,000	$ 300,000	$ 1,610,951	
Cooperative sales					1,223,726	(50)

	1956					
1	12	2			14	
2	19		1		20	
7	13	3			16	
8	18				18	
9	8	3	2		13	
10	4	1	3	1	9	
Sales manager			2	4	6	
Total number of sales	74	9	8	5	96	
Total value of sales	$ 738,216	$ 138,528	$ 462,843	$ 512,000	$ 1,851,587	
Cooperative sales					1,320,679	(48)

Listings obtained

	1954	1955	1956	Total
Salesperson 1	72	105	116	293
2	90	100	110	300
3	96	96		192
4	76			76
5	24			24
6		140		140
7		158	190	348
8			220	220
9			180	180
10			120	120
Sales manager	10	8	6	24
Annual totals	368	607	942	

The owner submits the following analyses. Would you recommend others? Why? Work them out and give your conclusions.

BROKERAGE OPERATING ANALYSES

Item of Analysis	*Year*		
	1st	*2nd*	*3rd*
Number of listings obtained per sale made	5.2	12.1	19.6
Commissions paid as % of gross commissions earned	50%	55%	57%
Commissions paid to other offices as % of commissions paid to own salesmen	22%	16%	19%
Administrative expenses (items 1, 2, 10, 12, 13) as % of total expenses	13.4%	11.7%	10%
Advertising as % of sales expenses	4.8%	8.5%	12.4%

CASE 69-R: BROKERAGE RECORDS AND RECORD KEEPING IN A SMALL BROKERAGE FIRM

The following represent six months of operations ending June 30. Arrange the items into a profit and loss statement and a balance sheet.

1. How would you measure the success of this office?
2. What would be your estimate of a year's profit? income? assets?
3. Would your calculations be different if this were a six-month period ending November 1?
4. Do you see any weaknesses or potential trouble spots?

Commissions paid, $25,844.27
Miscellaneous income, $182.63
Business promotion, $189.00
Accounts payable—trade, $225.00
Clients' deposits—property management, $29.73
Net worth, January 1, 1955: total, $17,858
Net worth, Jan. 1, 1955: Partner A, $8,942.46; Partner B, $8,916.07
Capital additions—total: Partner A, $1,000; Partner B, $1,000

Deposits, property management, $29.73
Deposits, C & G Apartments, $1,253.00
Trust account deposit, $50.44
Furniture and fixtures: Cost, $3,244.37; depreciation, $1,275.73
Leasehold improvements: Cost, $1,526.34; depreciation, $1,363.96
Rental income, C & G Property, $5,419; expenses, $4,916.12
Rental income, Bayshore Duplexes, $1,687.50; expenses, $2,272.93
Withdrawals from the business: Partner A, $6,236.96; Partner B, $9,478.18
Salaries, $2,633.80; Rent, $1,080.00; Advertising, $3,080.45
Stationery and office expense, $968.31; Telephone and telegraph, $1,446.70
Taxes and licenses, $204.30; Miscellaneous expenses, $476.19
Rental and management fees, $2,759.35
Rental income (net), $82.55
Commissions earned by the firm, $60,251.06
Commercial checking account, $602.84; Insurance account, $1,051.01
Petty cash, $45.00; Accounts receivable, $90.00; Prepaid insurance, $132.00
C & G property: Land, $6,246.99; Bldg., $61,420.82; Furn. and Fix., $4,175.58
Depreciation, C & G building, $3,133.15; furn. and fix., $726.89
Bayshore Duplexes: Land, $20,000; Bldg., $51,638.85; Depr., $376.53
Insurance on the office, $117.99; Legal and accounting exp., $400.00
Selling expenses, misc., $1,681.65
Miscellaneous other income, $182.63
Rental deposits, C & G Apartments, $297.50
Client deposits, $50.44; Long-term obligation payments due in next twelve months, $6,587.26
Client deposits on insurance, $1,051.01
Payroll and withholding taxes payable, $321.08
Long-term obligations due, $102,370.00

The next two schedules represent the rearrangement of items by one broker. How would you evaluate his arrangements? Would you recommend some changes?

What would you estimate as the gross sales by this firm?

If you were to create a financial budget for this firm, would you change any of the amounts? Why?

INCOME STATEMENT
FOR THE SIX MONTHS ENDED JUNE 30,
(Prepared Without Audit of the Records)

Income:		
Commissions	$60,251.06	
Rental and Management Fees	2,759.35	
Rental Income (Net), Schedule 1	(82.55)	
Total Income		$62,927.86
Expenses:		
Commissions Paid	$25,844.27	
Salaries	2,633.80	
Rent	1,080.00	
Advertising	3,080.45	
Stationery and Office Expense	968.31	
Telephone and Telegraph	1,446.70	
Depreciation and Amortization	205.30	
Taxes and Licenses	204.59	
Miscellaneous Expenses	476.19	
Insurance	117.99	
Legal and Accounting	400.00	
Selling Expense	1,681.65	
Business Promotion	189.00	
Total Expenses		$38,328.25
Net Income from Operations		$24,599.61
Other Income:		
Miscellaneous	$ 182.63	
Gain on Sale of 1244	4,812.29	
Total Other Income		4,994.92
Net Income for the Period		$29,594.53

EXHIBIT B

SCHEDULE OF RENTAL INCOME AND EXPENSE
FOR THE SIX MONTHS ENDED JUNE 30,
(Prepared Without Audit of the Records)

	A & G PROPERTIES		*SHORE DUPLEXES*	
Rental Income		$5,419.00		$1,687.50
Rental Expenses:				
Taxes	$1,294.30		$393.00	
Interest	1,893.40		690.14	
Telephone and Utilities	147.62		—	
Maintenance and Repairs	288.91		348.57	
Miscellaneous	5.34		73.22	
Depreciation	1,186.24		376.53	
Insurance	61.25		189.00	
Gardening and Cleaning	—		152.50	
Commissions	39.06		49.97	
Total Rental Expenses		4,916.12		2,272.93
Net Rental Income		$ 502.88		$ (585.43)

SCHEDULE 1

Chapter 9

EFFECTIVE ADVERTISING PRACTICES

Real estate is not a commodity that can be brought to the consumer; therefore, the potential consumer must be brought to the product. The best real estate salesman cannot sell if he has no one to whom to show his products. It is for this reason that planning, preparing, and executing effective advertising programs are a continuing and major problem facing the majority of real estate offices.

Many of the advertising problems of real estate brokerage offices stem from the fact that few firms have experienced advertising personnel on their staffs or consult experienced advertising agencies. The usual practice is for the owner or someone in his firm to prepare the advertising copy. Occasionally, advice is sought of the sales representatives from the advertising departments of the newspapers. Typically, however, advertising programs tend to be imitative and unimaginative.

In small firms, advertising copywriting and planning are usually kept under the direct and continuing supervision of the owner of the firm. In larger firms, this function may be delegated to one of the salespersons.

SETTING ADVERTISING BUDGETS

Advertising expenditures constitute one of the major expenses of the majority of real estate firms, yet these firms find great difficulty in controlling these outlays except within rather broad limits. These firms explain their inability to anticipate or regularize their expenditures as being due to the variations that occur from week to week in the number of listings that they obtain and the numbers of sales that are completed. The firms that have little variation in advertising expenditures usually have some type of advertising budget that they follow.

Almost all real estate firms report that advertising has contributed significantly to their growth, and almost all of them also agree that advertising is playing an increasingly important role in their profit positions. They believe that advertising is becoming more important because of the emergence of a buyer's market and the rapid increase in competition in all real estate markets.

Firms that were spending smaller amounts on advertising, or that felt advertising was less important now than in previous years, based their estimates on the facts that the firm had been in the community a sufficient number of years to have established a good reputation and a well-known name; that the firm had a continuous stream of referral business; and that the local markets were sufficiently active so that they felt little advertising was needed.

Opinions differ on how much should be spent in advertising a particular property. Among the most often mentioned determinants are:

a. The quality of the listing
b. The price of the property and the commission potential
c. Anticipated response to the advertising
d. The number of days the exclusive listing has to run
e. Whether the listing is an open or an exclusive listing
f. Actual responses to the advertising
g. The desires of the sales force

Two-thirds of the real estate firms plan the amounts they will spend on advertising from one week to one year in advance of the actual expenditures. The majority plan their expenditures on a month-to-month basis; the others on a week-to-week, six-month, or annual basis. The firms that do not plan expenditures prefer to increase their expenditures when business is good and cut their expenditures when business declines.

The firms that do plan their expenditures do their planning in a number of ways. The preferred method is to base expenditures on the volume of sales made in the previous year, assuming that, if they are to match the previous year's record, they must spend the same amount on advertising in the next year as they spent in the past year. If they anticipate an increase or decrease in sales, they change the budget accordingly. For example, if they spent $10,000 for advertising last year and wish to increase sales by 10 per cent in the next year, they will budget $11,000 for advertising. Others feel that a fixed amount should be spent each year no matter what business may be expected in the next year. The amount is changed only when a decline in business or an increase in competition indicates that more must be spent.

The most common method of budgeting for advertising is to allocate 10 per cent of gross income from sales or 15 to 20 per cent of the gross commissions received by the firm after the sales personnel have received their share of the commissions, with the amount to be spent determined by the amount of sales made in the previous month or the previous year. A few firms determine the amount to be spent by the number of listings that have to be sold. Usually they allocate a given amount to each listing on the basis of previous experience. Some simply allocate a given amount to each salesman and allow him to decide how much to spend at a particular time. All of these latter methods are basically trial-and-error methods and tend to produce erratic advertising expenditures.

The firms that use advertising most effectively recognize that advertising must be planned and budgeted carefully. They study their markets; determine which media are most useful and estimate the costs of using each; estimate the number of sales that have to be made; and, finally, plan their advertising budgets. The typical office that increases advertising when business is good and decreases it when business is bad fails to recognize the basic function of advertising. In the first place, advertising must be carried on consistently if it is to be effective, so that advertising heavily at times and then not at all at other times does not build the impact that produces constant sales. In the second place, if advertising is to be varied, then greater amounts should be spent when business is declining, as a means of increasing business, and smaller amounts should be spent when business is increasing.

SELECTING ADVERTISING MEDIA

Real estate firms use almost all types of advertising media that are available to them, although most of them prefer to use regularly either newspaper advertising or lot signs (Table 9–1). A listing of the various media that are used indicates the tremendous variety of materials that are used:

a. Personal or form letters
b. Brochures
c. Television and radio
d. Souvenirs and gifts
e. Postcards; Christmas, anniversary, and birthday cards
f. Billboards
g. Subscriptions to magazines carrying the imprint of the firm name
h. Bench advertising
i. Large advertising sheets
j. Film shorts or trailers
k. Direct advertising

Table 9–1

Types of Advertising Used by Selected Real Estate Offices

Type of Advertising	*Per Cent of Firms Using the Advertising*		
	Regularly	*Occasionally*	*Never*
Classified ads	100%	0%	0%
Display newspaper ads	35	28	27
Personal letters	41	31	28
Form letters	4	22	56
Brochures	9	16	75
Lot signs	78	9	13
Television	2	14	84
Radio	2	19	79
Souvenirs	24	22	56

Newspaper advertising, particularly classified advertising, is the most heavily used media; the other types are usually designed to support the classified advertising. This form of advertising may be used to call attention to a specific property or to the services that the real estate firm offers. Five out of every six real estate firms use newspaper advertising to call attention to a specific property, and limit the use of institutional advertising to special occasions.

Newspaper advertising is designed in a number of ways. Because no form of illustration may be used in a classified advertisement, firms seek to achieve individuality by varying the size of type and the amount of white space they use in each ad. Firms also seek to call attention to their advertising by scattering their advertisements throughout the classified advertising section of the newspaper, by grouping their advertisements in blocks within the classified advertising section, or by alternating these methods. The larger and more successful firms now follow a policy of placing all of their advertisements together on a single full page in the classified advertising section. The use of large display ads in the real estate sections of the large Sunday papers is usually limited by the firms to advertising new-development or tract homes.

The feeling among many real estate firms is that advertising media other than newspapers and property signs are useful only in special instances. Postcards, brochures, tear sheets, and billboard advertising are useful primarily to call attention to the name of the firm and the services that the firm offers. One firm, for example, experimented with sending monthly cards containing recipes to every household in its market area for one year, but produced almost no sales from this form of advertising. On the other hand, another firm gives a live plant to each new home buyer, with the thought that these gifts will constantly remind the buyers of the firm and its services.

One of the most successful real estate firms has the philosophy that it must constantly saturate the market that it serves without becoming annoying to future clients. For this reason it advertises heavily in local newspapers, directories, and similar media. It offers prizes at community events, sends special magazines to all householders, and in other ways keeps its name before the public while still calling attention to the properties that it has to sell and the services that it can offer to both buyers and sellers.

The advertising practices of the larger firms do not differ markedly from those of the small firms: classified advertising and property signs are considered to be the most important advertising media and are used quite frequently. There is, however, a marked difference in the types of media stressed by the low- and the high-income firms. The low-income firms stress the use of the more impersonal forms of advertising, such as newspaper display ads, souvenirs, and brochures; but the high-income firms make frequent use of form and personal letters and display advertising.

A comparison of advertising used by many firms shows the same pattern of limited objectives and unimaginative use of the various media. Classified advertising particularly is treated in a very routine manner, with one advertisement closely resembling another, and shows very little imagination in its preparation. These results stem in a large degree from the practice of placing responsibility for the preparation of advertising copy in the hands of one of the office personnel—usually the office manager, receptionist, or secretary. The sales manager or the owner may check the copy for accuracy or may suggest some small changes in wording, but neither contributes much more than this, except in the high-income firms, in which the owner of the firm usually prepares all advertising copy. In most instances, the inspiration for the copy materials is derived from a study of competitors' ads or from one of the many books continuously published that give suggestions for the wording and make-up of advertising.

A few firms have used advertising consultants to plan their advertising programs and to prepare advertising copy, but the results have never been completely satisfactory. This lack of effectiveness may be due in some measure to the fact that, when advertising firms were used, they were given very limited opportunity to prepare adequate programs and a very short time in which to produce results. Some firms also reported poor results when they used consultants because the consultants sold them a "package," standard program not adapted to the real estate business.

Undoubtedly, a great deal of money is being wasted on advertising by firms that imitate their competitor's programs without knowing whether the programs have been successful or without considering whether the programs are applicable. The majority of the owners of real estate brokerage offices do not become greatly upset or concerned about the preparation of advertising copy and the planning of effective advertising programs because they feel that advertising can produce only a given amount of business, and that additional sales will be due primarily to the effectiveness of their sales personnel.

The decision as to which media to use should be determined by reference to these questions:

1. Is a specific property to be advertised, or will the material in the ad be institutional in nature?
2. Is the purpose of the advertising to encourage prospective buyers and sellers to call or to visit the office?
3. Is the purpose to obtain names and addresses of potential clients?
4. It the purpose to keep the name of the firm before the public?
5. What media is the competition using?
6. How much time can be devoted to preparing the advertising copy?

CHECKING THE EFFECTIVENESS OF ADVERTISING

The same casual approach found in the preparation of advertising copy and the selection of an advertising medium is also prevalent in checking the effectiveness of the advertising. Small firms check productivity occasionally and the larger firms make some effort to regularize their checking, but none have found a consistently effective means of measuring productivity. The most often used method of checking productivity is to require the sales force and receptionist to keep a record of all calls received in response to any advertising used. Variations of this procedure consist of asking clients what attracted them to the firm or the property, whereas some firms merely add up the number of inquiries about an advertised property.

Of the 85 per cent of the real estate firms that stated that they do check their advertising, the following methods were used:

Method of Checking	*Per Cent of All Firms*
Checking telephone calls	50%
Asking clients	14%
Guest books signed by prospects	8%
Sales personnel reports of comments by clients	8%
Other methods: Number of persons visiting open houses, volume of sales, shifting ads from newspaper to newspaper, daily check sheet of callers and inquiries, report of consulting service, comparison of property sold with property advertised.	26%
Total	100%

Some firms use different types of very informal methods to check the productivity of their advertising. For example, some continue to advertise a property until it is sold or until inquiries about it are no longer received; some firms allow the sales personnel to decide when an advertisement is no longer effective; some continue to advertise until the budget for that particular property has been spent; some continue to advertise as long as there is demand for the type of property being advertised.

The checking of the effectiveness of any form of advertising must be done by the owner of the firm, because sales personnel and the sales manager will always feel that their failures to make sales are due to the lack of advertising or the use of the wrong type of advertising. Because the productivity of advertising is so difficult to measure, each firm should institute policies that insure the most effective use of each advertising dollar and the preparation of the best possible advertising copy. The firms that have had the most effective advertising programs recommend the following policies:

1. Make one person in the firm responsible for the preparation of advertising copy and the measurement of results.
2. Require each salesperson to turn in to the person in charge of advertising information on the size of the house, its condition, the sales terms, and the particular points of the house that should be advertised. Once rough copy has been prepared, it should be rechecked with the listing salesperson, or a salesperson should be asked to prepare three different types of ads for each property that he wants the firm to advertise. From these ideas the final copy can be prepared.
3. Acquaint the entire sales staff with the purposes for which your firm used advertising.
4. Furnish each salesperson with copies of all advertising in current use and require each person to become thoroughly familiar with each property being advertised.
5. Maintain in the office a log book in which are entered the names of all callers, telephone and in-person, the property about which they were inquiring, and their comments about the property and the ad.
6. Experiment with various media until you find the one that produces results for your office.
7. Before you copy a competitor's method of advertising, check on whether he is getting the results he wants.
8. A continuous series of smaller advertisements will produce better results than one large advertisement.
9. Each salesperson should be allowed at least a minimum to spend for advertising that he prefers, but he should be required to show results or lose his budget.
10. Assign the showing of an advertised property to a particular salesperson and ask him to make a daily report on the number of calls received inquiring about the property and the reactions of the clients who see the property. Sometimes these reactions indicate the changes that should be made in the advertising.
11. Discuss the use of classified advertising with the local newspaper classified advertising departments and let them help you prepare your advertising.
12. Study carefully the suggestions given in various publications distributed by such organizations as the National Association of Real Estate Brokers in such pamphlets as *Real Estate Advertising, Featuring the Realtor's Ad Writer,* that are revised and published periodically.

ADVERTISING AND PUBLIC RELATIONS

Effective advertising is only one part of the total program of continuing public relations that aid the high-income firms to secure 40 to 50 per cent of their sales from referrals by former clients. Advertising merely calls attention to the services and properties offered by the firm; public relations represents the follow-up that turns a casual caller into a satisfied client. The most successful firms, therefore, have a continuous and strong program of training in public relations for their entire sales and administrative staffs.

A survey of real estate offices to determine why they had lost clients indicated that clients calling the office had met with indifference, arrogance, and rudeness on the part of the sales staff. Clients also complained that the sales staff had been overly aggressive, tended to exaggerate and misrepresent information about the properties, made irresponsible promises, concealed mistakes they had made or refused to accept responsibility for them, or lacked information about the property. These are serious indictments that are made all too frequently; fortunately, they can be corrected with an intensive and continuing program of education in public relations.

A first step in developing a good public relations program begins with the advertising program. Some firms include in their listing agreement a statement of the amount they will spend in advertising the property, but others may simply agree to advertise the particular property or properties sufficiently to attract prospective buyers to the property. If a property will require special promotional efforts, the client may be asked to share in the costs of the advertising program.

The most effective use of the advertising program as a part of a public relations activity is in connection with the listing process. Many successful firms maintain a file of the most effective advertisements that they have and are running, and show this file to a client as an indication of what the firm does. If this display is then supplemented with a list of the steps that will be followed in attempting to sell the property, the client will be much happier, even if the property is not sold.

The desire of the owner of the firm to maintain good client relations must be impressed on all members of the firm; therefore, all public relations activities should be managed only by the owner. Constant surveys must be run to determine what clients do or do not like about the firm, and the results of the surveys must be used to develop public relations training programs for the staff.

In the larger firms, the owners usually say that their principal function is to develop good community relations for their firm. Such men participate actively in real estate board and community activities. They do not advertise their businesses, but they do gain acceptance for themselves, and eventually the business, by serving community organizations in a number of ways. Usually such firms also encourage every member of the sales staff to belong to at least one local service organization and to participate actively in its programs.

CASE STUDY

ADVERTISING AND PUBLIC RELATIONS

Identification

	1961	*1962*	*1963*
Gross income	$100,000	$115,000	$102,000
Net income	50,000	41,000	51,000
Net income as a per cent of gross income	50%	36%	50%
Commissions paid as per cent of gross income	12%	15%	14%
Brokerage income as per cent of gross income	n/a	19%	41%
Advertising as per cent of gross income	12%	14%	15%

Size of Firm: Single proprietorship; owner, sales manager, four salesmen, one nonselling person, one secretary.

Age: Operations were started in 1954.

The Owner: Previously owned a wholesale grocery business. Became interested in real estate and took tests which confirmed his interests. He was attracted to the business because of the high profits which could be made with relatively little effort. He started as a salesman in 1950, was promoted to sales manager, and worked at this for three years; then he decided that he could do as well in his own business, and started in January 1954.

Distribution of Firm's Activities

Real estate brokerage	50%
Land development and sales	20
Operations for own account	15
Building and sales	5
Loan negotiation	3
Misc., insurance, escrow, etc.	2

The Problem

The area in which this office is located was formerly a rich agricultural area. As the metropolitan center grew and freeways were extended, increasing numbers of families moved to this area, so that in approximately 1953 large-scale residential-tract development began and several areas were planned for industrial and commercial development. This type of growth provides many opportunities for land speculation and small-scale private construction speculation for the intelligent and alert individual investor.

The owner of this firm is one of these investors. Although he maintains a regular sales staff and spends one-half of his firm's efforts in brokerage of residential properties, the major portion of his income has been derived from the various kinds of transactions which he has been able to assemble. When asked how he undertakes one of these transactions, he stated that he usually just "dreamed them up." He has developed a wide acquaintance in the community and gathers a lot of information about projected commercial and industrial developments. Once he has discovered a transaction which he believes would sell, he buys or options the land, puts in the improvements, and then engages in a heavy program of brochure, sign, and newspaper advertising.

The owner is a strong believer in a vigorous advertising program as a means of achieving quick sales and high profits on transactions which he plans. He also believes that he must circulate widely through the community in order to discover new opportunities for development.

At the time of the interview, he had been reviewing his operations, and had found that brokerage was tending to become an increasingly more important activity in his office. Furthermore, his best salesmen had come to him expressing their dissatisfaction with his continual absence from the office and with the great amount of attention which he was devoting to his "speculations."

The owner is now faced with deciding whether he will continue as he is, listen to the sales force and devote more time to brokerage, or eliminate brokerage entirely and engage in nothing but "speculative developments." He feels that his greatest strength and much of his success derives from his emphasis on public relations activities and advertising. He doubts whether these would be an asset if he turned exclusively to brokerage operations. On the other hand, he is becoming increasingly concerned with the lack of opportunities in his community for developing the kinds of speculative projects which have been making him so much profit.

Organization

The sales manager is in complete charge of selecting, training, and retaining brokerage personnel. The owner prefers to be free to engage in his own activities. The firm is a member of the local realty board and cooperates actively with it. They do not belong to the local MLS, because they find that most of their business can be handled through normal channels and cooperation with other offices on exclusive listings.

The only real problem the owner sees is the stiff competition which some of the older, larger offices are able to offer. His relations with these offices are good. The broker participates actively in board affairs, Red Cross work, Boy Scout meetings, and numerous other civic activities.

Planning

Advertising is planned a year in advance, with the amount based on a percentage of the business obtained in the previous year. The owner writes at least one-half of all ads and checks the remainder, which are written by the sales force. All exclusive listings are advertised (these constitute the bulk of all listings held by the firm), but a greater amount of advertising is done for the more readily salable properties. The newspaper advertising is almost exclusively classified, and the bulk is placed on Sunday. The owner reports that "90 per cent of our prospects are attracted by classified ad." When asked how this was checked, he said that it was a mental calculation based on his observations.

He uses a small amount of radio and TV advertising from time to time, but has found these to be of only limited effectiveness.

When he has an attractive development to sell, farm properties which represent good opportunities for subdividing, or special commercial or industrial properties, he prepares attractive brochures which he distributes widely. He believes that these have been most effective.

The owner feels that the present location of his office is also a strong advertising factor. He states that he selected it only after studying the community carefully. The interviewer, however, had great difficulty finding the building, which is located off the main business district and on a minor side street. The owner had made no attempt to determine for himself whether his locational decision was a good one.

Controlling

The owner has never checked his advertising except through his personal observations. He classifies mentally whatever sales activity he observes occurring in his office and then recalls this when necessary. He talks to almost all of the prospects and sellers with whom his office is dealing, and feels that he knows how successful his advertising and public relations have been.

The only other records kept on the operations of the office are the financial reports based on a periodic audit of records by a CPA. The owner keeps all monetary records; the secretary keeps the escrow and related records. The owner would prefer to keep all records himself.

Directing

The owner holds weekly sales meetings, at which daily problems are discussed; the program rarely consists of any other topics. However, the owner insists that he will not lead sales personnel around by the head. He believes that the best way of keeping salesmen is by giving them good listings, ample advertising, and strong public relations programs. If a salesman demands an undue proportion of the owner's time, he is expected to produce more to compensate the owner for his time. If the salesman does not produce under these conditions, he is expected to leave.

The owner states that he would prefer having fewer salespersons, so that he could exercise more supervision over them, but at the same time he is making plans to increase his staff by two more salesmen shortly. Salesmen are expected to work at least eight hours each day; they must be ethical and above reproach; the first impression must be good; and they can speculate for their own account as long as they keep the owner informed.

The salesmen are expected to accept as their primary duty the protection and servicing of the seller. The highest offer only is submitted; offers which the salesmen believe are too low are not submitted. If the office sees a seller offering a bargain, the owner or the salesman will buy it, because the owner believes he must take advantage of every opportunity offered for profit-taking.

The owner does insist that the legal aspects of principal-agent relationship be followed scrupulously; however, the service due a client is often ignored. His failure to service his clients is reflected in the fact that few of his sales are ever completed because of referrals but principally because of the heavy advertising programs.

Chapter 10

MEETING COMPETITION THROUGH GROWTH

The numerous limitations which real estate firms face in attempting to grow do not discourage many owner-managers from experimenting constantly with larger and more varied operations. As previous chapters have shown, the majority of these owner-managers rarely have much success with any reasonably large scale of operations, so that the majority of brokerage offices usually consist of the owner-manager and two or three salesmen. The firms that do achieve a larger scale of operations rarely maintain this scale at a consistent level as they change the nature of their brokerage operations and add or delete related real estate functions such as property management, appraising, and building. The principal deterrent to consistent growth or stability in operations is the inability of the owner-managers to operate more as general business managers and less as sales managers.

THE IMPACT OF SIZE

Growth creates two principal kinds of managerial problems for the manager. In one form of growth, the firm limits its activities to selling properties—usually homes—and grows through the addition of residential sales personnel. The principal general-managerial problem in such a firm is that of staffing; therefore, the manager must be reasonably effective in selecting, training, and supervising persons. However, the majority of his time will be spent in acquainting these persons with the technical aspects of real estate selling. As the number of sales personnel in such firms increases, the size of the general-managerial problem increases but tends to remain in the area of staffing. For this reason, such a firm is classified as "small" in this study because the general-managerial problems are rather simple, usually being found almost exclusively in the area of staffing, and the major portion of the manager's time is spent in solving technical problems relating to selling real estate.

As a firm diversifies its operations, more and more of the manager's time must be spent in such nontechnical activities as setting profit goals, defining and assigning personnel responsibilities and authority, creating and enforcing operational policies, preparing and administering financial, sales, and advertising budgets, and in similar general-managerial functions. In the largest firms, the manager will be engaged primarily in policy decision making and will have department heads who assist him in carrying out both his general-managerial and technical-managerial functions.

Real estate brokerage offices face their most difficult growth problems in adding nonbrokerage activities. A few firms remain small because their managers are unable or unwilling to handle the problems associated with increased selling activity; however, the majority are small because they must add nonbrokerage activities in order to survive, and their managers are unable to handle the general-managerial problems introduced by these activities.

GROWTH PROBLEMS

The nature of the growth problems is best highlighted by a brief panoramic review of the growth process. This evolutionary process is often painful and erratic, so that stable income and profits at a reasonably high level are rarely achieved in much less than one or two decades. For this reason, there are few large, stable, well-respected real estate brokerage offices which have been operating for less than 10 years, with the majority having been operating for 20 or more years.

The preponderance of small brokerage offices can be ascribed primarily to the unhappy experience of many owner-managers with larger-scale operations and their firm resolve to keep their business problems and operations on a small scale and to concentrate on selling. This small size permits the owner-manager to build his operations around a few reasonably competent sales personnel whose efforts will produce sufficient income to pay operational expenses and a small profit, while leaving the owner-manager free to concentrate on his own sales opportunities. This is an ideal situation for the typical employing broker, because he can easily select, train, and supervise such a small sales force; his business costs are paid for completely by the staff, so that all of his personal sales are clear profit; and, if the sales force is at all effective, he will have additional profits.

The owner-manager who is determined to try a larger scale of operations usually sees only the greater profit potential but none of the problems associated with larger size. For the majority of firms, medium size (that is, a sales staff of 8 to 25 persons and one or two departments engaged in non-brokerage activities; see Figure 4–1) is a transitional size in which the owner builds up his brokerage operations while experimenting gingerly with such activities as leasing, rent collections, and insurance. As the owner-manager develops more confidence in his ability to handle this larger operation, he may decide to stabilize his operations on the larger scale or he may find the financial returns not commensurate with the added responsibilities, and so he returns to smaller-size operations.

Basic Managerial Problems

He must see that the sales and nonsales activities are properly coordinated, recognizing that selling remains the principal activity of the majority of even the largest real estate offices. He must also set goals, outline policies, create budgets, maintain financial and operational control, and do other things very far removed from his former sales supervision responsibilities. The ultimate complexity of the larger brokerage firms (see Figure 4–1) requires that the managers of these firms be basically good business managers and only secondarily good real estate sales managers.

Growth Problems of the Small Office

The majority of brokerage offices resolve their growth problems by staying small, concentrating on home sales, and building their operations around available sales personnel who can operate with minimum supervision or direction. The managerial problems of these offices revolve around staffing problems because the offices are almost completely dependent on their sales staffs for the continuity and level of their profits. For this reason, the manager in such an office is in continuous search for new sales talent and is willing to accept almost any person of promise. The selection process is very casual primarily because so few managers have developed criteria for selection, performance, and compensation of sales personnel, because the turnover of personnel is high, and because the number of really effective sales personnel is so small.

The growth of the firm, however, is directly proportionate to the ability of the owner to find effective, self-starting salesmen. Few owners attempt to develop such personnel, because the time taken for such training reduces the owner's personal selling time while offering no guarantees that the person trained will benefit from the training or stay with the firm if he does benefit. The training programs which are offered are typically minimal, repetitive, and directed essentially toward solving immediate daily sales problems rather than toward developing more effective sales personnel. For these reasons, growth through internal expansion is rarely possible, and staff problems are not solved.

When an owner is fortunate enough to secure a number of effective sales personnel, he is able to give some thought to expanding his operations; however, few offices ever reach this point because one-fourth to one-half of the sales force usually accounts for at least three-fourths of the properties sold. The financial and managerial drag created by the unproductive members of the sales force prevents the manager from giving thought to growth and usually demands such a high proportion of his time that he neglects the effective sales personnel, who can operate a large proportion of their time without direction. As a result, managers who are fortunate enough to have a high proportion of effective sales personnel may not be able to retain them because of the temptations open to such persons to open their own offices.

The interest of superior sales personnel in opening their own offices rises sharply as they observe that they are paid almost the same proportion of the commission as the poorer salesmen, yet their higher sales volume is vitally necessary to keeping the firm operating. Owners of the firms who are aware of these observations sometimes attempt to recognize superior performance by promoting the most effective man to the role of sales manager with the provision that he is to share in all commissions earned by the persons under his control. This device rarely works for very long, because the additional earnings are rarely sufficient to compensate for the increased work-load responsibilities accompanying the sales manager's job.

Chafed by the restraints placed on his activities in his role as sales manager, and still unhappy over his commission percentages, the sales manager finally feels compelled to open his own office. The new office is invariably small, sparsely furnished, and undercapitalized. Its pattern of operations is strongly imitative of the patterns of operation of the office which the new owner just left. The result is a strange potpourri of sales and advertising practices of limited effectiveness and profitability.

Sales in the newly opened offices are invariably slow initially and expenses rather high, so that the new owner-manager receives much less than his customary income. The new entrepreneur also fails to realize that his office overhead must be paid for largely by himself, because he does not have sales staff returning the commissions to the office from which expenses could be paid. He soon learns that, as long as his sales staff is very small and he is the only responsible person in the firm, he must work harder, longer, and more intelligently than ever before to earn an income equal to that of his former best selling days. Invariably this discovery leads him to seek more and more sales personnel and starts the cycle which we have just reviewed.

Sometimes the owners of small brokerage offices seek to grow by bringing in competent persons who can supplement or complement the work of the owners. These persons may be brought in as partners, with the total work load shared among the partners. Thus, some small firms are operated by partners, each of whom specializes in a particular activity, such as selling homes or industrial or commercial property, developing vacant land, or building homes. Other small firms invite independent operators to share the office and office expenses in return for their opportunity of sharing in the firm's business activities. These persons may be insurance brokers, builders, appraisers, loan correspondents, or anyone in a field related to real estate brokerage. The looseness of all such arrangements usually means that total sales volume and income of the original owner of the business do not pick up appreciably but business operational costs and problems can be shared to some degree, thus insuring some increased stability on operations and slightly higher income.

Owners of small brokerage offices are rarely able to hire the additional talent they need because they have almost no capital resources. The unpredictability of their income does not permit them to pay any type of fixed wage, and the high risks of their businesses, compared with the profit potential, are not attractive to prospective employees who might be hired on a profit-sharing basis. In addition, the owners rarely understand how to use such persons effectively and often require more from them than can be realized. For example, an owner may hire someone to operate a property-management department. Such a person would be expected to secure new management business, find tenants, set lease terms, do the maintenance and repair work, collect rents, and maintain a flow of business into the brokerage department. Firms which have added such departments have found that income from such operations rarely equals expenses until several months have elapsed, so that sometimes a substantial loss may have to be carried for some time when such a department is introduced. Only in rare instances is the owner of a small brokerage office able or willing to incur this loss; therefore, this avenue of growth is rarely tried and even more rarely successful.

There are, of course, other factors which contribute to the growth problems of small offices, but these are not necessarily peculiar to the real estate business. For example, owners of small businesses, including those in real estate, having founded and developed their businesses through their own efforts, are extremely reluctant to rely on or seek the counsel of others when difficult business problems arise. Almost all small brokerage office owners have supreme confidence in their abilities to solve their own problems. In addition, these men become accustomed to retaining full responsibility and authority for all phases of their business operations and are reluctant to delegate anything to subordinates. In these cases, growth is limited by the work capacity of the owner. Small brokerage office owners are always searching diligently for the technique or "gimmick" which will increase sales significantly without a proportionate increase in expenses or effort. The programs of local, state, and national real estate conferences are always heavily loaded with the latest "how to" items. This tendency diverts the manager from a careful study of his basic problems and leaves him with many, often inadequate, short-term solutions to his long-term growth problems. Finally, the owners of small brokerage offices are almost invariably eager and somewhat impatient in their business operations, so that they expect immediate profits from any new venture they undertake. Unfortunately, growth from small to medium size takes time, during which profits are often almost nonexistent, and the owners abandon their efforts to grow before they have allowed enough time for these efforts to bear fruit.

Finally, many small firms do not want to grow for fear that they will be over-committed in a declining real estate market. Many real estate men are acutely aware of the erratic nature of real estate market trends and feel that the flexibility in selling which is needed to survive in such markets is seriously impaired if the firm is too large and has excessive overhead. However, there are others who believe that operational and profit stability is possible only if the firm can get big enough to have a broadly diversified range of activities which will offset fluctuations in sales.

Growth Problems of Medium-Size Offices

The growth from small to medium-size operations does not begin until the owner has organized a reasonably large sales staff (8 to 15) which is consistently effective in its sales efforts (Figure 4–1). Many owners are discouraged rather quickly from building such a staff because they must reduce their own sales efforts while they select and train the sales staff. This, of course, results in lower income for the owners, because they are not selling and the new men are not immediately productive; however, if the owners persevere in their purpose and have made a wise selection of sales personnel, their firms' earnings will begin to rise to acceptable levels at the end of a 12- to 18-month period. If an owner is a good business and sales manager, and if he has the good fortune to be in a reasonably active market, his earnings will soon exceed the income he once earned in his smaller-scale operations and he will be free to concentrate on stabilizing his operations at this new, higher level or on planning for additional growth.

The first significant growth step is the appointment of a sales manager who is capable of relieving the owner of the bulk of the problems relating to selecting, training, and supervising sales personnel. Clerical and secretarial personnel are also added to take care of telephone-answering, record-keeping, correspondence preparation, and advertising planning. With the time thus saved from routine duties, the owner concentrates on setting sales policies, developing new sources of sales, and planning for more diversified operations.

The next problem facing the owner is how to use this extra time in the most effective way to achieve further growth. The majority of owners usually prefer to introduce the sales of apartment, commercial, and industrial properties. For many this becomes the moment of truth as they see their scale of operations growing at the expense of their own business freedom and personal independence. Once again many prefer to revert to small-scale operations rather than assume responsibility for directing the work of others and for solving the complexities attendant upon such responsibilities. Others realize the opportunities inherent in the situation and use them as a means to even greater growth. For this reason, the medium-sized, relatively new firm is basically a transitional operation in which the owner is experimenting with ways of keeping the growth already achieved and moving on to a large-scale operation.

Brokerage continues to dominate the activities of medium-size firms, but the problems accompanying this phase of the business are shifted to competent sales managers. This leaves the owner free to develop and stabilize insurance sales, leasing, the accumulation of funds from private investors for reinvestment in real estate equities or mortgages, for buying and developing raw land, and for increased public relations activities. As each of these operations develops into a consistent and lucrative profit source, it is placed under a departmental manager and incorporated into the normal operations of the business.

Growth Problems of Large Firms

Stability of operations and profits on a large scale are finally achieved as the owner recognizes his increasing managerial, as opposed to sales management, functions. He begins to spend more of his time providing policy and planning advice to his department heads. His role in public relations broadens as he circulates more widely through the business community. Occasionally he assists in sales training and may even cooperate from time to time with his sales personnel in particularly complex or difficult sales transactions.

Management of the large firm forces the owner to assume many new roles, although he still works as many hours and with even more intensity than the owner of a small firm. Setting objectives, stimulating personnel to greater achievements, and searching out new sources of business now replace time once devoted exclusively to selling. The increasing scope of the managerial problems often prompts owners of large firms to seek additional assistance at the managerial level through the formation of a partnership or corporation. This joining of forces is unique, because it does not represent an equivalent sharing of managerial responsibilities but a specialization on the part of each executive in particular activities. This is epitomized by the saying of one of two partners who, when asked about how public relations were handled, replied, "My partner goes to church while I play golf."

The owners of the large firms are well equipped to continue reasonably successful operations after having survived more than a decade of managing the smallest to the largest real estate brokerage operations. Problems of selling and sales management are never completely solved, and the search for solutions to them is continuous. These and other business problems are more often than not solved through a process of trial and error rather than through the use of good management practices and principles. Even though the businesses are relatively large, the owners continue to show the proclivity common to owners of small businesses to depend more on their own resources rather than on the counsel of a staff, to grab indiscriminately for pat solutions, and to be highly suspicious of any "outside" advice on the solution of their business problems. Almost invariably, however, the superior achievements of the high-income brokerage firms can be traced to the more efficient managerial as opposed to sales management abilities of the owners.

This, then, is the path by which a small office develops into a stable, highly profitable, large brokerage office. This path is one which the majority of small office owners would like to follow but which often presents them with insurmountable roadblocks and detours. The specific reasons why the majority of the offices fail in reaching the goal of a consistently profitable large-scale operation are presented in the following materials.

THE WILL TO FAILURE

Although poor sales management appears to be the reason for the failure of many brokerage offices to achieve either profit stability or growth, the reasons are much more fundamental. The principal reason can be traced to the unwillingness of the owner to face four important problems related to selling:

1. The need for defining future sales objectives on a realistic basis
2. The need for developing effective financial control over his sales operations
3. The need for developing adequate sales personnel programs
4. The need for developing imaginative, carefully planned and controlled advertising to supplement his sales programs

The inability of unsuccessful owners to anticipate and plan for growth stems in a large measure from their unswerving pursuit of immediate profits. A substantial proportion of the owners start in business with the primary intention of improving their income, and they see an immediate short cut to this goal through the development of a variety of sales gimmicks, techniques, and methods which are conducive to immediate sales. This fixity of objective is no better illustrated than from a perusal of the topics which appear year after year at any real estate sales conference. For example, annual favorites include how to close a sale when the buyer is reluctant to commit himself immediately, or how to write effective advertising copy, how to secure listings, and so on.

Typical of firms in this category is firm "K", which was just two and one-half years old at the time of the interview. The owner was a retired military officer who had observed the markets in his section of the country and decided to open an office in one of the smaller but more active communities. He selected his location to maximize his sales opportunities for both tract-development and older home sales. He immediately introduced some of the less desirable features of a semimilitary-type organization in handling his personnel. For example, he accepted any person who applied, gave them no training, placed no restrictions on their activities, did not require that they keep him informed of their activities, and allowed each salesman to decide how much should be spent to advertise a particular property. From time to time, he did help an individual salesperson complete a particularly difficult sale; otherwise, salesmen were left completely to their own devices. On the other hand, he was rather aloof and impersonal in dealing with his sales personnel and strict in setting rules of behavior and sales performance. In many ways he revealed a suspicion of the sales capacities of his men, which they could sense, so that he aggravated his personnel problems by insisting on doing a great deal of the selling himself.

The owner saw as one of his chief functions that of circulating widely through the community in order to secure listing and sales leads. In order to compensate for his continuing absence from the firm, he developed an excellent policy book; however, he did not enforce policy or explain it. He continually placed heavy stress on the need for his staff to operate "ethically," without interpreting what he meant by this.

The financial impact of this type of management was clearly evident. In the first year of operation, the firm produced $17,569 in gross commissions, paid $7,750 in commissions to salesmen ($6,000 to one salesman), and had a net income of $5,181. In the second year, the gross income was $23,927 and net income of $4,102. In the first six months of the third year, the gross income equaled $10,676 and the net income $87. One of the major factors in the declining net income was the rapid increase in unaccounted-for expenditures, which rose from $1,560 in the first year to $4,009 in the first six months of the third year. Another was general ineffectiveness of his sales staff.

THE WILL TO SUCCEED

The successful firms stand in marked contrast to firm "K." The owners invariably have had extensive technical experience in real estate, either as builders, contractors, or salesmen—which has very frequently been augmented by education at the collegiate level. These owners increase their business opportunities through multiple management and a carefully planned introduction of nonbrokerage income sources. They accept their responsibilities as managers and spend a planned period of time training and assisting their sales personnel.

These owners also generally have some rather concrete plans for expanding their operations and creating capital reserves for implementing this growth. These capital reserves are usually in the form of a checking account, from which are paid costs of extra advertising, financing unusual but profitable property sales, investing in land and income properties, and paying office costs in slack income periods. The ability to build these reserves stems in a large degree from the owners' capacity to develop effective sales personnel and to exercise close control over selling expenses.

Firm "H" is an excellent example of the latter type of firm. The firm, a husband-and-wife partnership, was started in 1935, after the husband had had four years of real estate experience in a Midwestern community. Their present main office was once a branch office which became the main office when the local markets shifted and necessitated the change. Sales brokerage constituted 80 per cent of the firm's activities, and a well-run property-management business an additional 10 per cent. The remaining activities were diversified in leasing and insurance, although the partners had plans under way for substantially increasing the insurance business as a hedge against declines in brokerage income. The owners were very flexible in their thinking and planning for the future, and they anticipated that they might have to make continuing changes in their planning as real estate markets in their community changed.

The sales staff consisted of 2 sales managers, 10 full-time and 2 part-time salesmen. The part-time men were sales trainees who were being groomed for full-time selling. Sales policies were outlined in a very complete manual which provided detailed statements on training and the need for rigorous scheduling of selling time on the part of all sales personnel. All new men, regardless of experience, were expected to spend six months in a probationary training program in order to learn about the firm and the local market. At the end of this period, if they were judged to be successful, they were offered a permanent sales position.

The principal weakness of the firm was the rigidity with which the husband enforced his personal standards of business ethics. This had caused him to lose sales managers who felt that he had assumed some of their prerogatives.

Advertising was planned but consistently related to the needs of the individual property sellers. Advertising included not only classified advertising, but also radio and television programs and extensive souvenir giveaway campaigns. Advertising costs were held to approximately 10 per cent of gross income, and all expenses were watched carefully and analyzed constantly.

The effectiveness of this type of program is reflected in the net income, which rose from $4,604 (exclusive of salaries and nonbrokerage income) on gross commissions of $36,146, to $16,357 on $95,233 in gross commissions in 1956. The net income would have been even higher in 1953 if the owners had not decided to experiment with doubling the advertising budget. The experiment was not successful, and advertising was reduced to the 10 per cent level in the following years.

The strength of the firm lies in the recognition by the partners of their managerial responsibilities. The rather rigid managerial approach of the one partner is softened and guided into more appropriate channels by the other. The strong accounting background of the one partner is balanced by the human-relations capacities of the other. The firm is not always successful in everything it attempts, but the partners expect this and are prepared to spend several years in developing operational and profit stability.

There are other elements in the operations of firms of this type which are not immediately apparent from casual analysis or observation. It is these elements, perhaps more than any other, which are the important determinants of success. These include an evident desire to grow and to develop business continuity, limitation of objectives, recognition of the human element as a major factor in growth, and a more realistic appraisal of the future.

A real desire for growth is expressed initially in the willingness of a firm to accept temporary reductions in earnings in order to build a solid program for future growth. For instance, as was previously mentioned, the introduction of an insurance department or a property-management function invariably creates a condition of operational costs in excess of income which will continue for 18 months or more. Any firm which tries these activities and abandons them in a year or less because they are not profitable has not given these activities sufficient opportunity to develop. These activities must be included eventually if the firm is to stabilize its profits, because specialization in sales brokerage produces erratic and unpredictable income returns. However, the introduction must be carefully timed so that the firm will have the resources to carry them during their unproductive period.

Growth must also be predicated on continuous effectiveness in the basic functions of finding prospective buyers and sellers, advertising, and sales management. These functions must be fitted to the needs of the local markets and reduced to largely a routine basis. These routines must then be forcefully impressed on all sales personnel so that the sales manager can see that they are followed and so that the owner of the firm can be freed to attend to other more important duties.

The need for this can be seen by comparing a sales organization to a football team. Assistant coaches spend their time teaching the individual members the fundamentals of blocking, kicking, running, and so forth. No man can stay on the team who is not expert in these fundamentals. The head coach spends his time planning the strategy needed to win, and his best strategy cannot succeed if the players cannot execute the fundamentals. If the coach takes his time to train individual members, the entire team suffers.

The continuous close, daily contact between the owner of the firm and his sales staff requires the owner to pay considerable attention to developing smooth working relations with everyone in the firm. The owner must understand motivation and must work continuously to find the combination of monetary and nonmonetary incentives which will spur the salesmen to consistently high sales-performance levels. The owner must also recognize that the highest morale in a sales force is present when the salesmen know that the owner is interested in seeing that each man develops to his maximum potential and that no one is retained on the force who is not interested in becoming a full-time, professionally minded salesperson.

Finally, an owner must develop a clear picture of the talents and capacities of his force and use them judiciously to obtain maximum results. He must be careful not to overextend his salesmen's efforts, or the men will become frustrated and disheartened; nor can he permit them to operate at less than capacity, because they will then become bored and lazy. Progress must be sought in the light of what has happened in the past, what the sales force is capable of at present, and what must be added in order for them to grow in the future.

Principles of Growth

1. *Management functions.* As a real estate firm increases in size, the management function changes from concentrating on staffing problems to those of organizing, directing, and controlling.
2. *Evolution.* Almost all real estate firms have grown slowly over time. Very few are able to start immediately at a large scale of operations and survive.
3. *Marginal size.* Firms with 15 to 25 sales personnel are usually in a stage of evolution from small to large size and cannot continue for long in the middle-size category.
4. *Selling.* Selling remains the principal activity of a real estate firm no matter how large it may become; types of properties sold and kinds of clients served do change, however.
5. *Small size.* The majority of real estate firms remain small in size because the owners of these firms either cannot or do not want to be concerned with nonselling activities.
6. *Competitors.* The number of real estate firms increases constantly because of the poor quality of management in the existing firms and the desire of ambitious salespersons to own their own firms.

7. *Expert counsel.* Many firms do not grow because the chief executives of these firms do not understand how to use expert management counsel, or because they distrust the advice given by management counselors.
8. *Work capacity.* The growth of a small firm is usually limited to the work capacity of the principal owner.
9. *Stability.* Few real estate firms can maintain a plateau of activity because their competitors will cause them to either grow or shrink in their operations.
10. *Will to failure.* The majority of firms fail to compete successfully because they (a) do not define realistic sales objectives, (b) do not develop effective financial controls, (c) do not develop adequate sales personnel programs, and (d) fail to use imagination in developing new advertising and selling techniques.
11. *Profits.* Growth is stifled if too much attention is paid to immediate profits.

CASE STUDY

The following case study represents an unusual brokerage situation but one which may become more common as various cities face problems of integration. See if you can answer all of the problems posed at the end of the study.

THE URBAN REALTY CASE

Author: Lee Burns
Editor: Fred E.Case

History of the Firm

The J. W. Evans Realty Company opened its doors in 1925, weathered the depression of the 1930's, and topped $2.5 million in residential sales in 1960. The sales record of that year has never been broken. The president-owner-manager of the firm, Mr. J. Walter Evans, organized the company with the avowed purpose of serving the public. The "public" in this case was the inhabitants and about-to-be-inhabitants of a neighborhood known in the 1920's as Willow Valley. The residents consisted mainly of bank presidents and mature members of the professions. The city of Metropole has shared in the burgeoning population problems of most other cities of this section. Its population of about one quarter of a million relies principally on income from agricultural production and the sales of farm-produced commodities to other cities across the nation.

J. Walter Evans is now 58 years old and has gray hair that complements an already distinguished appearance. He is a conservative dresser, has a congenial personality, and is generally regarded by his associates as a business leader who has grown and prospered with the community. He serves actively on the board of a national charity, actively participates in the governing of his Episcopal parish church, and has served three consecutive terms of office as president of a most influential local civic organization.

Evans had established himself as a successful business leader by 1959. He attributes his early success and the fact that his was the sole real estate firm in the area surviving the depression to the good will and respect he had created for himself in the community. Since the 1930's, the sales figures of the Evans Company, the only real estate office serving the Willow Valley area, have reflected the stability of land values and the respected position of the firm.

Although land uses have remained stable, the area could be properly regarded as transitional, because many of the former owners of the spacious, dignified residences on large lots moved out during World War II or in the five years that followed. Since then, the properties have changed hands often, with an average property turnover of about once every three years. In 1955 one house on the periphery was sold to a minority family by another real estate firm. Since then, other minority families have moved in, and the number of houses available for sale has increased substantially.

Until 1956 Mr. Evans had earned annually between $20,000 and $25,000 profits from the firm with a small residue retained in a reserve account to avoid the necessity of borrowing from the bank should the need arise. Although Evans has established a line of credit should he need working capital, he has relied on this form of financing only rarely. This is consistent with his personal policy of never borrowing unless absolutely necessary and reflects his attitude at the beginning of operations, when he financed the initial organization entirely with his own savings.

The office is located in a one-and-one-half-story building adjacent to the bank. The building was built by a friend of Evans in 1924 and has been leased to him since 1925, when the firm started business. The office has been changed little since then, because Evans believes that it is a local trade-mark, "almost an institution," and that any changes would also alter the confidence that the public has in the firm.

During the life of the firm, several competitors have come and gone, always frozen out by Evans's ability to maintain his old customers. Although offices located outside of the neighborhood have always competed with the Evans company, Evans estimates that he averaged at least four out of five of all the sales in the community—that is, until recently. In 1957 a new office, owned and staffed by members of the minority group, located about five blocks from Evans. At first they had sufficient buyers from their own group, but lacked listings, because most of the residents staunchly refused to sell to a minority-group member. At the same time, Evans was faced with the problem of disposing of a surplus of listings which grew as sales declined. The new firm, Urban Realty, employed 10 salesmen and netted about $35,000 in 1958, its first full year of business operation. Evans believes that he lost a number of listings in the past year to this firm; these listings were for homes being sold by the majority group.

Present Organizational Structure of the Firm

Until recent years, income from insurance and property-management activities has accounted for about 15 per cent of gross and sales of single-family homes accounted for the remainder. Although the total volume from non-real estate sales has fallen off since 1956 (see Table 10–1), this business has represented an increasing proportion of gross revenues, because it has declined at a significantly lesser rate than real estate sales.

The owner attributes the declining volume of real estate sales to several factors. First, he believes the panic which followed the first nonwhite sale in 1955 is partially responsible. The firm has consistently refused to broker sales to nonwhite families because of the risk of depressing property values. He also believes that another factor causing the decline in business is the reluctance of white families to move into the neighborhood because of its transitional nature. And third, Evans believes that what he describes as "the buyer's market" has taken its toll.

Table 10–1

THE URBAN REALTY CASE
Income Statements, 1945–1958

	1945	1950	1955	1956	1957	1958
Gross Income:						
Real estate sales commissions	$ 75,000	$ 80,500	$ 73,000	$ 65,500	$ 35,000	$ 21,000
Insurance and property management	8,000	12,000	10,000	9,500	9,000	8,000
Total gross income	$ 83,000	$ 92,500	$ 83,000	$ 75,000	$ 44,000	$ 29,000
Expenses:						
Commissions	$ 35,500	$ 37,000	$ 34,000	$ 31,000	$ 17,000	$ 11,000
Advertising	6,000	7,400	6,500	6,700	6,900	7,000
Occupancy expense	500	550	600	600	600	600
Salaries	2,800	3,000	3,000	3,100	3,100	3,100
Other	4,200	4,550	4,900	4,600	4,400	4,300
Total Expenses	$ 49,000	$ 52,500	$ 49,000	$ 46,000	$ 32,000	$ 27,000
Net income	$ 34,000	$ 40,000	$ 34,000	$ 29,000	$ 12,000	$ 3,000
Number of listings	75	85	90	110	125	90
Number of sales	60	60	50	55	30	20
Average sales price	$ 40,000	$ 45,000	$ 50,000	$ 40,000	$ 38,000	$ 40,000
Sales volume	$ 2,500,000	$ 2,700,000	$ 2,450,000	$ 2,200,000	$ 1,200,000	$ 750,000

Although Evans's income has declined, office expenses have remained relatively constant, declining chiefly through the decrease in commission expense, which parallels closely sales income. Advertising expense has increased steadily. Profit declined from a record of $40,000 before taxes in 1950 to $3,000 in 1958.

Staffing and Directing

The Evans office has employed an average of eight salesmen for many years. The typical salesman has been with the office for 18 years and is 52 years old. The office accommodates just ten desks: Mr. Evans' at the back of the office, the secretary's at the entrance, and the eight salesmen's desks located in between. Three of the salesmen joined the firm during the war. The youngest, now 35 years old, was hired when he returned from military service. In addition to his real estate sales, he has promoted the growth of insurance and, to a limited extent, property-management activities. Except for the death of the oldest salesman in 1953 and the resignation of another nine months ago, there have been no changes in the sales staff. The secretary has been in Evans' faithful employ for 33 years. Until the last several years, Evans has been able to count on an average of one sales job inquiry per month, which he usually turned down with the excuse that "we have no vacant desks." The recent resignation created a vacancy, but Evans had kept no waiting list of applicants and consequently did not seek out a replacement. About a month later, a member of the minority group approached Evans for a job and was refused.

Evans relates no problems in handling his sales personnel. He has always treated them as "professional businessmen," and he believes that he has been extremely fortunate in attracting salesmen characterized by their honesty, integrity, and dignity. He points out that the salesmen have always produced at their peak capacity, so that sales contests and quotas were never necessary. Until 1956, the least any of his salesmen had "taken home" in the past decade was $4,500 a year.

There is no policy book, although each salesman has a conference with Evans when he is employed, at which time Evans emphasizes the importance of ethics and standards when dealing with the public and reviews the procedures for closing a sale. Other than this, the salesmen receive no formal training and attend no sales meetings. When Evans wishes to make announcements, he does this informally in the office by personal contact.

A commission dispute, either between salesmen in the office or with other offices, is rare.

Planning

Evans keeps no formal budgets. However, he plans expenditures on a rough month-to-month basis. He believes that there is little or no need for a formalized budget or for sales goals. The budget takes care of itself, he says. The salary, for example, paid to the secretary is a constant amount. Occupancy expenses are almost as invariable. Commissions automatically adjust to sales volume. The only room for decision, according to Evans, is in the amount of advertising expenditures. Here Evans keeps a running record of the costs of advertising figured as a percentage of sales, but gears total advertising expenditures to the number of listings he is trying to sell (see Table 10–1).

Because he has always endeavored to operate a conservative office and prided himself on maintaining high ethical standards (and he says that the community was always aware of these standards), Evans has never been faced with the problem of deciding whether to cut commissions in order to put a "deal" together. "My clients are aware of this standard, just as they are aware of all of my standards, and they know that I would be insulted if they haggled over the five per cent."

Controlling

Evans keeps his own financial records, consisting of a ledger, a cash book, and a general journal, which are audited annually at tax time by a local accountant. He also keeps a duplicate record of each salesman's personal sales and listing record; however, he regards this as merely an information source rather than a method of checking performance.

Questions

1. What is Evans's principal problem?
2. If you were called in by Evans as a business consultant to correct his sales problem, what would you suggest? Why?
3. Should Evans stay in business?
   a. If so, should he maintain the same location? Should he change any external or internal policies? Which ones, and how will this affect his sales volume and his public relations?
4. What do you think of the local realty board's "code" regarding sales to nonwhites? Of the risk of depressed values from nonwhite infiltration?
5. What does Evans mean by the "buyer's market?"
6. Why had advertising expense increased? Is this good cause for increasing expenditures for advertising?
7. Why was Evans able to effectively resist competition?
8. What is Evans's function(s) in the firm? How well do you think he is performing this function(s)?
9. What principles of management are involved here? Which are violated?

Note: This case is a composite of several individual case studies of medium-sized firms. The income figures, names, and so forth, are fictitious.

Chapter 11

THE SEARCH FOR "PROFESSIONALISM"

In recent years, real estate brokers have been working to secure recognition as "professional" persons. An important outgrowth of this trend has been the development of a code of ethics by the National Association of Real Estate Boards. However, not all brokers agree that "professionalism" is a desirable goal. This chapter examines some of the issues to be faced in a search for "professionalism."

THE FUNCTIONS OF THE BROKER

The picture of inefficiency and low productivity which emerges from a study of some real estate brokerage offices raises the question as to whether real estate brokerage offices are really necessary. Perhaps the functions which they perform could be accomplished as satisfactorily by escrow companies, title companies, banks, lawyers, mortgage lenders, or others. There is even the possibility that public interest might be better served and the costs of commissions eliminated from current selling prices under such arrangements. In order to determine whether real estate brokerage offices are necessary, we should examine the functions which the brokers must perform in an exchange of ownership, the product which they sell, the manner in which they sell the product, and the pricing structures in real estate markets.

The market for real properties is an informal one in which the actions of the broker, the buyer, and the seller are determined more by tradition than by law or regulation. There is no particular starting point nor any necessary sequence of events, although custom has dictated a series of actions which are most efficient and most likely to yield a completed transaction. For instance, a prospective buyer could secure a mortgage loan commitment first and then find a property which would fit the commitment. He might also determine the terms of purchase which best meet his needs and search for a property which would fit these needs and terms. However, the normal sequence of events in the sale of a property would develop somewhat in this manner:

1. The broker searches out persons who have an interest in selling properties and negotiates with them on the terms on which the property is to be sold and the role which he is to play in the sale. The broker most often prefers an arrangement which will pay him a commission regardless of who may complete the final sale.
2. The broker searches out persons who have an interest in buying properties and exposes to their view those properties which best fit their needs and buying capacities. In the process, he usually establishes the physical space needs and desires of the prospective buyers, the amount of cash assets which they can devote to the purchase, and the amount of monthly income they can devote to the mortgage, insurance, and taxes on the property.
3. Once the broker has determined which buyers and sellers can be most appropriately matched, he brings them together for negotiation on final terms under which the property will change hands.
4. As a part of the process of bringing the buyer and seller together, the broker will also search out possible loan sources, if these are not already available, and seek to qualify the buyer for that loan which will not only sell the property but which can be most easily assumed by the buyer.
5. The broker will advise both buyer and seller as to the necessary legal documents which must be completed as well as the fees to be paid by each. Normally he does little more than complete standard forms; if more complex arrangements are necessary, he will call for the services of legal counsel.

In summary, then, we see the broker serving as the market place, in the absence of a central market place; working as a catalyst drawing buyers and sellers together more quickly; providing information on the quantity and quality of properties being offered and purchased; estimating prices at which properties will exchange hands; and providing financial and legal advice which will lead to a completed transaction. What he does is determined partly by the kind of market in which he operates, partly by the few legal requirements which must be met in a transfer of property rights, and, to a large degree, by the kind of product which he handles.

THE PRODUCT

The special characteristics of the product which the broker sells and the manner in which it determines the sales process and the duties of the broker can be best understood by comparing it with the ideal product in a highly competitive market.

The ideal product is available in large quantities, each unit is sufficiently like any unit so that purchases can be made from samples, the product is easily transported from one market to another, and the price is not too large to exclude a large number of buyers.

The housing product has none of these characteristics. Each product is unique either because it occupies a particular parcel which no other property can occupy simultaneously, or because the improvements to the land are put together in a unique combination. The supply of the product is relatively fixed, with no more than two per cent being added in any one year on an aggregate basis, so that, in any given period of time, fluctuations in price will be due more to changes in demand than to variations in supply. The product cannot be sold from a sample or even from pictures and word descriptions, but must normally be inspected in its setting. Furthermore, the processes of depreciation and community change will cause the characteristics of the supply to change constantly, sometimes in a marked degree. The product cannot be moved about easily, so that the broker must go to the product whenever he wants to inspect it and the buyers must be brought to the product if they wish to see what they are buying.

The price of the product is always large in comparison with the assets of the typical purchaser, and the purchase usually represents the greatest investment the typical buyer will make during his entire life. The price is also complex in its make-up, because it becomes a combination of the cash or other assets asked for a down payment, the monthly payments required for acquisition, the costs of maintaining the structure during use, and the total amount which must be invested. These factors can and are changed in relationship to each other not only for an individual buyer but for each of the buyers who inspects the property.

All of the special characteristics of the product, when taken together, mean that the broker must be an expert and adaptable negotiator—that he must know not only his product, but also price trends, construction costs, financial markets, and a variety of other information.

MANNER OF SALE

The sales of real estate are one of the few areas of economic activity remaining in which final terms of sale are open to a wide degree of bargaining. The unique characteristics of the product mean that even the most experienced buyer, seller, or real estate sales agent cannot be certain as to the best manner in which the property can be brought to the attention of prospective buyers, nor can he be certain what prices or terms should be set for the sale. Sellers will probably be the most experienced at any particular moment, because they will typically have been viewing a sufficiently wide variety of properties to know what is available and on what prices and terms. On the other hand, the seller will be the least certain as to what can be done, and he will be interested in protecting his position as much as possible.

Under these conditions, the broker must encourage the seller to offer the property on a basis which will at least invite inquiries from interested buyers. If the seller will not be reasonable in his demands, the broker may refuse to handle the sale, or, if the broker has determined that the seller must sell, he must obtain an agreement from the seller to change the selling terms if reasonable exposure to the market does not produce a qualified buyer. Once the broker has secured the "opening bids" from buyer and seller and determined their sincerity with respect to closing the transaction, he must then move between them, searching for the combination of factors which will produce a completed sale.

In the process, the broker may be required to search out more than one source of financing. He may be required to secure expert advice on repairs, title matters, tax rates, potential property uses, and a variety of other matters. The final price which produces a sale will usually be hedged with various limitations as to what the buyer, the seller, and the broker must do in order to have a completed sale. However, although all conditions and terms may have an important bearing on whether the sale is completed, price is usually the single most important determinant. Invariably our research indicated that a broker believed that a properly priced property, including financing terms as a part of price, would sell most easily and with the maximum equity given to the rights of buyer and seller.

PRICING STRUCTURES

Although real properties are normally offered for sale in terms of a single dollar price, they are purchased in terms of a series of limitations and combinations of terms of which the final purchase price is only an important incident. In some most desirable sections, the price terms are set under conditions of adequate supply and volatile and sustained demand. This creates the almost perfect classical condition in which no single supplier and no single buyer can set his price terms unilaterally. However, this condition is offset to a slight degree by the monopoly position created by location, so that properties offering the same services but located in different areas will have different prices because of the locational differences. In fact, in terms of residential properties, the locational differences serve to define the local market areas within which the same price tends to prevail for approximately the same kinds of property services. Within the local market area, properties will enjoy little monopoly advantage, except in the minds of the individual purchasers, because the numerous brokers in the area keep buyers and sellers reasonably informed on price trends. The prices between local markets will also tend toward uniformity as the mobility of the families provides them with numerous locational selections.

As the numbers of licensed sales personnel increase in an area, the competition among them to secure clients keeps the market information circulating constantly as each offers his services and bids to secure a property listing. Any inflated price tendencies due to offering the listing properties at higher prices is offset by the number of sales completed at lower prices. These actual sales prices will be communicated quickly to other prospective buyers and sellers as brokers seek to nullify the unrealistic listing prices. High net sales figures and proven ability to sell within a close percentage of the listing price will develop as the most effective arguments for securing new clients and serve to keep both asking and sales prices within reasonable bounds.

Under the highly competitive conditions prevailing in our metropolitan sections, the real estate markets' brokerage offices are forced into offering more services without being able to raise their commission rates. Furthermore, as the market becomes increasingly supplied with new units, as compared with demand increases, the prices of all homes will tend to lower and the commission per unit sold, which is always based on a percentage figure, will drop. In addition, in highly active markets, owners will be alert to opportunities to sell their properties without paying the brokerage commission, and they will be encouraged in this practice by the degree to which the sales can be routinized so that the major services can be performed by escrow and title insurance companies.

Commissions and House Prices

The nature of the product, the characteristics of the buyers and sellers, and the structuring of the market mean that the price of any single parcel of real estate can vary within rather broad limits. The ultimate selling price will be determined by the knowledge of the buyers and sellers, their bargaining strengths, and the compulsion they are under to complete the transaction. For these reasons, it is impossible to assert that the price in a particular transaction would have been lower or higher merely because of the presence or absence of the amount paid for a broker's commission.

In fact, there is every reason to believe that the total price of a property will have no effect on the decision to purchase. The most important influences will be the down payment required and the size of the monthly payments. Under such conditions, the brokerage commission would influence the completion of the sale only by the degree to which it added to either the down payment or the monthly payments, and in the ordinary transaction it affects neither of these items.

On the other hand, the functions which a broker performs must be performed by someone because of the present characteristics of the product, the buyers and sellers, and the market structure. None of the services which he performs could be eliminated entirely. The costs might be reduced by a more efficient organization, but if the broker is eliminated, these services would be scattered among a variety of organizations, so that they might be performed less efficiently and at greater cost. However, the highly competitive nature of real estate selling suggests that the competition for business among brokers forces them to meet the prices of their competitors and to charge no more for their services than their competitors charge.

Because the brokers perform the minimum services which must be performed at a minimum cost, their commissions could not be eliminated by transferring the brokers' functions to other organizations. The ability of these organizations to perform these services at lower costs is highly debatable because of the degree to which these costs are minimized under the present brokerage system of selling.

Are Real Estate Brokers Necessary as Marketing Agents?

Both empirical and theoretical evidence suggests that brokers are necessary as marketing agents, and that their commissions do not represent excessive charges which raise housing prices. The arguments in favor of this proposition may be summarized as follows:

1. Brokers serve as a central clearinghouse for information on housing prices and price trends.
2. Brokers serve as catalysts bringing together inexperienced buyers and sellers.
3. Brokers provide the information by means of which the unique qualities of properties can be balanced against each other and reasonably rational decisions can be made by buyers and sellers as to comparative prices.
4. The large numbers of licensed brokers and sellers produces a keenly competitive situation in which their services must be priced low to meet competition.
5. The present commission charges represent the minimum costs incurred in completing a property sale in today's markets.

THE SEARCH FOR "PROFESSIONALISM"

Real estate brokerage operations have undergone little basic change since the eighteenth century, when the introduction of private ownership of real estate gave rise to specialized legal and business services relating to transfer of property. Although the real estate brokerage business has gained increased recognition since that time through its numerous professional organizations, today the small office and the autonomous local real estate board remain supreme in the field. Small-scale operations, relative to the huge scale of business and industrial size which are commonplace today, have remained a characteristic of the business, chiefly because of the nature of the business, the product which is sold, the market in which the business is transacted, and the legal complications of transferring ownership.

Birth and Growth of Real Estate Brokerage

The function of transferring property rights has been an important segment of business activity since colonial days, when royal ownership of lands was removed and ownership by individuals was permitted.[1] The function grew rapidly as the rights of royal proprietors were reduced and exploration and seizure of land moved on apace.

In this early environment, the real estate business was concerned essentially with legal aspects, with the lawyer playing a dominant role in all property transfers. However, the rapid growth of cities in the early 1800's and the emergence of several large cities by the 1840's introduced complexities in the transfer of real property which created a need not only for legal talent, but for business ability as well. The status of real estate brokers as basically businessmen rather than lawyers was recognized early in the nineteenth century with the creation of local real estate exchange organizations, the first of which was started in New York in 1847. Similar types of exchanges were created in other major cities, and correspondence and discussion of common problems between these groups soon made evident a need for some type of national organization.

In 1908 the National Association of Real Estate Exchanges was formed, in order to "unite real estate men of America for the purpose of exerting effectively a combined influence upon matters affecting real estate interests." The need for such an organization grew out of an increasing number of grievances which were being leveled against those who engaged in various aspects of real estate brokerage operations. For instance, one of the early speakers at a convention of real estate dealers stated that anyone could call himself a real estate agent, and "only public opinion and criminal courts could see that the business was conducted on ethical lines." The need for professional business organizations was indicated also by the increasing complexity of the functions of the real estate broker, which by the early 1900's included such activities as appraising, negotiating and making leases, collecting rents, making sales of real estate, and negotiating mortgage loans.

The growth of real estate brokerage as an organized business since these early days has continued chiefly through the formation of local real estate boards, started by individual small real estate offices, and through the association of local boards in state and national organizations. Local boards continue to maintain a high degree of autonomy, and none of the boards

---

[1] Pearl Janel Davies, *Real Estate in American History* (Washington, D. C.: Public Affairs Press, 1958), pp. 1–4. The historical materials of this chapter are based on this reference.

is dominated by any single or small number of large business organizations. Rather, the importance of the individual broker and his influence on community development are stressed and given chief recognition.

At the same time that the many local businessmen were attempting to create standards of ethical operations and to organize real estate boards which might enforce these regulations, numerous opportunities for profits in land speculation attracted a growing number of unscrupulous dealers. For instance, the Los Angeles Board in 1908 asked for laws against such practices as "selling land to which the vender did not possess title, purchasing worthless land at about $2 an acre, mortgaging it heavily to a confederate and then selling the mortgage to unsuspecting persons, and selling land owned only on contract for sale, the contract being on terms the vender never intended to fulfill." The problems arising from such practices were further complicated by the "ignorant and incompetent operator who could do quite as much damage to the buyer." The growing adverse opinion with respect to real estate brokerage operations was further accentuated by the excesses of land speculation which occurred in the 1920's.

In order to overcome increasingly adverse public reaction, local boards began to codify and strengthen their standards for business operations, and the state organizations and the National Association of Real Estate Boards developed increasingly explicit statements of ethical standards. However, state and local organizations could only be as effective as the local boards, because membership in NAREB continued to be based on board membership or, in cases where no local board existed, on individual membership. NAREB's goal of giving increasing recognition and a special designation to men handling real estate sales could only be accomplished through the effort of local real estate boards. As a result, one of the earliest announced objectives of NAREB was to see that real estate owners would be required to buy and sell properties only through local real estate agents who were members of local real estate boards.

These efforts resulted in the slow evolution of community recognition that the real estate brokerage business was actually a full-time business occupation. As this recognition increased, local board membership grew, and the activities of the boards became more numerous and more effective as members were required to pay dues and subscribe to codes of ethics.

Early in the 1900's, the states began passing licensing laws which required some evidence of competency to perform as a real estate broker. However, almost all of these requirements were extremely minimal and rarely prevented any but the most unscrupulous or incompetent from entering the business.

The specialized activities which required greater competencies than those associated with brokerage were recognized through the formation of various types of affiliated national organizations for persons engaging in appraising, property management, building management, and similar activities. Today the National Association of Real Estate Boards, its member state associations, and local boards and the affiliated specialists' organizations stand pre-eminent in the organization of this type of business activity. However, in spite of the increasing influence and size of these organizations and the growth in the number of persons licensed to sell real estate, the small real estate office remains the dominant form of business enterprise in real estate brokerage operations.

Scope of Real Estate Brokerage Activities

The scope of present real estate brokerage operations can be gauged from an examination of real estate activity in the State of California, which represents one of the largest and most active real estate markets in the United States. The importance of brokerage activities to the economy of the State of California can be deduced from the number of persons who have been licensed to sell real estate in the state, the number of deeds recorded annually, the number of dwelling units started, and the number of mortgages recorded.

In 1927, when licenses were first required in California for persons selling real estate for a commission, the total number of licenses issued was 65,970. The depression period and the period following World War II caused a small decline in the annual number of licenses issued; but at the close of the war, the number began to grow rapidly, until in 1964 approximately 200,000 persons were licensed to sell real estate. That the real estate brokerage business has grown much more rapidly than the increase in population is indicated by the fact that, in the early years of licensing, there was one broker for about every 200 persons in the population; but by 1964 this ratio had grown to one broker for every 100 persons of population, despite the growth of California in absolute numbers.

The growth in the number of persons in real estate brokerage operations has been associated with the startling increase in real estate activity in the state, particularly in the postwar period. For instance, in 1950, 2,359,982 instruments relating to some aspect of real estate ownership or transfer were recorded in California. Only eight short years later, the number of instruments recorded had increased by almost 30 per cent to something over 3,000,000. Although there are no statistics available to indicate what percentage of the transactions represented by these instruments was handled by real estate brokers, we may nevertheless infer from the number of persons licensed that the real estate broker played an important role in the transactions.

The need for a large number of real estate brokers in the State of California can also be deduced from the number of new dwelling units which have been started annually in California in response to the large influx of population into the state since World War II. The postwar high rate of building, which began in approximately 1950 with over 196,000 units constructed, reached a peak of 214,700 units in 1955. Although there has been some decline in the rate of construction since that peak, new units have approximated the 200,000 mark almost every year since. Each year since 1952, total housing construction in California has equaled at least 15 per cent of all such construction in the United States. This activity, thus, has resulted in a tremendous demand for persons who are skillful in securing buyers and financing for new residential and nonresidential properties.

An idea of the value of business transacted by real estate brokers can also be obtained from mortgage recordings of $20,000 or less in the State of California. The Census of 1960 indicated that at least 80 per cent of all sales of homes required some type of mortgage financing. Because mortgages today represent a fairly high percentage of purchase price, the amount of mortgage recordings gives at least a clue to the value of business transacted by real estate brokers. Even though refinancing and other mortgage transactions may be handled without the assistance of a real estate broker, this possible source of overstatement is likely to be offset by the excess of purchase prices over mortgages and by the number of transactions involving mortgage loans exceeding $20,000. Since 1950, mortgage recordings of $20,000 or less have risen from $2.4 billion to $6 billion in 1964.

Dominance of the Small Office

Real estate brokerage operations will probably continue to be characterized by numerous small offices, chiefly because: the business can be entered so easily; there is a lack of established clientele; the employment of salespersons is usually tenuous; there is no effective way of developing a competitive distinction; and sales opportunities are concentrated in local markets. The need for a license in order to conduct real estate brokerage operations is not a significant hindrance, even though the licensing requirements are becoming stricter, because anyone of reasonable intelligence and diligence can secure a license by attending a special course for licensing purposes or by study on his own. Once the license is secured, only a small outlay of cash is needed to secure a desk and a telephone and to do some minimum advertising in announcing the opening of a new real estate brokerage office. Brokers in this study, for instance, indicated that a man with a good credit rating could start a real estate brokerage office with as little as $50 or $75 in cash, and that a man with $3,000 to $9,000 in cash could not only open an office but could underwrite his activities for several months while developing an adequate sales volume.

The ease of entering the business and opening an office creates a high degree of competition between persons in the business itself. As Maisel's study showed, there are multiple small offices competing not only among themselves, but with buyers and sellers who have found ways of completing transactions without resort to real estate brokers. The minimal quality of the licensing requirements permits lawyers, housewives, retired businessmen, and others to secure a license in order that they may from time to time earn small commissions by handling the transactions of their friends, relatives, and casual acquaintances.

The typical real estate brokerage office is unable to develop much of an established clientele on which growth could be based, chiefly because buyers and sellers are in the market so infrequently. Because of this infrequent market participation, buyers and sellers have little basis for judging the qualities of one real estate office as compared with another; therefore, they are likely to be completely capricious in the selection of an office to handle their transactions. Because of the general lack of knowledge of buyers and sellers with respect to the complexities of real estate property transfers, and because of the requirement that they pay a percentage of the purchase price for the services of someone who apparently does nothing but insert a small advertisement in the paper, they are easy prey for unscrupulous dealers who promise them almost anything in order to handle their transaction. These assumptions may even encourage buyers and sellers to attempt to complete their transactions without the services of a real estate broker, lawyer, or other professional assistance.

The typical real estate brokerage office also faces difficulties because the average salesperson is considered to be basically an independent contractor and not subject to reasonably close control by the employing broker. The body of legal opinion, for instance, holds that a real estate broker can do little more than set general selling goals for his real estate personnel or he would be interfering with their status as indepedent contractors. As a result, the working agreements between employing brokers and their sales force are extremely tenuous and often not reduced to writing. The broker, in fact, is never certain from day to day as to the number of persons he may have working for him. In addition, sales personnel are paid, not salaries, but commissions based upon sales actually completed. Employing brokers have little financial hold over their sales force. All of these factors add up to a condition in which the real estate broker finds extreme difficulty in developing a permanent personnel organization of any size.

Some local real estate firms attempt to develop a competitive distinction by becoming members of trade associations, real estate boards, special institutes, or multiple-listing agencies. Although these affiliations add to the reputation of a local real estate office, the general public is often unaware of them and may be unwilling to pay the extra price for using a specialist in a real estate transaction. Moreover, membership in these organizations is usually based on minimum or moderate educational or business qualifications, so that the distinction which might be acquired by membership in a professional organization is reduced by the large number of persons who are able to qualify for membership.

Product Variety

The nature of real property as an object of commerce, even more than the way in which the business is organized, will probably continue to maintain the presence of numerous small organizations. Each parcel of real estate is a distinct quantity, not only because the improvements on it are rarely similar to those of other improvements, but also because each location is unique. As a result, the market is characterized by numerous heterogeneous products which require that each be especially appraised in terms of its unique quality and traded as an individual unit. Moreover, each parcel, in comparison with most market goods, is large in size and high in price, so that financing must usually be arranged for each property. Consequently, numerous negotiations must be conducted between the buyer and one or more lenders, and the services of a local real estate broker who is well acquainted with that particular property and the neighborhood is often helpful to the buyer in successful completion of the transaction.

The market for a product can always be increased if buyers can purchase the product from samples or if the product can be taken to the buyer; but neither of these conditions prevails in real estate. A person who wishes to buy a particular property must view it in that location and he must be satisfied with the environment which surrounds that property. If he takes a fancy to the improvements on the land, these may be duplicated to some extent on another site. However, the prospective buyer will have to go to that area and see the site before he can appreciate all of its qualities and plan properly for its development.

Because real estate markets are characterized by numerous submarkets in terms of neighborhoods, type of property, and price class, the local real estate broker finds it difficult to obtain information about transactions being completed in these markets. There are few adequate indicators of local real estate market activities. As a result, any firm which plans to expand beyond its own local market must proceed by trial and error until it has learned something about the new markets which it has entered. Moreover, the few indicators of real estate market activity which are available suggest that the markets are volatile, sensitive to numerous business and other influences, and therefore difficult to predict. All of these factors militate against the growth of a real estate brokerage office and provide formidable barriers to an office that plans to operate much beyond its own real estate markets.

A final and important limitation on the ability of real estate offices to grow to reasonable size lies in the legal complexities which surround the negotiation for and the final sale of real property. The salesmen are confined in their activities by various aspects of the law of agency. The transaction itself must be completed according to both contract law and real estate law. The actions of the salesmen in dealing with both buyer and seller are usually closely circumscribed by real estate licensing law. As a result, each transaction becomes a matter of often complicated legal negotiations, and a single office would find it difficult to develop any large volume of business on a routine basis.

AN ESTIMATE OF THE FUTURE

In time, the various forces which currently are adverse to the creation of larger-scale operations may be mitigated. Moreover, this study indicates that some large firms are evolving. This finding suggests a number of important questions. For instance, what opportunities exist for the growth to larger size? To what degree is the small-sized firm, in terms of either salesmen or facilities or some other measure, efficient? What steps should be taken if a firm does want to increase its size? What kind of problems does a firm face if it plans to grow? Should a firm join a multiple-listing system? What role should the owner of a real estate brokerage firm play in guiding the growth of his community and land uses in it? Should professionalization be the goal toward which all real estate brokerage should strive? Can real estate brokerage offices ever become anything more than efficient sales organizations? To what extent should a college degree or equivalent education be established as minimum entrance requirements for the real estate brokerage business? Should real estate brokerage firms provide more support for research that will help them understand their own operations and improve the quality of the services that they offer the general public?

CASE STUDIES

The two case studies presented in the following pages represent marked contrasts to each other. The first, 15-L, has been earning a very low income and seems destined to fail. Firm 17-AL has an excellent earning record and seems destined for increasing success. You are given the raw notes of the research reporter, including his comments. After studying the two firms, indicate whether you agree with the analyses and recommendations made by the researcher and prepare a report that you would submit to the owner of firm 15-L and that you believe he could use in improving his operations. Can you recommend anything for 17-AL?

CASE 15-L: SUMMARY OF FACTS

I-S. *Identification*

Classification: Small firm, low income
Start of operations: 1951
Income: See income and expense statement.

II-S. *Organizing*

A. Location: The firm is located in a small agricultural, college community of about 20,000.
B. Competition: Most real estate offices in the town are small.
C. Community consciousness: He retains membership in the local real estate board, the CREA, NAREB and NIREB, and Rotary.
D. Activity: 95 per cent brokerage, 5 per cent leasing. An insurance department was added. Broker thinks escrow service is good because it eliminates much detail work. Broker does some business on the side, such as speculative buying in sacrifice cases. He also once built a house and sold it.

III-S. *Staffing*

A. Size: Two owners, two salesmen, and a part-time secretary; one owner's wife sells part-time.

B. Salesmen:

1. Selection: The most important criterion in this firm is education and intelligence (his one salesman at the time of the interview had only a high school education). How he measures these qualities we do not know. Owner also stressed personality and gregariousness. He would hire an inexperienced salesman over 60—age is no criterion. "A salesman solely dependent on his real estate earnings will have greater incentive. He should have enough saved to carry himself for 'a while.' "
2. His first salesman was over 65 and worked part-time. The owner had to assist him to finish and close a deal, and still had to pay the salesman a commission.
3. Turnover: Two good men left to go into business for themselves. (This is reflected in low net income.) One left and was replaced in 1956.
4. Commission: Split 50–50 after 15 per cent deduction for listing. Owner says that the office cut of the commission is the bare minimum he can accept and still show a profit.
5. During an interview with the highest producer (who was chiefly concerned with the relative merits of the Audograph), it was learned that he sold about three per cent of the people to whom he showed property, and this was a high figure! He was attracted to 15-L's firm because he liked the way they did business. He plans to go on his own as soon as he is eligible to take a broker's license. This is an efficient office that costs plenty to run, he says; he thinks "real estate is O.K. if you devote full time to it." (This man has another income and works only part-time.) When queried whether he would recommend this business to young men, he instructed the interviewer to turn off the recording machine before he would answer.

C. Owner:

Is sorry that he wasted 10 to 15 of his best years raising fruit when he could have been selling real estate, because he likes it so well. Yet he later mentions that he "might be better off if he had just stayed as a salesman, because then he wouldn't have all this overhead and expense."

2. Has a bachelor's degree in agriculture, which he believes has been useful because he is located in an agricultural community.
3. Age, about 45
4. Occasionally in the course of the interview, he sounds as if he were going to sleep. There is frequently a long pause after questions, and answers are usually poor and do not reflect the intention of the question.

D. Secretary: No information on functions or responsibilities. Owner seems to perform most secretarial and routine duties himhelf.

IV-S. *Directing*

A. Relations with salesmen:

1. The broker competes with the salesmen (particularly likes to sell orchards), but few important problems arise, because there are always too many prospects, anyway. If a prospect comes to the office and a salesman has time to handle him, the salesman gets the prospect. The important problem is qualifying prospects to determine which ones are capable of translating need into purchases.
2. There are no written policies. Broker believes that a salesman must work full-time, but part-time people are O.K. "for tract-development work on weekends."
3. Training: If he hired a man with some education but inexperienced in real estate, owner would have the man "follow him around" for at least a month. At the end of 30 days, he would be capable of a simple selling job.

B. Relations with customs:

1. Broker says that the best source of listings is word-of-mouth reference plus personal contact (equals reputation). Yet, less than 50 per cent of his sales result from contact or referral. Also, "familiarity with the firm is built through advertising, and listings are gained this way."
2. Listings:
   (a) Accepts both open and exclusive listings. They seldom advertise a listing immediately after it is obtained in order to give the listing salesman a fair chance to sell it.
   (b) Would prefer to take an exclusive listing at a higher price rather than take it as an open. Reason: property owner will realize that it is overpriced after 60 days and lower the price anyway.
   (c) How he decides on proper listing price: He makes a mental appraisal of the property in terms of market prices of similar properties and reproduction cost. Sometimes he will review replacement costs with the owner so that he will see that it is being priced right.
   (d) When asked what advantages he mentioned when attempting to get a seller to list with him rather than with a competitor, he was unable to reply. He finally mentioned that his advantage rests on community reputation rather than on a specific service he offers.
   (e) They sell few tract-development homes. The commission is a flat rate of $100 to $150 per house.
3. There is no problem in attracting customers. The community is sharing in the

rapid growth of this section of the country, and is changing from a small agricultural community to an urban suburb.

V-S. *Planning*

A. Except for advertising, there are no budgets.
B. Advertising:
1. Expenditures are budgeted; they range between four and eight per cent of gross.
2. Media: Classified ads, letters, and post cards
3. Broker believes that advertising is a principal problem. He would like to know more about it.

C. Broker feels that entrance into real estate business is easy: Office rental of about $30 per month plus $200 to join the Multiple-Listing Service, which provides a bunch of good listings to work on, is all that is necessary.
D. Goals: He does not believe in setting quotas, yet he expects to receive a minimum of $250 to $300 per salesman per month.
E. Standards: Will deviate from the standard five per cent commission, but has seldom found this necessary. In one or two cases they have absorbed costs of a termite bill.
F. He tries to keep in contact with business trends by reading the *U. S. News*, *CREA Journal,* and the *National Real Estate and Building Journal.*
G. Broker's biggest problem is planning his time efficiently. He has wished he could hire a good office manager to take care of petty details, such as small commission rentals and friends that come in to visit.
H. Success and failure:
1. Broker's reasons for success: Hard work and doing a conscientious job of service. He believes that real estate is primarily a service function, that service and profit are equally important.
2. Believes the measure of success is (a) good reputation, and (b) good income. When asked if size was any indication of success, broker replied that all he is after is a comfortable living. He does not care to be the biggest firm. Later he mentions that a good reputation is *not* a requisite to success: he knows of a fellow broker, a very foxy character that people should beware of, who has made much money in the real estate business; however, he is not sure whether this fellow made all of his money in real estate.

INCOME AND EXPENSE STATEMENTS

	Year 2 *19—*		*Year 3* *19—*		*Year 4* *19—*	
	Amount	*As % of total gross*	*Amount*	*As % of total gross*	*Amount*	*As % of total gross*
Total Gross Income	$ 13,386	100.0%	$ 21,933	100.0%	$ 27,337	100.0%
Expenses:						
Occupancy			$ 600E	2.7%	$ 884	3.2%
Commissions			8,869	53.0	9,539	35.0
Advertising			1,990	9.0	1,281	5.0
Other expenses			4,429	20.2	4,280	15.7
Total Expenses	$ 12,879	96.0%	$ 15,888	72.0%	$ 15,984	58.0
Net Profit Before Taxes	507	4.0	6,045	28.0	11,353	42.0

3. Broker believes that other firms fail by "not knowing enough to do the right things." He has been amazed by some brokers who seem inept and not at all able or intelligent, but who are making a good living.

VI-S. *Control*

Of records: The firm prepares profit and loss statements and an accountant draws up a balance sheet periodically. In addition, they keep a general ledger, journal, cash book, and other records.

ANALYSIS

I-A. *Organizing*

A. Despite its haphazard organization, the firm has doubled its net income every year since 1953, moving from $600 to $23,000 net in three years. The partners are therefore earning better than $11,000 each per annum. Increasing profits may be attributed to changing from a sole proprietorship to a partnership (of two) fairly recently and the resulting injection of new ideas.
B. From 1951 to 1955, all income was derived from brokerage and leasing activity. Reference to nonbrokerage income indicates that during the past year 13 per cent of gross income was derived from the addition of an insurance department.
C. Broker belongs to several trade and service organizations. Whether this membership is held for amenity or public relations purposes is unknown; we might presume the former (II-S, part C).

II-A. *Staffing*

A. Criteria: The owner seems unrealistic in his choice of selection criteria, mentioning that education and intelligence are most important (III-S, part B-1). He also prefers salespeople who are dependent on their sales income, yet the salesman interviewed depends rather on an outside income and is not very concerned over his low brokerage production (III-S, B-5). The owner is probably not very careful to apply any criteria in selection, but will try "any comers."
B. Turnover: The high rate of turnover in relation to staff size suggests that the firm may seem like a happier place to work from outward appearances than is true (III-S, part B-3); lack of direction, policies, and training (see IV-S), coupled with an apparent lack of inspiration from above, is not conducive to long tenures (III-S, C-4). The fact that several left to go into business for themselves suggests that this broker does not alert his employees to the costs of a brokerage operation. On the surface, the broker does not seem concerned, rationalizing turnover with, "It's O.K.; that's how I got my start," that is, he quit as a salesman to go into business for himself. The turnover problem cannot be caused by lack of sales potential, as there are sufficient customers (IV-S, B-2), but undoubtedly by poor management and lack of services. Note that the owner complained that he had to help an older salesman complete a deal (III-S, B-2), indicating a lack of interest and unwillingness to give assistance.

C. The salesman regards his three per cent sales-to-total prospects ratio as good. Obviously, this is not good, but the salesman has no measuring stick, because he came into the firm inexperienced in sales work (III-S, B-5).

III-A. *Directing*

A. Referral business: This broker knows what is right, but is too reticent or indifferent. For example, he knows and recognizes that the best source of business is reference, yet is unconcerned with building up his referral business (IV-S, part B-1). Further, he gives no indication in the interview of attempting to biuld reputation: despite the fact that less than 50 per cent of his sales are the result of referrals, he mentions (IV-S, B-2-d) that he offers reputation rather than "any specific services." Owner then contradicts himself, saying that his real estate business involves primarily a service function (V-S, part H-1).
B. This broker does not seem wont to analyze or think too seriously. For example, he has not considered the competitive advantages of his firm (IV-S, B-2-d). Yet he is quick to "analyze" reasons for other brokers' success or lack of it. In the former, he may be a "foxy" operator (V-S, part H-2); in the latter, by "not knowing enough to do the right things," for ineptness or lack of intelligence. Again, this broker suggests that intelligence is responsible for success.
C. Listings: They seem to take any property that they are fortunate enough to receive. As sales have increased, the ratio of advertising expense to gross has also increased, indicating that they are becoming increasingly aware of the importance of advertising their listings conscientiously.
D. Owner competes with salesmen in selling orchards (IV-S, part A-1). As the community changes from an agricultural to an urban community, he must of necessity either change his specialty to some other form of property or be forced into managing the firm properly!
E. Training is minimal if not a total waste of time. We wonder what a trainee would learn from this broker despite personal exposure to him for even so long a period as one month. This is probably a mere token, or an attempt to give the trainee a "feel for selling" (IV-S, part A-3).
F. Policies: We would venture to say that lack of policies has led to numerous disputes and may be partially responsible for losing salesmen (IV-S, part A-2).
G. It would seem that salesmen are required to scout up their own prospects rather than to service drop-ins and call-ups (IV-S, part A), which they receive only "if they have time to handle them."

IV-A. *Planning*

A. The only difference this owner implies between a broker and a salesman is that the former pays operating expenses. This is implied by his statement (III-S, C-1) to the effect that he might prefer to be a salesman once more just to get rid of expenses, and (V-S, part C) by his mentioning that he feels entrance into the business is easy—all it takes is enough to join the Multiple-Listing Service and rent a desk!
B. The broker is a poor planner and recognizes the problem (V-S, part G). Yet most of his personal planning problems could be solved if he made an effort. He could easily delegate certain authority to his secretary and sales-

people, schedule his own time much as he would expect a salesman to plan his day, and so forth.

C. Lack of strict standards (V-S, part E and IV-S, part B-2), such as enforcing the five per cent commission rigorously and accepting only exclusive listings, may be responsible for this broker's lack of strong reputation and, correspondingly, of referral business.

V-A. *Control*

We are inclined to believe that control is very weak.

A. Strengths:

1. The growing, transitory nature of the community
2. Increasing profits
3. Membership in community organizations
4. Diversification into nonbrokerage activity

B. Weaknesses:

1. Lack of interest in management
   a. Inability to direct
      (1) Prefers selling
      (2) Poor training program
      (3) Lack of policies
   b. Inability to plan
   c. Inability to control
2. Lack of interest in building reputation
   a. Nonenforcement of standards
   b. Disinterest in service
3. Lack of imagination

SUMMARY OF FACTS

I-S. *Identification*

Classification: Small firm, high income.
Start of operations: 1950.
Income: See balance sheet and expense statement.

II-S. *Organization*

A. Scope:		
	Brokerage	90%
	Rentals	10%
	TOTAL	100%

B. Size: Brokers have purposely limited the size of their organization and staff in order to be free to sell property themselves without becoming entangled in managerial problems.

C. Their principal problem is meeting competition. Although they feel that there is sufficient potential to support all of the licensees in this area, they find that it is difficult to compete with other salesmen who refuse to maintain the same high standards to which they subscribe.

D. Favorable organization factors:
1. Good location
2. Good profits record
3. Good reputation, standards, ethics
4. Good relations with other firms
5. Strong advertising program

III-S. *Staffing*

A. Staff includes two partners, two salespersons—both female (one who handles only rentals), no secretary. The partners, aged 52 and 48, have had many years of real estate experience and selling. They divide work about evenly and cooperate on own deals. Their relations with each other have always been happy.
B. Have kept sales staff small to minimize managerial problems, freeing owners to sell. (See "Organization.")
C. Owners feel that clerical help is unnecessary, owners performing duties of correspondence and record-keeping.
D. Hiring: When they hired their last saleswoman, they investigated her background, church affiliation, family situation, and source of supplementary income. Although they feel that education is important, they do not delve into an applicant's educational background but "appraise her use of English through the interview."
E. The successful salesman must, they believe, earn at least $500 a month. He must gross $3,000 per annum in addition to cover his desk. Their present two salesmen are meeting this requirement. The two salesmen earned $5,000 each in 1954; Each salesman specializes in properties in the area in which he lives. The owners feel that the salesmen are most interested in and informed about their home area.
The area has a large number of retired and semiretired people with real estate broker's licenses and a supplementary income. This is the source of its salesmen. Still, the owners say they prefer women between the ages of 30 and 50, and will not hire an inexperienced salesman.
F. There is a waiting list of applicants for jobs when a vacancy occurs. Salesmen are attracted to the firm by its extensive advertising program (see V-S, "Planning").
G. Salesmen feel that they are maximizing their income with this firm and are, in general, satisfied with the working conditions.
H. Although there has been no turnover problem for several years (because of the small size of the staff), the owner reports that he has had frequent experience with salesmen leaving as soon as they become really successful. They were usually dissatisfied with the commission arrangement or left to go into business for themselves.

IV-S. *Direction*

A. Rather than directing the staff, the owners dictate policy to them.
1. Most of the staff's actions must be approved.
2. Owner takes over closing details.
B. Only experienced salespeople are hired. New employees are briskly indoctrinated and supervised until they are familiar with the policies of the firm.

There are no sales meetings or group meetings of the staff, but the owners are willing to help and lend an ear when needed.

C. Hire only women—"fewer headaches."

V-S. *Planning*

A. Advertising:

1. At the start of operations, owners agreed to spend $200 per month for advertising regardless of the number of sales, and planned to increase this amount each month. They now spend in excess of $400 monthly and find that the program has paid off.
2. Advertising copy is planned week by week and changed weekly.
3. The firm mails out mimeographed circulars to other brokers describing exclusives and enlisting their cooperation in selling them.

B. Reputation:

1. They strive to be ethical, and they feel that their high standards have secured referrals, especially from banks and other business people.
2. Their new office contributes to their enviable reputation. It was designed to

BALANCE SHEET

	Year 4–5	*Year 6*		*Year 7*	
Assets					
Cash			$ 50		$ 50
Bank—Commercial Account			1,513		925
Bank—Trustee Account			101		125
Savings Account			98		98
Furniture and Fixtures		$ 5,336		$ 5,788	
Less Reserve for Depreciation		1,560	3,776	2,153	3,634
Building and Improvements		$ 21,288		$ 21,288	
Less Reserve for Depreciation		160	21,128	1,118	20,170
Land			17,010		17,010
Total Assets	$ 38,405		$ 43,676		$ 42,012
Liabilities					
Payroll Taxes Payable			$ 120		$ —
Trust Deed Payable			$ 23,404		$ 22,263
Owners' Liability			1		26
Notes Payable			9,000		9,000
Contracts Payable			1,087		351
Total Liabilities	$ 31,259		$ 33,613		$ 31,640
Capital					
Partner 1—Capital		$ 3,973		$ 5,532	
1/2 of Annual Earnings		7,618		7,624	
Less Drawings on Account		−6,060		−7,320	
Net Capital			$ 5,531		$ 5,836
Partner 2—Capital		$ 3,173		$ 4,532	
1/2 of Annual Earnings		7,618		$ 7,624	
Less Annual Drawings		−6,260		−7,620	
Net Capital			$ 4,532		$ 4,536
Total Capital	$ 7,146		$ 10,062		$ 10,372
Add Liabilities	$ 31,259		$ 33,613		$ 31,640
Total Liabilities plus Capital	$ 38,405		$ 43,676		$ 42,012

conform with existing styles and represents an attractive addition to the community.

3. 17-AL refuses to cut commissions. They lost one $40,000 deal because they refused to cut their commission by $500. Furthermore, they will not pay for gifts, additions, lawns, paint, and so on, in lieu of cutting commissions.

C. Goals:

1. They have short- and long-range goals; for example, in one past year they did $900,000 of business, so they set their sights on attaining $1,000,000 the following year.
2. Their long-range plans include expansion of the size of the enterprise. They anticipate expanding the rental department and establishing a building department and two branch offices. (N. B.: These were mentioned in the 1954 interview; to our knowledge, this had not been done by 1957.) They are considering forming a separate partnership for speculating in buying and selling properties. They calculate a potential profit of $70,000 on a deal that requires $150,000 credit.

VI-S. *Control*

A. The merchandise, records, expenses, and deals are carefully controlled.
B. An outside accountant analyzes records; the records are kept by owners.

INCOME AND EXPENSE STATEMENTS

	Year 4	*Year 5*	*Year 6*	*Year 7*
Income				
Sales Commissions	$ 32,723	$ 37,952	$ 30,975	$ 35,888
Rental Commissions	3,852	4,057	4,304	1,466
Rents	1,069	845	438	—
Other (principally, capital gains)	—	(595)	6,312	—
Total Income	$ 37,644	$ 42,258	$ 42,049	$ 37,354
Expenses				
Accounting and legal	$ 122	$ 65	$ 143	$ 110
Advertising	4,292	4,707	4,547	5,337
Automobile	1,200	1,200	1,200	1,200
Brokers' commissions	1,547	815	0	36
Depreciation	724	834	1,088	1,552
Dues and subscriptions	315	262	210	211
Entertainment	29	10	0	—
Insurance	192	86	326	77
Interest	—	—	205	1,680
Janitor and cleaning	182	222	271	42
Miscellaneous	181	342	312	205
Postage	107	105	106	61
Rent	3,000	3,000	3,663	—
Repairs and replacements	87	59	112	81
Supplies	717	513	665	441
Taxes and licenses	208	259	326	523
Utilities	1,298	1,256	1,157	1,408
Wages and commissions	6,020	10,562	12,461	9,143
Total Expenses	$ 20,221	$ 24,295	$ 26,792	$ 22,106
Net Profit Before Taxes	$ 17,423	$ 17,963	$ 15,237	$ 15,248

C. Cumulative sales totals are maintained, to keep a running tabulation of their business to date.
D. They are compiling a record of properties in the area for comparison purposes.
E. All records and details pertaining to a given deal are kept in a separate envelope, which has on the front a summary of the important facts. This envelope is kept up to date while the deal is in progress, held in suspension while it is in escrow, and filed permanently when sale is completed.
F. They are very particular about the exclusive listings they take. In an area where listings are scarce, they turn down many which are poorly located or unreasonably priced. An owner must inspect and approve every listing before it is accepted. Only one deal in their five years of operation has fallen through.

ANALYSIS

II-A. *Organization*

A. Scope: The firm is sufficiently diversified for the area and size of the community in which it is located.
B. Size: Limitation of size may be the result of ineffectual management in the past and failure to cope successfully with problems.
C. Organized well to compete with the strong competition of the area (where there is one real estate license per 75 people), at the same time, cooperating with them whenever possible, for example, enlisting their help selling listings (thus acting in the capacity of a multiple, inasmuch as there is no such organization in the community). They have a standing reciprocal agreement with an old insurance agency in town. In return for hiring their real estate saleslady when they closed their real estate department, the insurance agency refers all real estate business to 17-AL.

III-A. *Staffing*

A. The partnership is an ideal combination, with each operating in accord with and to the satisfaction of the other.
B. Overlooking clerical help has meant that owners must devote to clerical tasks much of their valuable time that could (or should) be spent guiding a larger sales staff, or (if they felt it wise) selling, or more effectively managing the firm.
C. The owners admit that the principal reason for the all-female staff is that women are easier to manage. It might be added that another reason could be that women are less likely to object to competition from their managers.
D. The staff is kept in a state of ignorance. (a) Because they do not keep floor time and prospects are distributed at the owners' discretion, the salesladies are unable to plan their time well. (b) They are not asked to share in management decisions, a procedure that many firms have found successful. This rather unnatural management attitude probably results from the fear of competition from the salesmen.

IV-A. *Direction*

A. Direction is weak. (a) Owners dictate rather than direct, probably feeling that their staff is not competent; instead of helping, they take over. (b) Training is superficially done (only experienced salesmen are hired).
B. No training program is necessary, because only experienced salespeople are hired.
C. Rather than limiting the size of the staff because of headaches in order to have time to sell (as the owner stated), it may be that he is an ineffectual director. Possible reason for hiring only saleswomen: for easier control and because they will tolerate competition of owners. Owners want to be sure the saleswomen do things their way and follow tight policies (unwritten) that will keep them out of trouble and that will free the owners for selling.

V-A. *Planning*

A. Planning and control are the strongest management functions in the firm.
B. Reputation: An enviable reputation has been established because of their ability to plan:
1. Extensive advertising has created a name for servicing listings.
2. An active public relations program has paid off.
3. High ethical standards have secured referrals from good sources.
C. Goals:
1. They are farsighted in approach, as is evidenced by their plans. Whether these plans are realistic is another matter. If plans for expanding mentioned in 1954 were short-range, it seems that they have not been accomplished.
2. We might suggest that, in addition to setting an absolute sum as their annual goal, they also strive to capture a certain percentage of the market each year. This is important in striving to meet competition and even more important when there are only a few firms in the community who are of a caliber to compete actively with this firm.

VI-A. *Control*

A. Although adequate controls are maintained over merchandise, records, and expenses, the staff is too rigidly controlled. (See "Staffing:")
B. Records are adequate and well kept. The principal drawback is that owners waste time keeping them up to date.
C. As a result of their policy of accepting only salable listings and their extensive advertising program, they sell about 75 per cent of the exclusives.
D. Their enviable record of completing deals is due to their careful qualification of prospects.

VII-A. *Conclusions*

A. Strengths:
1. Diversified operation
2. Farsighted planning
3. Reputation in community

4. Control of merchandise, deals, and records
5. Advertising campaigns
6. Ambition of owners

B. Weaknesses:

1. Overcontrol of staff; poor relations
2. Possible fear of growth
3. Lacking ability in certain managerial areas
4. Poor direction

C. Recommendations:

1. Overhaul training program.
2. Hire secretary.
3. Establish policy book.
4. Owners, if they must sell, should specialize in a type of real estate different from that which the salesladies sell, to avoid direct competition.

INDEX

D

E

F

G

Q

R

S

T

U

V